REMAKING AMERICA

PUBLIC MEMORY, COMMEMORATION, AND PATRIOTISM IN THE TWENTIETH CENTURY

John Bodnar

PRINCETON UNIVERSITY PRESS   PRINCETON, NEW JERSEY

Published by Princeton University Press, 41 William Street,
Princeton, New Jersey 08540
In the United Kingdom: Princeton University Press,
Chichester, West Sussex

Library of Congress Cataloging-in-Publication Data

Bodnar, John E., 1944–
Remaking America : public memory, commemoration, and
patriotism in the twentieth century / John Bodnar.
p. cm.
Includes bibliographical references and index.
ISBN 0-691-04783-9 (alk. paper)
ISBN 0-691-03495-8 (pbk.)
1. United States—History—20th century. 2. Public history—
United States. 3. Patriotism—United States.
4. United States—Popular culture. 5. United States—Anniversaries.
6. Memorials—United States. I. Title
E741.B64 1991
973.9—dc20 91-17830 CIP

This book has been composed in Linotron Palatino

Princeton University Press books are printed
on acid-free paper and meet the guidelines
for permanence and durability of the Committee
on Production Guidelines for Book Longevity
of the Council on Library Resources

First Princeton Paperback printing, 1994

Printed in the United States of America

3 5 7 9 10 8 6 4

http://pup.princeton.edu

REMAKING AMERICA

To John Chellino and the Memory of Martha Chellino and Joseph Bodnar

Contents

List of Illustrations

Preface

THIS BOOK about the past is a product of the present. It originated from the intersection of professional and political concerns in the 1980s which influenced my thinking a great deal. Professionally I had been engaged in a long period of research and reflection in the field of American social history. I had always assumed that social history—the study of small worlds and individual lives—had contributed much that was new to the field of American history. I found the examination of the lives and concerns of ordinary people an exciting prospect and, must confess, found myself in empathy with the struggles and goals many of these people pursued. Therefore, I was somewhat surprised by the growing criticism social history received in this country by the 1980s. Reviewers, for instance, complained that works in the field left out the politics of the past and focused too much on "middle-range" questions.

Scholarly reservations about social history were reinforced by political attacks upon a history that failed to stress national and traditional values and truths. It seemed that ideology had made a comeback in the 1980s, but this time it emanated from conservative rather than liberal sources. Patriotism was discussed a great deal by Ronald Reagan and members of his administration; calls for a return to the study of a national and unified past were widespread. It became impossible to ignore this contemporary discussion and not reflect on the ways in which the small worlds of ordinary people were linked to the larger realm of national politics and on the political uses of the past in the present.

Ordinary people usually react to problems by looking for practical solutions; scholars write books. My book began by reflecting upon the political expressions of patriotism in the 1980s and the manner in which this cultural defense of the nation so freqeuntly used historical stories and symbols. Ronald Reagan transformed symbols such as the Panama Canal and the Statue of Liberty into evocations of patriotism. Cultural leaders continually called for a return to a more inspiring and unified story of the past. Lynne V. Cheney, chairman of the National Endowment for the Humanities, criticized American schools for failing to preserve the past in 1987 in *American Memory: A Report on the Humanities in the Nation's Public Schools*. She saw the past—history—as a monolithic entity that taught lessons of nation building and patriotism and a "kind of civic glue" that would help all citizens feel part of a common undertaking. As a social historian my reaction was to think about how such evocations may have affected ordinary people in the past. What type of past was most meaningful to them? What exactly was patriotism? What role did particular social groups play in constructing versions of the past? Perhaps the past that Cheney feared was disappearing had been replaced by something else, or perhaps it was never as neat and tidy as she recalled. Gradually I began to think that patriotism and memory might become subjects that could link the small realms of ordinary people to the larger world of political structures. I thought I could begin to discuss the concerns of ordinary people and political events at the same time. Perhaps the designation "middle-range questions" used by some critics to describe the study of personal lives unnecessarily diminished the importance of everyday concerns and obscured any attempt to understand the intimate links between everyday life and political issues.

The resulting study of public memory, however, was more than a product of my imagination. A broad range of friends, scholars, archivists, and supporters contributed to the completion of this effort. Valuable financial assistance came from the Spencer Foundation and a grant-in-aid funded by the American Association of State and Local History, the National Endowment for the Humanities, and the Indiana Historical Society. Graduate students including Hannah Griff and Naomi Lichtenberg helped me locate relevant material on several centennial celebrations. Archivists who assisted me are too numerous to mention. But I must thank Jeffrey Flannery of the Library of Congress; John Grabowski of the Western Reserve Historical Society; Charles Hay of the Eastern Kentucky State University Archives; Lloyd Hustvedt of the Norwegian-American Historical Association; David Nathan and Ruth Harris of the National Park Service archives at Harpers Ferry, West Virginia; Barbara Thisesen of the Mennonite Library and Archives; Kermit Westerberg of the Swedish Immigration Research Center; and the staff of the Illinois State Historical Society, the National Archives, and the Ohio History Center. The Indiana University library at Bloomington processed countless interlibrary loan requests for newspapers, and Barry Mackintosh generously gave me access to historic files and a copier at the offices of the National Park Service in Washington, D.C.

A number of scholars gave me specific references and ideas. I would especially like to thank Jon Gjerde, John Jenswold, Dominick Pacyga, Roy Rosenzweig, Todd Stephenson, and Rudolph Vecoli. David Glassberg and Robert Weible generously read the chapter on the National Park Service. Longer portions of the manuscript were read by Thomas Bender and Gary Gerstle, and I benefited from their comments. In addition to lengthy criticisms from anonymous readers for Princeton University Press, I received valuable readings from John Gillis and my colleague, Michael McGerr. Gillis organized an especially informative conference on collective memory at Rutgers University in 1990. Periodic discussions with colleagues like Richard Blackett, Casey Blake, William Cohen, and especially James Riley left me with much to consider. Cohen and Riley taught me a great deal about the process of public memory in France. And few scholars are fortunate enough to have access to the insights and friendship of someone like David Thelen. Finally, I learned from the experience of this book that editors like Gail Ullman at Princeton University Press can be nurturing individuals.

REMAKING AMERICA

1. "Heroic soldiers" look toward the wall containing the engraved names of their fallen comrades in the Vietnam Veterans Memorial, Washington, D.C. Courtesy of the National Park Service.

PROLOGUE

The Vietnam Veterans Memorial

IN 1979, Jan Scruggs, Tom Carhart, and other Vietnam veterans in the Washington, D.C., area began to formulate a plan to build a memorial to the casualties of that conflict. They were not interested in reviving the political arguments over the merits of the war or lauding their fellow soldiers for their patriotism. They wanted, like ordinary people before them, to connect the past and the present in a personal and manageable way. Moved by the attitude of many Vietnam veterans that the nation had betrayed and neglected them after their return home, Scruggs and Carhart sought to give consolation and recognition to their fellow soldiers. Many of the veterans who endorsed their cause were equally intent on removing the "stigma" they felt their actions had evoked in fighting an unpopular war. They wanted to remember the dead and reinterpret the role they had played in the conflict itself.[1]

The path that Scruggs, Carhart, and their supporters followed to build their memorial was not only fraught with difficulties but provided a graphic illustration of the various interests that had to be served in any attempt at public commemoration. First, they had to solict the support of prominent leaders in the government. John Warner, who as Secretary of the Navy during much of the war had signed orders sending thousands of Marines and sailors into combat, promised to help. Senator Gary Hart of Colorado backed the group and cited the need to memorialize the act of sacrificing for the nation. Other senators and leaders talked of the need to promote national solidarity and healing after the discord of the Vietnam era in the United States, something that had not motivated the veterans who conceived of the memorial in the first place. Senator Jake Garn said that the merits of the war could be debated by historians and statesmen, but it was important now to promote a national sense of reconciliation and loyalty to the nation. In fact, Scruggs and other veterans who worked on the memorial's behalf stressed how important it was for them to argue that the monument would promote healing and reconciliation in their discussions with government officials. Ultimately, Scruggs and the Vietnam Veterans Memorial Foundation accommodated the interests of government leaders in unity by selecting a site for their monument near the Lincoln Memorial. They felt that the ability of Lincoln to represent the oneness of the union would help generate support for their own cause.[2]

The publicity generated by the proponents of the memorial elicited support not only from influential political leaders but from ordinary citizens throughout the country. In letters sent to the Vietnam Veterans Memorial Fund in Washington these people explained their reasons for contributing to the memorial project. Few mentioned the need for national unity that dominated the thinking of many leaders but some used the symbol of patriotism for reaching a sense of personal understanding about the loss of loved ones. A man in Delaware, whose only son had been killed in the war, wanted "to honor those who have given their best and their all for the security of our country." Others desired to commemorate those who demonstrated "The Love of Our Country."[3]

Most letter writers, however, claimed to be motivated neither by a desire for unity nor patriotism but by empathy for the soldiers who suffered and died. Many indicated that they saw their contributions as a way to relieve grief. Parents remembered dead sons. One couple sent funds to Bob Hope, who helped the veterans solicit money, and said that the loss of their son was still a "real heartache." Wayne Buchner of Worthington, Ohio, indicated what the reality of the war's aftermath felt like for many when he claimed that Vietnam veterans "living and dead received a 'raw deal' from their country and its people," and deserve "recognition for their valiant efforts." One woman exclaimed that her "heart broke" thinking of "how awful these men were treated." Many added that while they wished to express sorrow and respect for living and dead soldiers, however, their contributions in no way reflected their support for the war itself. A woman from Michigan saw the soldiers as courageous but victims of "needless sacrifice." One man sent funds for the "war I hated and the friends and loved ones I lost."[4]

The final design for the memorial was more of an expression of grief and sorrow than a celebration of national unity or the glorious triumph of the nation. Skewed toward the personal interests of ordinary people, this design glorified neither the nation nor the sacrifices of foot soldiers for magnificent national causes. The veterans had left the design up to a committee that included a number of people with artistic and design expertise. The result was two long, black granite walls that intersected to form the shape of a chevron. Inscribed in the stone were simply the names of each of the fifty-eight thousand men and women who gave their lives in Southeast Asia between 1957 and 1975. No national symbols were used in this design and no particular references were made to the ideal of national service. Rather the motif was a testament to ordinary people who had lived and died, not to any idea of national greatness or heroism. The designer, a young art student at Yale University, Maya Ying Lin, thought the memorial conveyed the idea that war was sad. In many ways it resembled the cemeteries that were erected in the South immediately after the Civil War where people could honor those they had lost and express their grief. It would be several decades after the war before the South began to celebrate the nobility of the "Lost Cause" and Civil War military leaders such as Robert E. Lee who were praised for their efforts at promoting national reconciliation.

The selection of an actual design, however, forced monument promoters to consider the symbolic meaning of their plans more than they had done previously. This reassessment revealed fundamental differences among leaders of the monument project and other supporters that revolved around the issue of the power of large political structures such as the nation-state. Scruggs and others were satisfied that the monument commemorated their comrades. Others, however, were angered by what they perceived to be a lack of patriotism and glory. James Webb, who had served as an officer in Vietnam, felt the design looked like a "mass grave" and that it needed a flag and white walls. Wealthy Texas businessman H. Ross Perot, who had funded the design competition, did not like the plan either and felt it only commemorated the "guys that died." Tom Carhart now reconsidered his staunch support for the memorial because it seemed "anti-heroic" and failed to promote the notion of duty to the nation, an ideal he was certainly exposed to in his training at West Point. Carhart called the design a "black gash of shame" and pleaded for patriotism and nationalism when he explained, "We want something that will make us part of America."[5]

Letters to officials of the memorial fund added to the public outcry over the lack of patriotism and the failure to interpret the past deeds of soldiers in other than heroic terms. A woman from Ohio, whose son did not return from Vietnam alive, felt that the memorial should portray "the courage, the bravery" of the soldiers and not "denigrate our men in black marble." Another grieving parent wanted a monument "symbolic of the courage and patriotism of the young men of the Vietnam experience." A man from Virginia queried, "Can't we find a patriot to design this memorial?"[6]

Most citizens who protested wrote directly to President Ronald Reagan and asked him to assist them in obtaining a more explicitly patriotic design. One retired Air Force officer argued that the memorial must be one that can be "looked up to, not fallen into." Another man asked Reagan if he would like to be remembered by a "black hole in the ground." John Gustafson of Elgin, Illinois, compared the proposal to past monuments: "I suggest that a memorial be built that is similar to the Iwo Jima memorial in Washington, D.C., that shows the true heroism that American G.I.'s displayed in Vietnam. There were many examples of heroism in Vietnam and any of these would be a fine tribute to all Vietnam veterans."[7]

Several people went so far as to submit drawings of their own for the memorial. Regis Brawdy, a disabled veteran who argued that a "hole in the ground" did not conform to his idea of being honored, submitted a sketch of a large "V" for victory rising into the sky with an American flag in the middle of the structure. Brawdy proposed that the names of living vets be placed on one side of the monument and the names of the dead be inscribed on the reverse side. An Army officer, G. S. Robinson, thought the black granite proposal was not "inspirational like the Washington Monument" and suggested a white marble column carved in the form of a bamboo stalk that was entangled in a strand of barbed wire. The stalk stood for Southeast Asia, and the wire represented tyranny. In this rendition both the stalk and the wire were broken to symbolize the American effort to break the Communist stronghold on the Vietnamese people.[8]

A compromise eventually worked out between conflicting sides was announced by Scruggs and Warner in 1982. The original design with names of the dead would stand. Added to the site, however, would be an American flag, a "heroic statue" of three soldiers from the Vietnamese conflict, and the inscription "God Bless America" on the monument itself. The powerful and dominant interests of patriots and nationalists could not let a text composed only by and about ordinary people and ordinary emotions stand alone. The profane was clearly a threat to the sacred. Scruggs incorrectly argued that the original design represented neither victory nor defeat but simply the acknowledgment of those who served. He was more insightful when he commented that aesthetically the design did not need the additional statue of the "heroic soldiers" but "politically it does."[9]

Thousands of Vietnam veterans converged on Washington during the week of November 7, 1982, for the monument dedication ceremonies. This commemorative occasion would witness the expression of the same conflicting set of interests, however, that had marked the discussion over the promotion and design of the monument itself. Patriotic language and symbols punctuated the entire affair, but most people—veterans, relatives, and friends—came to voice their personal sentiments: grief for fallen comrades, a desire to recognize the ordinary soldiers, and sorrow over the loss of loved ones. Expressions of national greatness, unity, and loyalty to the nation were not only infrequent but often contradicted.

Personal feeling and private agendas were powerfully articulated. The parents of Robert Rosar who was killed in the Mekong Delta in 1968 came from Colorado to honor the memory of their son. Wilma Rosar explained: "It [the monument] means so much to us. It's a very deep thing, our loss, it was absolutely devastating." Rosar's father said the memorial provided a sense of honor concerning Bob's death that he had never felt before.[10]

Other veterans came to the commemoration for personal reasons. Jack Ferrier came from Hartford, Connecticut, "to find peace with myself and spend some time with my memories." He explained that he lost many friends in a military offensive in 1969. Jim Everett of Orlando, Florida, came to the commemoration out of a sense of frustration, "Nobody understands me," he told a reporter for the *Washington Post*, "not unless they've been through it." Everett said that the main reason he came was that he had lost contact with every friend he made in Vietnam. David Gray drove with three veteran friends from Indianapolis to Washington because he felt a tribute to the soldiers who fought in Vietnam was long overdue. "And all these guys who were wounded in Vietnam got no recognition," he asserted. "We couldn't separate the politics of the war from the veterans themselves."[11]

A massive parade of veterans that preceded the monument dedication on November 13 was disorderly when compared to the normal civil and military parades that marked American commemorative activity. Respect for authority, order, and unity were less in evidence as men and women marched in and out of uniform, brought along pets, and carried either small American flags or placards that criticized political decisions from the past: "We Killed, We Bled, We Died for Worse than Nothing"; "No More Wars. No More Lies." This presentation of views in opposition to the ideology of national unity and reconciliation and national power was another indication that the public discussion over the memory of this war involved significant contention and debate. The parade's theme, "Marching Along Together Again," actually expressed sentiments of loyalty to a community or brotherhood of soldiers rather than loyalty to a nation of patriotic citizens.[12]

From the moment the monument was dedicated, expressions of personal pain, grief, and loss were manifested. People who visited the wall touched the names of loved ones and wept openly. As evening fell some veterans kept a vigil and handed out flashlights so people could find the names for which they were searching. One night, shortly after the dedication, the parents of one fallen soldier apparently left an old pair of cowboy boots at the base of the black granite monolith. Shortly after that, Elanor Wimbish of Maryland left the first of more than twenty letters she would write to her dead son. She said that she wanted to bring something personal to the wall. By 1985 the National Park Service began to collect the thousands of personal mementos that were being left behind. These small remembrances said little of national greatness but much of what dominated individual memories. They included yellowed pictures of teenage soldiers, plastic roses, childhood teddy bears, baseball caps, worn Army dogtags, diaries, postcards written from war zones, and love letters. A park service technician who helped catalog the items left behind told a reporter that the mementos left him "a little misty." He claimed that these objects were "not like history" but had an "immediacy" about them.[13] What he might have added was that they were not really like the history that was usually commemorated in public.

This effort to restate the human pain and sorrow of war rather than the valor and glory of warriors and nations, moreover, originated in the experience of war itself. The monument to the veterans was not only a simple memory invention of survivors moved by feelings they had after the war but represented a continuance of a conflict that had originated in Vietnam. That dispute was rooted in the contradictory perceptions of ordinary soldiers and powerful political structures such as the nation-state. The former felt mostly pain and frustration while government or official statements about the war talked of military progress, often expressed in terms of "body counts," and the need for international security against Communist expansion.

Soldiers did not always experience the conflict as the government described it. In an incisive examination of many of the literary accounts of the war, Christie Norton Bradley has demonstrated how much of that literature was produced by writers who were actually in Vietnam and who felt a sense of duty not to the nation but to the individuals they knew who fought and died. They were intent on providing not histories of the war but accounts of how the war felt and was perceived by those who were there. The most powerful of these writers shared the sense of the soldiers that official reports of the war—by the government and news-gathering agencies—failed to accurately relate what it meant to be there. To the extent that survivors restated the war experience in ways that did not directly serve the interests of the nation-state, they were not simply feeling guilt for having survived but were sustaining an oppositional attitude that had been created by the warriors themselves.[14] Scruggs, wounded in action as a "grunt," reflected much of this war experience and this antagonistic attitude toward those in authority. Not surprisingly, key critics of the original design such as Webb and Carhart were graduates of service academies where they had been fully exposed to the ideologies of national service and glory.

Despite concessions to the demands of patriots and nationalists, the Vietnam memorial clearly represented the triumph of one set of interests over another. It could be viewed by people as an embodiment of the ideals of patriotism and nationalism and as an expression of comradeship with and sorrow for the dead. But unmistakably the latter theme predominated over the former, a point which troubled opponents of the original design.

Part One

MEMORY IN THE PRESENT AND THE PAST

Collective memory . . . is a current of continuous thought
whose continuity is not at all artificial, for it retains from
the past only what still lives or is capable of living in the
consciousness of groups keeping the memory alive.
—*Maurice Halbwachs*

Fairy tales are told for entertainment. You've got to
distinguish between the myths that have to do with the
serious matter of living life in terms of the order of society
and of nature and stories with some of those motifs
that are told for entertainment.
—*Joseph Campbell*

It will be seen that the control of the past depends
above all on the training of memory.
—*George Orwell*

Nationalism usually conquers in the name of a
putative folk culture.
—*Ernest Gellner*

CHAPTER ONE

The Memory Debate: An Introduction

THE STORY of the Vietnam Veterans Memorial underscores a very fundamental point. The shaping of a past worthy of public commemoration in the present is contested and involves a struggle for supremacy between advocates of various political ideas and sentiments. It is the creation of public memory in commemorative activities celebrating America's past and the dramatic exchange of interests that are involved in such exercises that constitute the focus of this book.

The debate over the Vietnam memorial involved two main sides. The dominant interest expressed in the memorial originated in the consciousness of ordinary people most directly involved in the war: veterans who fought there and people who cared about them. In the context of American society they represented a vernacular culture which formulated specialized concerns during the war, such as their critique of official interpretations of the conflict, and after the war, such as their reverence for the dead. They manifested these concerns in the memorial itself. Standing opposed to their concerns and ultimately accommodating them were the defenders of the nation-state. The structure of national power was safeguarded by national political leaders who saw in the monument a device that would foster national unity and patriotism and many veterans and other citizens who celebrated the ideal of patriotic duty. These guardians of the nation were representatives of an overarching or official culture which resisted cultural expressions that minimized the degree to which service in Vietnam may have been valorous.

Public memory emerges from the intersection of official and vernacular cultural expressions. The former originates in the concerns of cultural leaders or authorities at all levels of society. Whether in positions of prominence in small towns, ethnic communities, or in educational, government, or military bureaucracies, these leaders share a common interest in social unity, the continuity of existing institutions, and loyalty to the status quo. They attempt to advance these concerns by promoting interpretations of past and present reality that reduce the power of competing interests that threaten the attainment of their goals. Official culture relies on "dogmatic formalism" and the restatement of reality in ideal rather than complex or ambiguous terms. It presents the past on an abstract basis of timelessness and sacredness. Thus, officials and their followers preferred to commemorate the Vietnam War in the ideal language of patriotism rather than the real language of grief and sorrow. Normally official culture promotes a nationalistic, patriotic culture of the whole that mediates an assortment of vernacular interests. But seldom does it seek mediation at the expense of ascendency.[1]

Vernacular culture, on the other hand, represents an array of specialized interests that are grounded in parts of the whole. They are diverse and changing and can be reformulated from time to time by the creation of new social units such as soldiers and their friends who share an experience in war or immigrants who settle a particular place. They can even clash with one another. Defenders of such cultures are numerous and intent on protecting values and restating views of reality derived from firsthand experience in small-scale communities rather than the "imagined" communities of a large nation. Both cultures are championed by leaders and gain adherents from throughout the population, and individuals themselves can support aspects of both cultures at once. But normally vernacular expressions convey what social reality feels like rather than what it should be like. Its very existence threatens the sacred and timeless nature of official expressions.

Public memory is produced from a political discussion that involves not so much specific economic or moral problems but rather fundamental issues about the entire existence of a society: its organization, structure of power, and the very meaning of its past and present. This is not simple class or status politics, although those concerns are involved in the discussion, but it is an argument about the interpretation of reality; this is an aspect of the politics of culture. It is rooted not simply in a time dimension between the past and the present but is ultimately grounded in the inherent contradictions of a social system: local and national structures, ethnic and national cultures, men and women, young and old, professionals and clients, workers and managers, political leaders and followers, soldiers and commanders. Its function is to mediate the competing restatements of reality these antinomies express. Because it takes the form of an ideological system with special language, beliefs, symbols, and stories, people can use it as a cognitive device to mediate competing interpretations and privilege some explanations over others. Thus, the symbolic language of patriotism is central to public memory in the United States because it has the capacity to mediate both vernacular loyalties to local and familiar places and official loyalties to national and imagined structures.[2]

Public memory is a body of beliefs and ideas about the past that help a public or society understand both its past, present, and by implication, its future. It is fashioned ideally in a public sphere in which various parts of the social structure exchange views. The major focus of this communicative and cognitive process is not the past, however, but serious matters in the present such as the nature of power and the question of loyalty to both official and vernacular cultures. Public memory speaks primarily about the structure of power in society because that power is always in question in a world of polarities and contradictions and because cultural understanding is always grounded in the material structure of society itself. Memory adds perspective and authenticity to the views articulated in this exchange; defenders of official and vernacular interests are selectively retrieved from the past to perform similar functions in the present.

Adherents to official and vernacular interests demonstrate conflicting obsessions. Cultural leaders orchestrate commemorative events to calm anxiety about change or political events, eliminate citizen indifference toward official concerns, promote exemplary patterns of citizen behavior, and stress citizen duties over rights. They feel the need to do this because of the existence of social contradictions, alternative views, and indifference that perpetuate fears of societal dissolution and unregulated political behavior.

Ordinary people, on the other hand, react to the actions of leaders in a variety of ways. At times they accept official interpretations of reality. Sometimes this can be seen when an individual declares that a son died in defense of his country or an immigrant ancestor emigrated to build a new nation. Individuals also express alternative renditions of reality when they feel a war death was needless or an immigrant ancestor moved simply to support his family. Frequently people put official agendas to unintended uses as they almost always do when they use public ritual time for recreational purposes or patriotic symbols to demand political rights.[3]

Most cultural leaders in the United States come from a broad group of middle-class professionals—government officials, editors, lawyers, clerics, teachers, military officers, and small businessmen. They are "self-conscious purveyors" of loyalty to larger political structures and existing institutions. Their careers and social positions usually depend upon the survival of the very institutions that are celebrated in commemorative activities. The boundaries of the leadership group are permeable, however, and can be crossed by rich and very influential individuals. Seldom are they crossed by factory workers, homemakers, millhands, farmers, and others whose work and social position allow them little time and access to the organizations that shape most public commemorative events.[4]

The term "ordinary people" best describes the rest of society that participates in public commemoration and protects vernacular interests. They are a diverse lot, are not synonymous with the working class, and invariably include individuals from all social stations. They are more likely to honor pioneer ancestors rather than founding fathers and favor comrades over patriots as some did regarding the Vietnam memorial. They acknowledge the ideal of loyalty in commemorative events and agree to defend the symbol of the nation but often use commemoration to redefine that symbol or ignore it for the sake of leisure or economic ends. There is certainly patriotism in much of what they honor, but they do not hesitate to privilege the personal or vernacular dimension of patriotism over the public one. They are less interested than cultural leaders in exerting influence or control over others, and are preoccupied, instead, with defending the interests and rights of their respective social segments.

Because numerous interests clash in commemorative events they are inevitably multivocal. They contain powerful symbolic expressions—metaphors, signs, and rituals—that give meaning to competing interpretations of past and present reality. In modern America no cultural expression contains the multivocal quality of public commemorations better than the idea of the nation-state and the language of patriotism. On a cultural level it serves as a symbol that "coerces" the discordant interests of diverse social groups and unites them into a "unitary conceptual framework" which connects the ideal with the real. Officials use it as a powerful metaphor that stimulates ideals of social unity and civic loyalty. And its very real structure of local, regional, and national government constantly seeks loyalty and respect. But the component parts of the nation-state—its families, classes, ethnic groups, and regions—also attract loyalty and devotion. Citizens view the larger entity of the nation through the lens of smaller units and places that they know firsthand. And they frequently see the nation as a defender of their rights rather than simply a source of obligation.[5] The symbols of the nation-state and the patriot do what all symbols do: they mediate both official and vernacular interests. By themselves they do not privilege one interest over another. That task is performed admirably by men and women living in space and time.

Public commemorations usually celebrate official concerns more than vernacular ones. This does not mean that cultural differences are removed from the discussion over memory. Most citizens can honor the basic political structure of the nation, for instance, and still vigorously disagree with cultural leaders about what the nation stands for and what type of devotion it merits. They often express this disagreement not in violent terms but in more subtle expressions of indifference or inventive historical constructions of their own. For instance, the pioneer was a popular historical symbol in midwestern commemorations during the late nineteenth and early twentieth centuries. Its appeal to ordinary people resided in its vernacular meaning of sturdy ancestors who founded ethnic communities and families, preserved traditions in the face of social change, and overcame hardship. These defenders of vernacular culture were especially important to midwesterners who were anxious about the pace of economic centralization and the impact of urban and industrial growth upon their local places. Their commemorations of pioneers were so pervasive, in fact, that officials attempted to redefine these figures from the past as builders and defenders of a nation rather than of small communities or staunch supporters of local institutions.

Because the expression of patriotic and nationalistic texts, moreover, reflects both the interests of cultural leaders and ordinary people, it does not follow that an equitable compromise is reached. Negotiation and cultural mediation do not preclude domination and distortion. Usually it is the local and personal past that is incorporated into a nationalized public memory rather than the other way around. Local, regional, class, and ethnic interests are sustained in one form or another in the final product, but the dominant meaning is usually nationalistic. And this does not seem to be particularly wrong to most citizens. In fact, it appears to be "fundamentally true." As Maurice Godelier argues, it is when ideologies do not appear to the "exploited" as illusions or as instruments of their exploitation that they contribute effectively to persuading people to accept them. They can only do this if they incorporate—as the symbols of the pioneer and patriot do—meanings dear to a number of social groups that participate in the memory debate.[6]

One implication of the argument that the abundant patriotic messages of American public memory are rooted partially in the quest for power by leaders of various sorts is that patriotism is invented as a form of social control and that it does not naturally find resonance within the hearts and minds of ordinary people. Obviously this study cannot pretend to explore private hearts and minds. But it does present clues as to what the masses think and feel when they demonstrate loyalty to the nation-state. They certainly respond enthusiastically to patriotic messages and symbols with referential connections to their immediate environs and group. National commemorations such as the 1976 bicentennial, for instance, celebrated both local, ethnic, and national history. But are they performing? Do they exhibit patriotic sentiments in the dramatic exchanges that take place in commemorative activities because they know that is what those in power want them to do? Or is the observation that American patriotism is "indigenous" and not fabricated as it is in Europe correct?[7]

This study of commemorative activity suggests several points on the matter. Leaders in the period under review here expended a very substantial effort to stimulate loyalty to large political structures. Ordinary people demonstrated a considerable interest of their own in expressing attachments to structures of a smaller scale such as local and cultural communities. Ordinary people also exhibited indifference to patriotic messages at times, especially when it came to paying for monuments, and a periodic determination to use commemorative time to pursue personal rather than civic interests.[8]

More suggestive is the widespread effort on the part of ordinary people to celebrate symbols such as pioneer ancestors or dead soldiers that were more important for autobiographical and local memory than for civic memory. In fact, because the vernacular dimension of memory would not go away it was susceptible to reformulation by officials. Constantly they honored pioneers for building a nation and fallen soldiers for defending it. But the patriotism they evoked on the part of ordinary people was not always grounded in official expressions but in the power of vernacular meanings officials tried to constrain.

Ordinary people do two things when they affirm loyalty to the nation. They do what leaders expect of them, but they also insist that much of what they value on a smaller and less political scale is important to them. The prominence of patriotism in American commemorative activities does not signify the complete triumph of the power of the nation-state. Patriotism itself embodies both official and vernacular interests, although most patriotic expressions tend to emphasize the dominance of the former over the latter.[9]

Indeed, a striking comparison could be made with French history. The pioneer symbol, regardless of the extent it served the interests of the nation, originated in the attempts of local communities and ethnic enclaves to mark their communal origins. In a similar fashion, Maurice Agulhon shows how the most powerful symbol of the French Republic by the late nineteenth century—a female figure named Marianne—originated in the vernacular culture of peasants in the south of France before it came to serve the official interests of national culture as well. The cognitive power of both Marianne and pioneers was certainly due in part to their ability to link the official and vernacular interests of political structures and ordinary people.[10]

It is not surprising to see several interests connected in the symbols that were most powerful, if we can accept the argument that the symbolic meaning of ideological systems emerges from a communicative process. Thus, both the pioneer and patriot symbols do what all symbols do: they restate social contradictions in a modified form. To the extent that public memory originates in discourse or the presentation of divergent viewpoints, it is not simply manipulated. Discourse can simultaneously be a servant of and a hedge against hegemonic interests. To put it another way, manipulation and invention do not go far enough in explaining how certain symbols assume dominance in public memory. In the United States, since the early nineteenth century, commemorative activity involved considerably more than manipulation of the past by officials. It involved the presentation of multiple texts or numerous kinds of symbolic communication.[11]

Discourse or communication over the past, moreover, is not only vital but pervasive. Forums for discussion exist in the commemorative activity of ethnic communities, towns and cities, states and regions, and nations. Invariably the interests that are exchanged are numerous, and those most powerful in the social structure are influential in the discussion and the construction of memory. The fact that forums are numerous actually insures that a number of interests are articulated. The multiplicity of forums, however, does not prevent some interests from distorting the discussion to a considerable degree.

Regardless of the number of forums that exist or the complexity of communication over the past, the commemorative activities examined here—anniversaries, monument dedications, landmark designations, reunions, and centennials—almost always stress the desirability of maintaining the social order and existing institutions, the need to avoid disorder or dramatic changes, and the dominance of citizen duties over citizen rights. Accounts of fundamental change in the past such as the American Revolution, industrialization, migration, or war are usually reinterpreted in ways that soften the idea of transformation and promote stories of patriotism and national growth. Dramatic episodes of citizens asserting their rights, with the exception of the colonists of 1776, are almost never commemorated. The point is that although public memory is constructed from discourse the sources of cultural and political power are not simply diffuse. They are also unequal. Public memory came to be what it was in the United States because some interests exerted more power than others in the discussion and actually distorted public communication to an inordinate extent. Thus, distortion took place not through simple coercion but through a more subtle process of communication which Leslie Good suggests involves the "prevention" of certain statements being made in public in a meaningful way. Heavy doses of patriotism frustrate the expression, for instance, of state obligation toward its citizens. The power of large political structures and what Stuart Hall calls "cultural leadership" coexists with and dominates the power of smaller structures—communities, regions, groups—in the process of constructing public memory.[12]

By the latter part of the twentieth century public memory remains a product of elite manipulation, symbolic interaction, and contested discourse. Leaders continue to use the past to foster patriotism and civic duty and ordinary people continue to accept, reformulate, and ignore such messages. Because many had been so accepting for a very long time, in fact, the original design for the Vietnam Veterans Memorial came as something of a shock to some and raised the possibility that vernacular interests might be more powerful in the future. The deep emotional response evoked by the monument also revealed the continued power of vernacular culture and the fact that it had been sustained in symbols of commemoration that appeared to be more hegemonic than they actually were. This tension between official and vernacular memory and how it was resolved in commemorative events forms the core of the analysis in the following chapters. It will be explored in the communal forums of ethnic communities and large cities, the regional forum of the Midwest, the national forums of the National Park Service, and historic anniversaries relevant to the history of the nation. The intent here is to peel back the mask of innocence that surrounds commemorative events and reveal the very vital issues they address.

CHAPTER TWO

Public Memory in Nineteenth-Century America: Background and Context

PUBLIC MEMORY in American commemorative activities was formed by the public presentation of multiple texts in both the nineteenth and twentieth centuries. To an extent the evolution of this cultural exchange conformed to the arguments of Jürgen Habermas. It became less combative over time as the power of the nation-state came to mediate vernacular interests and dominate public communications. At the same time the supremacy of state power by the twentieth century should not obscure the fact that at times this power served the interests of one political group more than another.

Essentially, the balance of political power in the United States—the context of public memory—was shifting and fragmented before World War I. The nation-state, a growing business class, regional and local interests, and the concerns of ordinary workers, immigrants, and farmers all asserted themselves vigorously. No interest dominated the entire nineteenth century, but the nation-state was very influential in the aftermath of the American Revolution until the 1820s. It regained political and cultural power for a time after the Civil War. Its power, in terms of asserting its dominance over various vernacular interests, was effectively rivaled, however, in two periods and, unlike in the following century, could not be effectively sustained. Beginning in the late 1820s a rise in regional and class divisions led to sharp exchanges in commemorative activities and to something of a decline in the singleminded focus on patriotism and national unity that had reached a peak in 1825. Similarly, by the 1870s the consolidation of interests behind the effort to save the union in the North and leave it in the South gave way to a blatant drive for power by a growing class of businessmen and entrepreneurs and the efforts of workers, farmers, and ordinary people to restrain and control that effort. In the end this contest would help bring back the political and cultural power of the nation-state itself.

PUBLIC MEMORY IN THE NEW NATION

Robert Wiebe has argued that nineteenth-century America was a society "without an institutional core." Clearly it had fundamental organizations in which all citizens participated—political parties, a court system, and schools. The cornerstone of the century's public philosophy, however, was unregulated competition, individual liberty, and local and regional autonomy. Political power was decentralized in local communities and regions and the influence of the nation-state was something to be feared and limited.[1]

Despite the essential correctness of much of Wiebe's argument, his notion of a weak or underdeveloped nation-state must be modified. To the extent that public commemoration is a clue to the nature of political power itself, an argument can be made that the state, as a symbol and as a political structure, exerted considerable influence over politics and culture in the century. This influence was tenuous and often challenged by a variety of vernacular interests but was very real both because the nation-state was viewed as a resource for the attainment of leverage by various smaller interests from time to time and because it sometimes gathered a force and power of its own that could not be easily resisted.

In the first half-century of the new nation the major symbols of public memory in this country were associated with the American Revolution. That struggle not only represented the origins of the nation-state but produced a number of leaders, documents, and dates that served as important subjects for commemoration. Symbols had to serve needs in the material world, and no greater political need appeared to exist at the time than to ensure that the new nation survive. Consequently, symbols that generated loyalty and respect for the new structure of political power became widely honored including George Washington and, more slowly, the Declaration of Independence.[2]

The symbolic transfer of loyalty from the King of England to the new nation, something that began in ritual form before the Revolution, was solidified after 1776. In part this process was facilitated by the creation of a new "king" or symbol of central authority—George Washington. Scholars like Catherine Albanese have insightfully pointed out that these symbols of the Revolutionary era became less religious and more "humanocentric." She felt that "Jehovah" had stopped making history, and "the nation of patriots was obligingly making it for Him." Grounded in higher authority, the symbol of Washington and the new nation left little cultural space for competing symbols such as Thomas Jefferson or loyalties on the part of citizens. Sociologist Barry Schwartz has reinforced the notion that Washington replaced George III as a symbol of leadership and civic authority partially because of the religious nature of American society at the time. He became a source of good in opposition to the malevolent English king. By 1781 Washington's birthday was celebrated with special dinners and "demonstrations of joy."[3]

Not all Revolutionary War symbols gained the relatively rapid approval that Washington did, although he was certainly not without detractors on the political level. The Declaration of Independence was not generally considered a sacred document at all before 1800. On Independence Day, which was commemorated immediately after 1776 to some extent, orators saw the day and the document as important reminders of the break with the mother country and not as a symbol of political rights such as "liberty." The document acquired its later meanings when it became embroiled in the political contests between the Republicans and the Federalists. Once Jefferson became leader of the Republicans, the party celebrated everything with which he was associated. This adoration not only concerned Federalists because they naturally wished to discredit a political opponent, but because they were troubled by the possible link between the Declaration, individual rights, and political rebellion that had been suggested in the French Revolution. Prior to 1817 it was not uncommon to find separate Republican and Federalist celebrations on the Fourth of July.[4]

In the 1820s the decline of Republican and Federalist factionalism and the rise of historical interest in the Revolutionary era led to a more cohesive view of the Declaration of Independence and the celebration on the Fourth. A certain amount of unity and reverence was achieved by a growing sentiment for aged soldiers and leaders who had participated in the actual Revolutionary conflict itself. The fact that both Jefferson and John Adams died on July 4th, 1826, as nearly every historian of the period has noted, lent an almost mythic quality to the date. The Jubilee of the Declaration of Independence became a "solemn moment," according to Merrill Peterson, that stimulated the growth of American self-consciousness and patriotism.[5]

The establishment of the Revolutionary era as a centerpiece for public memory in the early Republic and the movement to generate loyalty to the new nation was furthered by the triumphant return visit of the Marquis de Lafayette in 1824–1825. Touring towns throughout the United States, Lafayette's appearance evoked much discussion about the past and the present as well as genuine public affection for the figures and events of the Revolution itself. Fred Somkin has demonstrated that Lafayette's pilgrimages to Revolutionary battlefields, his reunions with aged comrades, and the receptions arranged for him throughout the nation generated much public enthusiasm and interest. In New York City "overzealous patriots" actually attempted to unhitch horses that drew Lafayette's carriage and pull it themselves. Somkin was quick to point out, however, that Lafayette was not only a symbol of patriotism but a representation of political liberty for ordinary citizens as well, many of whom worshipped him for having left family and wealth in France to fight for liberty in America.[6]

The exaltation of the origins of the nation-state, however, did not come entirely from vague expressions of emotions but was also consciously expedited by the actions of cultural leaders. This was exactly the case when men of "social influence," part of the rising patriotic tide of the 1820s, formed an association in Charlestown, Massachusetts, to erect a memorial to the Revolutionary battle of Bunker Hill. These men were mostly from the class of entrepreneurs and professionals who were helping to make a new social order and appeared anxious to associate themselves with the heroic makers of the new nation. They planned to do this in ways similar to the rising commercial and professional classes of Albany, New York, that David Hackett found attempting to employ patriotism "to bolster entrepreneurial activity."[7]

The New England leaders argued that the new nation and its origins should be honored because it had provided the framework for the rapid increase in material progress. Public response to calls for contributions to the project were slowed, however, by a lack of interest—especially outside New England—and a lack of "progress" for working people in the Boston area. Although several years passed before sufficient resources were available, the groundbreaking ceremonies for the monument in 1825 turned out to be a major civic ceremony. Over two hundred veterans of the Revolutionary War and forty survivors of the battle of Bunker Hill marched in a long parade. "Glistening eyes" constituted the response of the marchers to the enthusiastic cheers of the grateful multitudes who lined the parade route and cheered," according to one account.[8]

The central event of the groundbreaking was an oration by Daniel Webster. His speech contained powerful exhortations for patriotic loyalty and further reinforced the attempt of a rising professional and merchant class to place their pursuit of material advancement and personal reward within the context of patriotic activity. Webster reasoned that his generation could win no laurels in a war for independence but could, in fact, accomplish other patriotic objectives. Specifically, they could preserve and defend what the Revolutionary generation had achieved. They could also improve upon the past by working toward material advancement. "Our proper business is improvement. . . . Let us develop the resources of our land, call forth its powers, build up its institutions," Webster exclaimed. Arguing that Americans were now much better fed and clothed and had more time for leisure activities since the Revolution, Webster insisted that the expansion of material progress must continue for "Our Country, Our Whole Country, and Nothing But Our Country."[9]

Seventeen years later in 1843, at the dedication of the monument, another elaborate celebration was held in Boston. President John Tyler and his cabinet attended and participated in a long parade that consisted of Revolutionary War veterans, military units, fraternal associations, and groups representing local educational institutions. The parade restated reality according to the desires of social and cultural leaders. It portrayed a highly ordered and unified society in which all citizens respected figures and institutions of authority. As Tyler, the veterans, and other prominent people moved along the line of march to the music of "The Union," men and women cheered and waved handkerchiefs in a symbolic display of patriotic and social unity. In this public ritual and space, all were expected to honor leaders of the present structure of power and believe that these officials were the heirs of the Revolution itself.[10]

A crowd reported to be about one hundred thousand people gathered near the recently completed monument to hear Webster again. Passages from his 1826 oration were said to have gained wide circulation and have become "household words throughout the nation." Webster again called for loyalty to the union. To him the monument stood for "patriotism and courage" and for "civil and religious liberty." But in his recounting of the past that led up to the Revolution and the monument to patriotism he reserved a special place for his favored middling classes. He claimed that among the colonists of English America liberty first manifested itself among the "middle, industrious, and already prosperous class," and the inhabitants of commercial and manufacturing cities. Webster compared American progress in commerce and liberty to the tyranny that he saw in South America at that time and declared, "Thank God, I, I also am an American." Several months later, in a speech before the New England Society of New York City, he again celebrated "eminent merchants" such as John Hancock and asserted that no class had shown "stronger and firmer devotion" to the preservation of the Union than the "great commercial masses of the country."[11]

EXPANDING THE CONTENT OF PUBLIC MEMORY, 1830–1870

By the 1830s the exacerbation of class, ethnic, and regional tensions caused by economic growth and the rise of a strong Democratic party led to the expression of a greater variety of positions in public commemoration. Ironically, the war to save the union and consolidate national power further enhanced the multivocal quality of commemoration and stimulated the expression of even more interests that had been rather quiet earlier in the century. The effort at civic instruction and the promotion of loyalty to the new nation continued, of course, but it now had increased competition. More commemorative attention was given to local, state, and regional pasts, so much so that historian Wesley Frank Craven suggested that parochial attitudes made it difficult to muster sufficient public support for an appropriate celebration of the centennial of Washington's birth in 1832.[12] Virginia, in fact, expressed its state pride by resisting a plan to move Washington's body to the base of a monument that was being built for him in the nation's capital. Pride in local and state pasts were further honored by the formation of state historical societies in Connecticut in 1825 and in Indiana in 1830.[13]

Davy Crockett represented a new cultural symbol that now competed with Washington. As Daniel Boorstin noted, Crockett was vulgar and crude compared to the "dignity" and "sober judgement" of the first president. But Crockett also represented a definite break with the almost monolithic patriotic symbolism of the early nineteenth century. He stood for common people rather than leaders and for a frontier or regional rather than national community. Certainly the spread of the frontier contributed to the growth of the nation-state itself, and, thus, the Crockett symbol contained patriotic dimensions. But the vernacular rather than the official dimension was more powerful in this particular construction of patriotic symbolism than in earlier ones.[14]

As American society became increasingly stratified by class, ordinary people demonstrated greater independence in the use of their commemorative time. A good deal of evidence from the 1830s and 1840s suggests that Fourth of July celebrations were used by the working class to pursue leisure-time activities rather than express civic loyalty to the nation-state. In the mill village of Rockdale, Pennsylvania, in the 1830s, where "rowdy men and women" filled the roads, the Fourth consisted of "disorderly, political picnics." During the same period in Philadelphia such celebrations, according to Susan Davis, included disciplined marches and "fine rhetoric" about civic values by voluntary militias and disorderly "tavern frolics" and informal excursions by members of the laboring classes. In Milwaukee native-born inhabitants spent the evening of the Fourth listening to serious orations about moral and civic values. German immigrants, on the other hand, gathered at local beer-gardens for fun and merrymaking.[15]

Ordinary Americans in this period not only exhibited some disinterest in patriotic rituals but also began increasingly to use the patriotic symbols and language of the Revolution for their own economic ends. Thus, some reformers and working-class organizations after 1830 began to celebrate the heroes of the Revolutionary era as defenders of individual rights rather than heroic builders of a nation. Instead of calling for deference to structures of national authority, they used patriotic language to support their claims for greater political power and social equality. Thus, it was the leaders of the early labor movement in New York and Philadelphia in the 1830s that revived the memory of Tom Paine and celebrated his notions of the right of workers to receive the full value of the products they produced and the need for all classes to share in the economic abundance of the nation. Opponents of labor claimed that such associations were disloyal because they were detrimental to the national interest. But some historians have insightfully revealed how groups of workers, especially craftsmen, marched through streets during this period proclaiming that the nation-state was not a symbol of patriotic duty but one of the rights of ordinary people to political equality with elites and economic justice. In many instances, as Sean Wilentz has noted, proud artisans and journeymen proclaimed that the continued survival of the Republic itself depended on the well-being of proud, independent producers such as themselves. In Cincinnati in the 1840s workers carried the American flag along with appeals for public support for their economic demands during Fourth of July parades.[16]

Although the Civil War stimulated considerable patriotic fervor in the North, it actually sustained rather than reversed the growth of a more contentious and complex public dialogue over memory. The war drew thousands of ordinary people into dramatic episodes of tragedy and sacrifice. In a sense it furthered the politicization of ordinary lives initiated by the intensification of class differences. It had reconstructed the experiences of individuals and families in a way that the normal passage of time usually did not and, consequently, created a tremendous imperative to understand the drastic changes that shook people's lives and express how that reality felt. More on how individuals came to terms with a recent past of war and dislocation in the South will be presented below. But the aftermath of the war created countless possibilities for commemoration that had not been so noticible before.

People who experienced the war instituted a broad range of commemorative activities that viewed the wartime experience of ordinary people—the soldiers and those that grieved for them and supported them—in terms of a "cult of sacrifice." But the metaphor of sacrifice was defined in two ways. It could relate to the grief and sorrow people felt over the loss of friends and ancestors. This was its vernacular meaning. It could also stand as an act of loyalty or a contribution to the salvation of the nation itself. The creation of the medal of honor program during the war allowed the government to play a more direct role in official commemoration and in the creation of heroes than had been the case prior to 1860 when heroic symbols emerged in less rationalized and, perhaps, democratic ways.

Commemoration immediately after the war was preoccupied with a vernacular interest: grieving for the dead. Memorial Day became a time not only when ordinary people expressed their personal feelings toward ordinary people from their past but, as Mary Ryan has demonstrated, when women assumed prominent roles in public commemoration. In the South, just after the war, memory was placed not so much in the service of cultural leaders or structures of government but directed toward the needs of people to come to terms with death, defeat, and devastation. Beautiful cemeteries, "cities of the dead," were the monuments that people built. In Richmond Memorial Day became an occasion when normal activity ceased and thousands of citizens walked toward Hollywood Cemetery carrying floral arrangements. In time the officers of this memorial place raised funds to bring back over twenty-nine hundred Confederate dead from Gettysburg for burial.[17]

National monuments to obscure fallen soldiers were created in the decade of the 1890s when Congress established national battlefields at Chickamauga, Chattanooga, Antietam, Shiloh, Vicksburg, and Gettysburg. Railroad companies were able to exploit these battlefields to stimulate tourist traffic and veterans from the North and the South gathered at some of them to demonstrate national unity, but the underlying interest served by the original construction of these symbols was the need of ordinary people to express sorrow and honor for the dead.[18]

UNREGULATED MEMORY

Raw political and economic conflict dominated the final quarter of the nineteenth century. A growing business class in the North and the South sought to nationalize the economy and expand corporate power. Workers, farmers, immigrants, and other ordinary people struggled to regulate that effort in ways that would temper the breathtaking pace of change and allow for their participation in the formation of public and economic policy. The resulting clash of interests produced not only class and political conflict but sharp cultural exchanges over the issue of public memory.

Cultural leaders, especially entrepreneurs, intellectuals, and professionals, in the North and the South intervened in the discussion over memory in ways that celebrated the role of elites who came before them and ideals such as material progress that they cherished. Prominent members of New York society organized a lavish celebration of the centennial of Washington's inaugural in 1889 partially because they saw the first president as a product of "colonial nobility" and a representation of how important all elites were to American society. During the celebration of the four-hundredth anniversary of the landing of Columbus in 1892, businessmen and civic leaders organized massive parades in Chicago and New York that reinforced notions of civic order with large contingents of military units and orderly citizens marching in the various fraternal and ethnic units. In a period of intense class conflict, it was Italian-American businessmen riding in carriages that led the Italian parade in Chicago and not lowly immigrant workers.[19]

The 1876 centennial exposition held in Philadelphia to commemorate the birth of the nation revealed just how influential business leaders in the late nineteenth century could be. The chief organizers of the event were mostly "self-made men" so dominant in the public and economic life of the late nineteenth century. General Joseph Hawley, a newspaper publisher and former congressman, was president of the centennial commission. John Walsh, a Philadelphia merchant, was head of the centennial's board of finance and, along with others, represented Philadelphia's very real interest in promoting itself as well as commemorating a national event. Other exposition planners included manufacturers, lawyers, and prominent officials. The majority of the financial support for the event came from the city of Philadelphia and private supporters; little was forthcoming from government on any level. The planners, moreover, were quite conscious of expositions that had been recently held in Vienna, Paris, and London, which received more public financing, and wanted above all else to impress citizens here and abroad with the nation's achievements in technology. Progress, a concern close to the heart of the rising industrial elite, was paramount here not patriotism, although no one for a moment proposed that patriotic rituals be forgotten.[20]

Patriotic ritual and history were abundant at the centennial. At the opening ceremonies President Grant spoke and was escorted into the grounds by over four thousand military personnel. An orchestra played "Hail Columbia" as the nation still did not have a national anthem. On July 4, 1876, patriotic oratory and a parade of Civil War veterans took place much as would be expected. And visitors viewed a nine-foot working model of George Washington rising from his tomb at regular intervals.

The central feature of the event, however, was not a historical or patriotic relic but a technological marvel. Machinery Hall was the exhibition's most spectacular attraction, and the Corliss Engine was the centerpiece of the hall that everyone came to see. Many considered the steam engine to be the "prime symbol of the centennial," the ultimate manifestation of American technological progress. The message for public memory here was that the past had been a prologue to the attainment of a sophisticated material civilization; working-class interpretations of a past supportive of equal rights were not to be heard at this event. It was American material progress, and inferentially, the group of industrial leaders supposedly responsible for it, that merited citizen loyalty and respect.[21]

In the four decades following the 1876 centennial celebration, American industrialists continued to organize giant expositions and fairs. In this period over one hundred million people attended events like the Chicago World's Fair (1893), the Pan American Exposition in Buffalo (1901), and the St. Louis World's Fair (1904). Created by leading merchants and entrepreneurs in their respective cities to promote local economies and celebrate technological progress, they were intended, in the words of Robert Rydell, to "organize the direction of society from a particular class perspective."[22]

These exhibitions were more than commemorative activities but contained ample amounts of interpretations of the past. Native American life, for instance, was presented in exhibits of tepees, artifacts, and dances. The object, however, was not ultimately to study culture but to use Native Americans as a baseline for measuring the extent of material progress that a business class felt it had created. It was partially for this reason that the ethnological collecting of Native American artifacts became "frenzied" in the late nineteenth century. American and European museums bought and hoarded these objects in order to accentuate the material achievements of the present and offer an understanding of the "historical trajectory" in which they resided.[23]

Visitors to the fairs received a version of the relationship between the past and the present that primarily served the interests of cultural leaders. The past was essentially a story of enterprising individuals improving upon what they found. Change was constant but desirable and purposeful. Most of what had come before, in other words, had only one aim: to prepare the way for a technologically sophisticated society led by industrialists and entrepreneurs. In this late century triumph of a business class and a national economy, the symbols of progress, were treated in a manner that was not restrained by very much patriotic symbolism and rhetoric. In such an atmosphere memory became largely a servant of a particular social group.[24]

Business and commercial interests were not only redesigning public memory in northern cities but in southern ones as well. In literature, schooling, and in public commemorative activities, Southerners began, by the 1880s, to devote an immense amount of attention to the formulation of a memory narrative called the "Lost Cause." In this public version of the Civil War southern soldiers had fought bravely but were simply outnumbered by the forces of the North. Southerners had a noble cause and had no reason to feel ashamed. Indeed, their leaders such as Robert E. Lee had preached sectional reconciliation after the war instead of continued resistance and, thus, could be counted as patriots to the nation-state.

This explanation of the past, which Gaines Foster has called a "public memory," served not only the psychological needs of defeated Southerners but especially the powerful interests of a rising class of southern industrialists who were anxious to resume activity with the North and who were assuming roles once played by the region's aristocracy. In their attempt to absolve the region of guilt and resume commerce with a growing national economy, they de-emphasized commemorative activities centered on grief and sorrow for the dead and defeat itself and fostered a memory designed to speed the process of reunification while preserving something of a sense of regional pride. Conveniently they were able to link, in the view of Morris Janowitz, loyalty to a region to loyalty to a nation and maintain a traditional respect for the military and for authority.[25]

No southern military leader and authority figure achieved greater status in this construction of public memory than Robert E. Lee. By 1900 this former leader of the revolt against the nation-state was becoming a patriotic hero and, in some areas of the South, more popular than Washington. The image of Lee was promoted not only by southern business leaders but by educators, clergymen, and other professionals in the region who shared their desire to rehabilitate the image of the South in the nation. Lee's picture was placed in southern schools, statues were erected to him, and celebrations of his birthday in Richmond attracted crowds in excess of one hundred thousand people.[26]

Ordinary people took part in many of the commemorative events orchestrated by business classes and cultural leaders during the era of national economic expansion. Because they might have derived gratification and enjoyment from these activities and took solace in some of their interpretations of past and present reality, however, did not mean that they abandoned their continuing attempt to state commemorative interests which were more directly related to their political and personal needs. This was especially evident in the many activities of the Knights of Labor in the 1880s. Leon Fink, in his examination of the group, described how the Knights formulated a political ideology that selectively drew its tenets from the Republican ideals of the Revolutionary era. Specifically, they attacked the growing inequality in society by invoking the Revolutionary era's calls for equal rights for all citizens rather than a vision of a community pursuing progress under the leadership of a business class. Fink revealed that the Knights often organized the only Independence Day parade in a town as a means of promoting their political goals. He claimed that their celebrations of Independence Day and Memorial Day were so "conspicuously sentimental," that their leaders frequently felt compelled to defend the organization from "spread-eagleism" and "Yankee doodleism."[27]

The longstanding tension between the classes over the proper celebration of the Fourth of July was resumed with vigor in the following century. Ordinary people frequently used the day to pursue leisure-time activities rather than to honor historical symbols; cultural leaders continued to exhibit a sense of uneasiness over the neglect of patriotic commemorative activities and the potential for disorder that appeared to them implicit in the behavior of ordinary people on such occasions. In Pittsburgh historian Frank Couvares explained how local fire companies, which were at the heart of strong, working-class neighborhoods, assumed the task of organizing Fourth of July celebrations in the 1870s and 1880s. In such activities patriotic speeches were brief and most attention was directed toward the enjoyment of events like balloon rides, chariot races, and parades which allowed various groups of tradesmen and craftsmen to display their products and skill. In Worcester, Massachusetts, during the same period, newspapers actually complained that the working class had "desecrated" Independence Day by chasing "lubricated pigs." Drinking was so widespread in the town that local papers claimed that the day was devoted only to "liquid patriotism." Residents of Worcester's middle-class neighborhoods were even victims of pranks and vandalism on the day. And French-Canadian residents actually displayed more interest in celebrating St. Jean Baptiste Day ten days prior to the Fourth of July.[28]

The proliferation of ethnic and class antagonisms in the late nineteenth century in fact stimulated a broad effort on the part of many civic and cultural leaders, especially from the business and professional classes, to regulate public behavior during commemorative periods. In Pittsburgh public ceremonies and games were staged by community leaders to replace the events formerly run by fire companies and neighborhood associations. After 1900 a Safe and Sane Fourth of July movement attempted to regulate rowdy behavior and accidents by regulating the use of fireworks. In many locations social workers and educators organized festivals and pageants for immigrant groups to encourage them to demonstrate their loyalty on the Fourth rather than simply have a good time.[29]

Ordinary people not only put commemorative time to "unintended uses," but articulated historical messages of their own. The most powerful historical symbol they expressed in the later century was that of the pioneer. As it was used and generally understood in commemorations and reunions, pioneers stood for ordinary people from the past who were praised not so much for founding a nation but for starting families and local communities. They were recognized for the role they had played in preserving traditional values, even if they had actually fostered change, instead of promoting a hasty rush toward material growth. Pioneers certainly could be patriots, but they were also strongly loyal to vernacular structures such as towns and ethnic communities. Above all, however, they were the antithesis of business leaders who were promoting rapid change and the centralization of economic and political life. Not surprisingly, the symbol was expressed most strongly where economic and professional elites had the least influence—in the small towns and ethnic settlements of the Midwest and in the Great Plains.

Pioneers competed effectively for symbolic space with patriotism and progress during the celebration of the nation's centennial anniversary in 1876. In Des Moines, Iowa, on July 4, 1876, Old Settler Associations held picnics and reunions of local residents, and German immigrants sponsored a centennial ball to honor ancestors. In a major parade and civic celebration, organized by local officials and businessmen, themes of patriotism and progress had to share the line of march with those of pioneer life. Moving under an arch that held six-foot portraits of Washington and Franklin, the parade contained floats and groups of marchers that represented sturdy pioneers building cabins and settling the virgin prairie, ethnic and fraternal societies, farmers carrying banners that proclaimed pride in Iowa agricultural progress including statistics on the number of bushels of corn produced, and finally, representations of George Washington and his bodyguards dressed in "full Continental uniforms and mounted" passing in review. The national celebration of progress and patriotism could not be presented in a local ceremony in nearly as narrow a manner as it had been at the centennial exposition in Philadelphia.[30]

Commemorations in some places excluded celebrations of patriotism and progress completely. In 1876 Congress passed a resolution asking citizens to compile brief histories of their particular localities for deposit with the Library of Congress. Contrasting one local record from rural Iowa with the celebrations in Des Moines and Philadelphia revealed slightly different views of a past worth commemorating. Instead of the attention devoted to technological progress and the effort to promote notions of advancement, the "Centennial Sketch History of Grant Township, Lyon County, Iowa" was much more concerned with recording the achievements of ordinary people and ancestors. The handwritten manuscript left behind at the Library of Congress listed the names of the first child born in the township in 1871, the first person to die, and the first couple to be married. An attachment to local place rather than a nation was evident in the account of the settlement of the first white colony. The report indicated that settlers first came from Wisconsin in 1871 to establish homes on the "beautiful prairies" and indicated that they had received reports in advance of the "wonderful beauty and fertility of the soil." The local history described in vivid detail how the settlers suffered during the first winter in Iowa. They were ill prepared for the cold and endured frostbite and food shortages. These pioneers were called "courageous" and praised for their cooperative spirit (rather than individual achievement) in helping each other through difficult circumstances. Pioneer women were especially lauded for overcoming adversity.[31]

Pioneer celebrations and special anniversaries held throughout the Midwest at the end of the nineteenth century invariably focused primary attention on the first generation of white settlers in a particular place. A pioneer picnic in Muskegon County, Michigan, in 1882, exhibited pioneer artifacts such as a knapsack and a mortar for cracking corn. At the "Great Pioneer Picnic of 1887," in the same county, over five thousand people attended, and a reporter was on hand to actually record the reminiscences of the early white settlers. The obligatory orator recalled that in his youth he used to read history and mythology and "did not know where history began and mythology ended." He declared now, however, that the reminiscences and gatherings at pioneer picnics would preserve "history, so far as possible." Similarly, at the centennial celebration at Gallipolis, Ohio, in 1890, local people celebrated pioneers by filling a "centennial relic room" with items handed down in their families, from a grandfather's hammer to a shawl made by a citizen's mother seventy years ago and candlesticks brought by immigrant ancestors from Europe.[32] On the twenty-fifth anniversary of the arrival of Dutch immigrants to Holland, Michigan, in 1872, a parade was held. Included in the line of march was a wagon carrying the thirteen "surviving pioneers" who had come to the "kolonie." In 1887 at Zeeland, Michigan, townsfolk erected a permanent memorial shaft in the center of the village carrying the names of the first pioneers "as well as the names of the first who died in the hard struggle against the primeval forest."[33]

It was also during the late nineteenth century that Abraham Lincoln slowly emerged as a major historical symbol. Certainly Lincoln, as any symbol, served a number of interests at once. He could rival Washington in his patriotism and service to the nation and exceed him in his martyrdom. Blacks often honored Lincoln for his role in emancipation, but such a symbol could also suggest that black people needed to be deferential to whites. But in the late nineteenth century, the Lincoln symbol was also a pioneer symbol. He was an ordinary man from humble beginnings, unlike Washington, who retained some of his pioneer mannerisms and ways of thinking. It was, in fact, a book by Lincoln's law partner, William Herndon, published in 1889, that solidified Lincoln's image as a pioneer hero. Herndon, according to historian David Donald, attempted to deliberately distinquish Lincoln from his "eastern contemporaries" and actually interviewed pioneer settlers in Illinois and Indiana to acquire just enough facts to enhance his pioneer status.[34] It may very well have been the ability of the Lincoln symbol to mediate the interests of ordinary people in pioneers and the interests of cultural leaders in national loyalty that ultimately explained its wide appeal.

A POLITICAL CULTURE FOR THE NEXT CENTURY

The unrestrained drive of a business class for political and cultural power in the late nineteenth century and the powerful defense of local and vernacular interests it provoked actually created a willingness on the part of many social groups for some form of cooperation. A political vision emerged that emphasized the interest all social groups had in maintaining the viability of an evolving national economy and the need for a more powerful nation-state that could mediate and regulate both politics and culture. The move toward national integration was led primarily by leaders of growing corporations whose fate was increasingly tied to the new national market. But they were not alone, as Martin Sklar has argued, and were joined by the burgeoning ranks of professionals who derived much prestige from their national ties to peers, reformers who sought to limit the excesses of class conflict and economic deprivation, and workers and farmers in numerous locales who saw the need to maintain some form of regulation over both the growing economy and corporate leaders. Inevitably the collective desire to influence a national economy led to a related need to enhance the power of the nation-state—an entity that many perceived to be an ally in their quest for moderating the unregulated change and competition of the late century.[35]

The movement toward the centralization of political power led to the formulation by the early twentieth century of what Sklar calls "corporate liberalism," a political vision that dominated American politics and public discourse through much of the twentieth century. At the foundation of this vision was the belief that a powerful nation-state could regulate economic life without destroying the essential power and privilege of large corporations and that a need existed for a pluralist political process that would allow the participation of a number of groups—laborers, farmers, professionals—in the fashioning of public policy. Although cooperation was emphasized more than competition, a pluralistic system did not foreclose the possibility that some interests would dominate others from time to time. By implication, consequently, the discourse over public memory in the twentieth century would be shaped to a greater extent than it had been in the century before by the administration of state power over pluralistic interests.[36]

The reconstruction of the political system was accompanied by other forms of national consolidation. Voters were mobilized increasingly by centralized educational campaigns. Community-based political parades and rallies, the basis for the vast public support for political parties in the nineteenth century, declined in importance as locales were flooded with publications from distant offices. Intellectuals and other citizens in the North even transformed the meaning of American nationalism and patriotism after the Civil War by creating an "organic theory of nationalism." As Merle Curti explained, this new definition celebrated the nation as the "highest form of human association" and discounted arguments that individuals and locales had any right to break their ties to it. Curti located the impulse for this cultural defense of national power in the search for social unity and cohesion that was exacerbated by the intensified class and ethnic struggles of the late century.[37]

Few supporters of the new order of corporate liberalism and central power, however, could have forseen the expansion of state power that took place during World War I. State control was extended into areas of economic planning, labor relations, and public opinion. Put simply, World War I enlarged the statist dimension of corporate liberalism at the expense of the pluralist dimension. Groups at odds with the nation-state's war agenda—usually labor and ethnic leaders—were prevented from participating in public exchanges. The trend toward educational politics was accelerated by the launching of a systematic propaganda effort to defend the interests of the nation-state and the importance of unquestioned patriotism. Although the exercise of state power subsided considerably after 1920, its presence did not shrink in ways that it had in the century before.

Corporate liberalism survived the postwar period and business, labor, agriculture, and the state all worked to exert some regulation of the economy and public policy. But few would argue that the corporate body, or what Ellis Hawley has called the "associative state," was composed of representatives with equal amounts of power or influence over state action. In the 1920s business interests stood above those of labor which had been weakened during the war. In the following decade the situation was reversed as New Deal policy simultaneously responded to the demands and needs of the working class and regulated those calls and the claims of other groups by further consolidating state power. These trends would be evident in the expressions of memory as well.[38]

The culmination of a long historical process that consolidated the power of the nation-state and liberal corporatism came with the Cold War. The enforced consolidation and centralization of American life during World War II was maintained during years of Cold War tensions. Armed conflict was followed by ideological battles with the Soviet Union and national pride in the achievement of defeating Germany and Japan. Yet, the period after 1945 witnessed a greater degree of pluralist politics than the one after 1918. Extremism of any kind could not be tolerated if some degree of consensus and unity were to be achieved to resist the Soviet threat. Labor radicalism had already been tempered somewhat in the war itself, and McCarthyism would eventually be restrained. The 1950s and the early 1960s essentially witnessed a period of relative equilibrium among vernacular interests in the public sphere and an agreement that the nation-state must be defended and supported.[39]

It was not until the later 1960s that the "decorum of the liberal consensus" was shattered.[40] The power and the policies of the nation-state and the national economic system, the foundation of the consensus, were bitterly attacked by Vietnam War protestors, angry youth, alienated blacks, and women. Vernacular power for blacks, neighborhoods, and even whites was espoused. Public discourse was characterized more by discussion over citizen rights than citizen duties, something that had not taken place for a considerable amount of time. Reservations over a structure of power that had slowly drained strength from local communities, ethnic groups, and ordinary people were expressed in a determined fashion. Links between personal lives and the nation-state, solidified during the past five decades, appeared weakened.

In the nineteenth century the power of the nation-state as a cultural and political symbol was effectively challenged by vernacular interests. Its ability to dominate the discourse over the past was frequently in doubt, and vernacular interests clashed in very direct ways. Indeed, it was the unregulated nature of both political and cultural conflict between vernacular interests that helped explain the rising power of the nation-state in the twentieth century and its ability to dominate collective memory. The political structure that fostered a patriotic and nationalistic public memory in the first half of the twentieth century was the result not only of contemporary events but of debates and arguments that had come in the century before.

Part Two

COMMUNAL FORUMS

We are gathered here today as representatives of the second and third generations, to lay a wreath of tribute on the graves of the first born here, as the connecting link between an arduous past, and let us hope, an honorable future; here as Americans by birth to honor the memory of our parents, Americans by choice.

—Speech at commemoration of the Swedish immigrant settlement at Bishop Hill, Illinois, 1916

Nothing can ever take away the love a heart holds dear. Fond memories linger every day. Remembrances keep him near.

—Memorial Day statement published by family of Korean War casualty, Indianapolis, 1968

CHAPTER THREE

The Construction of Ethnic Memory

THE CULTURAL POWER that patriotic and nationalistic symbols enjoyed in the nineteenth century was reinforced in this century by the expansion of government power on both state and national levels. At the beginning of this century vernacular and official cultures competed for cultural space without significant interference from governmental structures. Government, however, would take a more assertive role in mediating and ultimately dominating the various interests that had a stake in the discussion over public memory. Led by a broad band of professionals and bureaucrats, the promotion of official culture and its dogmatic stress on nationalism, patriotism, unity, and social order, eventually diminished the influence of businessmen and the celebration of material progress in commemorations. Buttressed by periods of war and economic crisis, the political and cultural power of the nation-state grew to a point in the twentieth century when it distorted all expressions of vernacular memory.

The impact of growing federal power and the consequent stress on patriotism and civic duty had a distinct impact on local commemorations in ethnic communities, cities, states, and regions. In the decade after World War I heightened attempts were made to replace vernacular interest in immigrant and local pioneers with expressions of loyalty to the nation-state. The effort on the part of cultural leaders to incorporate vernacular cultures into official ones actually accelerated during the 1930s and during the years of warfare in the 1940s. These attempts did encourage creative responses on the part of subcultures themselves in a valiant attempt to preserve something of their own interests. That response and the actions that prompted it took place on a number of communal levels, in fact, and constitute the focus of this chapter and the next.

The thrust toward the nationalization of culture and the contest over the definition of public memory was carried out in no uncertain terms in American ethnic communities. Ethnic and minority groups certainly had interests in ancestors and historic places that did not conform specifically to official visions that increasingly stressed loyalty to the nation. These groups came at different times to the United States, experienced uneven patterns of material advancement and possessed recollections from disparate homelands. It is not too much to presume that the public memory they discussed and constructed in the United States contained ingredients unique to the representative groups, and symbols and messages at variance with those found in national and state commemorative activities. At the same time the dialogue over memory in ethnic communities could not ignore the discussion that took place in the larger society or the various interests that asserted themselves within ethnic communities. The manner in which ethnic and official constructions of culture affected each other is little understood.

In general most scholars have viewed ethnic culture and heritage as a strategy by which people organized their lives. For some ethnicity is a source of identity or "genuine culture" from which people create a community based upon shared perceptions of "primordial attachments." Historians such as Kathleen Conzen have shown how such ethnic solidarity was pursued as an end in itself in order to retain a spirit of community that was perceived to have flowered in the homeland and insulate group members from criticisms of their cultures made by outsiders. For other scholars, ethnic identity is merely a means or a "strategy" by which groups mobilize their members to pursue scarce resources in society or political power. In both of these instances ethnic communities come together in a somewhat autonomous fashion to pursue objectives of their own choosing.[1] By inference, therefore, they are fully capable of creating a culture and, consequently, a memory separate from that which exists in the dominant society.

This brief survey of ethnic commemorative activity, however, suggests two points relevant to our current understanding of ethnic culture. First, the construction of memory in ethnic enclaves could not be completed without the participation of powerful interests outside the ethnic communities and negotiations between various interests within the community itself. Secondly, the mobilization of ethnic communities for economic or political objectives never took place without the simultaneous pursuit and interpretation of "primordial attachments." To put the matter another way, the discussion over ethnic memory, whether it was based on the need to commemorate a unique past or secure influence and acceptance in the present, almost always involved a reconciliation of personal and political, vernacular and official, agendas, and was invariably distorted by powerful interests.

In a related discussion Werner Sollors has explained that the construction of ethnic culture was always fashioned from the tension that existed between people's desire both to honor and break their ancestral and familial ties of *descent* and to express their *consent* to a new culture of individualism and new political structures. Although Sollors overemphasizes the extent that this tension resulted from a purely personal conflict and underestimates the degree that it was fought on social and political ground, his notion of cultural tension can reinforce the larger argument made here that ethnic memory and ethnic culture were the result of an "interweaving of cultural threads" in the present.[2]

American history is replete with examples of minority groups mounting spirited defenses of their own versions of the past and resisting pressures to acquiesce to nationally dominant traditions. Thus, one can cite the oration in 1852 of Frederick Douglass that proclaimed that blacks had no reason to rejoice over America's Independence Day. "We have to do with the past only as we can make it useful to the present and the future," Douglass explained in a statement that came close to actually defining public memory. He told whites that the inheritance of justice and liberty bequeathed "by your fathers is shared by you, not by me." He asserted that the Fourth of July is "yours" but "not mine." Not surprisingly, blacks continued to express a language of descent rather than consent and celebrated a number of independence days including the day that marked the abolition of slavery in the West Indies (August 1, 1834) well into the twentieth century. Scholars did find, however, that eventually black historical celebrations and pageants began to show evidence of a mixture of minority and nationalist themes. Thus, a glorious African past was as likely to be celebrated as were elements of American history pertaining to blacks such as Lincoln's decree of emancipation.[3]

This chapter seeks to probe the nature of ethnic memory as revealed in commemorative activities held largely during the first half of the twentieth century. The attempt here is not to be all inclusive but to suggest fundamental points about the origins and functions of collective memory within ethnic communities by looking selectively at ethnic celebrations in a number of rural and urban regions. Thus, the commemorative activities of Swedes in Illinois, Mennonites in Kansas, and others are examined for clues as to what may have taken place in most minority communities. Symbols and messages relevant to the "genuine culture" are viewed as well as those that may have been manufactured by interests inside and outside the ethnic group for purposes of mobilizing political sentiments.

SWEDES

Between the beginnings of Swedish immigrant settlement in the Midwest in the 1840s and World War II a good deal of commemorative activity took place at Bishop Hill, Illinois. On that site in 1846 a small band of Swedes, fleeing religious persecution in their homeland, founded a colony under the leadership of a religious dissenter, Eric Janson. Moving to the United States through a long and perilous ocean voyage and following stage routes and canal routes inland, the expedition arrived at Chicago and then moved to this spot on the prairie in western Illinois.

Throughout the next century, the story of the Bishop Hill settlement came to resemble a point of origin for Swedish-American history in the Midwest. Swedes, of course, had settled in colonial America, but most members of the ethnic group in this country traced their direct lineage to the migration stream that flowed into the Midwest beginning in the 1840s. The reference point for Swedish-American memory went back to the homeland and to the pioneers who left it for the Midwest in the middle parts of the nineteenth century. It did not inevitably begin with the birth of a new nation and heroes who fashioned it.

Early commemorative activities at Bishop Hill suggested that Swedish-Americans held a deep respect for their immigrant ancestors and made them the most important symbol of their past. These pioneers, of course, stood for many things. They were, after all, ordinary people who overcame difficult problems of geography, climate, and politics, and as such were always an inspiration to ordinary people who struggled with life in the present. They also represented people who initiated significant changes in their lives and defied religious authority when they left Sweden. Sollors' discussion on the use of "generations" as a metaphor suggests that the very act of constructing a "pioneer generation" was also a move of separation by younger Swedes who now saw themselves as a new group and, therefore, part of a different culture. It remained to be seen what, if any, of these themes predominated in the ceremonies that celebrated pioneers in ensuing years.[4]

The first occasion to formally mark the significance of the Bishop Hill settlement was a semicentennial celebration in 1896. Formal activities focused upon the dedication of a monument "to the memory of the hardy pioneers." The degree to which the image of these first settlers may have represented the desirability of social change or the need to make a commitment to the new nation was not made explicit at this event. Rather, the focus here was on ordinary people—the hardy pioneer overcoming obstacles and maintaining his or her faith and the "ritual" of reaffirming familial and communal ties through visiting and talking. Indeed, such rituals of reunion were increasingly important in a new culture that fostered individual mobility.

The impetus for the 1896 celebration came not only from the de-

2. Old Settlers Reunion, 1896, Bishop Hill, Illinois. Courtesy of Bishop Hill Heritage Association.

scendants of the pioneer band, the second generation, but from surviving members of the original colony such as John Root. Pioneer relics including old plows, spinning wheels, grain cradles, linen goods, and guns were displayed with respect not shame. And several thousand present and former residents of the settlement and other Swedish-Americans from the region gathered to hear speeches praising the newcomers of 1846.

A key address was delivered by the minister of the Swedish church in the community, which now numbered several hundred. The Reverend Axel Gabrielson justified the historical importance of Bishop Hill and dedicated a monument that served as a symbolic presentation from younger Swedish-Americans to the representatives of the pioneer generation still alive. He called Bishop Hill a "celebrated place" and praised the "brave men and women from the distant Northland" who built it. Showing no signs of alienation between the first and second generations, Gabrielson reaffirmed the notion of continuity over change and the intense interest of the assembled group in their personal past when he exclaimed: "In behalf also of the young manhood and womanhood of Bishop Hill, who have shared none of the hardships of the pioneers of forty-six, forty-eight, and fifty, but who today consciously enjoy, in the heritage they possess, the fruit of the privations and labor of those heroes, living and dead, I bid all present here, welcome to the fiftieth anniversary of the founding of Bishop Hill."[5]

John Root, who was born in Bishop Hill in 1849, stood for all of the pioneer generation and accepted the monument. Root's address was a ringing defense of the movement of these Swedes to Illinois. Claiming that Bishop Hill was the Scandinavian Plymouth Rock, he recited the obstacles that the immigrants overcame. He expressed amazement how they had endured starvation and pestilence and cleared the forest and turned the soil. He described for his listeners in detail structures that had been built by these pioneers that no longer stood. Root recalled a "grand obelisk" of a chimney on the flouring mill that towered one hundred feet above the ground. He lamented, in fact, its ultimate destruction and felt that it could have served as a "fitting monument for the admiration of coming generations."[6]

But even so staunch a defender of the pioneer past as Root could not end his oration without some acknowledgment of the role these pioneers played in the process of building a nation. Although their historical movement was rooted in religious dissent rather than in nation building, Root claimed that these early settlers had always been "true to their adopted country and its flag." They formed a company of soldiers immediately at the outbreak of the Civil War and "bravely defended the union." He recalled their participation in various battles and how some of them had failed to return "while their memory is ever kept sacred by kindred and friends on each recurring Memorial Day." Just three years after Root's speech another monument was erected in Bishop Hill to "The Loyal Sons of Bishop Hill" who fought for the union.[7]

On the seventieth anniversary of the founding of Bishop Hill in 1916, celebrants revealed the coexistence of both vernacular and official cultures by expressing continued pride in the accomplishments of the pioneer generation and awe at the "relics" which were again brought out for display. On this occasion paintings done of the earliest settlers were completed and displayed and "old colony buildings" were opened to the public for several hours so that visitors could view the old church and other structures. Visitors could look at Swedish Bibles brought to America, the autobiography of Eric Janson, prayerbooks, a Swedish hand loom and shuttle for weaving, candlesticks, money chests, and two ox-yokes. A much smaller amount of space was devoted to objects of a patriotic nature but the exhibition did include an army canteen and rifle from the Civil War. The 1916 ceremonies were held in a grove of trees, some of which were planted by the original colonists. Speechmaking largely celebrated the first generation and, by implication, cultural links to the homeland and the ethnic past. Henry S. Henschen, for instance, declared:

> We are gathered here today as representatives of the second and third generations, to lay a wreath of tribute on the graves of the firstborn here, as the connecting links between an arduous past and, let us hope, an honorable future; here, as Americans by birth to honor the memory of our parents, Americans by choice; here, to learn for ourselves and to teach our children the history and traditions of our fathers; here, to remind each other of that little country [Sweden], . . . which our fathers knew so much.[8]

Celebrations continued periodically at Bishop Hill until World War II. A slight change in the character of the events became noticeable, however. The major attention and reverence given to the first pioneers, their perseverance in an inhospitable environment, and their search for religious freedom was supplemented by a growing number of leisure-time activities. Formal ceremonies were increasingly followed by forms of entertainment, thus allowing Swedish-Americans to use these occasions as opportunities to reaffirm social ties and pursue personal pleasure as much as to honor their ancestral past. In 1926 short reminiscences by survivors of the original colony were followed by a band concert. A decade later a historical parade with participants in pioneer costumes and a formal address commemorating the pioneers were followed by a baseball game and a dance. The next day the issue of material progress during the difficult times of the 1930s was addressed with an "Industrial Parade" which allowed for an expression of hope that the industrial economy would soon return to a healthy state. Baseball and dancing again followed the symbolic activities.[9]

In the period after World War II Swedish-Americans throughout the Midwest mobilized their resources to commemorate an entire century of Swedish settlement in the region. Shifting focus from the small point at Bishop Hill to the entire group, the centennial celebration of 1948 attracted the support of a large and diverse ethnic community and cast the discussion and commemoration of ethnic memory into a more complex mold than had been evident in the rather localized and personalized activity at Bishop Hill. In a striking manner, moreover, the growing body of Swedish professionals and other members of the group's middle class took an exceedingly active role in the event and, consequently, expanded the patriotic content of the celebration considerably beyond the role it had played at Bishop Hill.

Plans for the 1948 celebration grew out of conferences of church leaders of the Augustana Lutheran Church at Rock Island, Illinois, in 1940. Church officials were motivated not so much by a desire to honor the immigrant pioneers or reassert familial ties as they were to use the pioneer symbol as a means of revitalizing the spiritual values of church members. They placed the language of descent into the service of institutional leaders themselves. The interests of these religious leaders were taken up with even more vigor by a group of Swedish-American businessmen, editors, and educators in Chicago. Meeting regularly at the Swedish Club in the city, this group organized a Swedish Pioneer Centennial celebration under the direction of a chairman, Conrad Bergendoff, the head of Augustana College, and prominent Swedish-Americans such as Arthur Appleton, a Chicago industrialist, and E. A. Anderson, editor of a leading Swedish-American newspaper.[10]

For these members of the ethnic middle class any such celebration had to take into account not only the traditional interests of the group in their ancestors but issues of consent such as the close ties the leadership class had already established to American political and economic institutions. These leaders were manifestations of success and prominence in an American social structure, despite their deep ties to their ethnic past. For them the past most relevant for the present and worthy of celebration was one that included the values and institutions of the dominant society to which they were inextricably tied as well as those of a more distant past that could both provide inspiration for ordinary individuals and fulfill longings to honor personal ancestors. In letters to governors of midwestern states and other public pronouncements these centennial planners articulated their reasons why they felt the anniversary of Swedish settlement in the region should be celebrated and how desperately they wanted to link the personal interests of ordinary people to the political considerations of the state to which their lives and fortunes were so closely connected. In the political atmosphere of the Cold War, when public debate discussed potential threats to American values, centennial planners argued that the "sturdy folk" of the immigration era were "devoted to democratic principles." Planners announced that they desired not merely to recall events of a century ago, but to "emphasize the qualities and virtues that made America great." They also expressed a strong desire to strengthen the attachment to American values in the "present generation which is faced with the task of preserving our democracy in America."[11]

Honoring immigrant pioneers for their patriotic ideals and contributions to nation building may have been a concept pushed heavily by the ethnic middle class by the late 1940s, but the older pride in ancestors and interest in the homeland remained visible. Patriotic language actually mediated both official and vernacular interests, although the former was privileged over the latter. Centennial planners also insisted that American historians had neglected the role minorities such as the Swedes had played in building the "great valley of the Mississippi." Actually this "contributions" approach reinforced the mediating power of patriotism and furthered the objectives of leaders to transform the meaning of vernacular stories rather than eliminate them. Conrad Bergendoff explained that "Plymouth Rock is but one of the foundation stones of the New World." The planning committee also reiterated the traditional middle-class theme of material progress by again expressing admiration for the pioneer achievement of transforming the rural landscape into farmhouses and productive farms. This later message served the nationalist framework of placing the American past into a progressive pageant and managed to reduce the pattern of immigrant success and failure to one of collective achievement.[12]

Although planners hoped for a decentralized celebration throughout the Midwest, the major focus of attention in 1948 was Chicago. In early June a celebration took place in the city that in content and form clearly resembled the influence and predilections of the urban, middle-class leaders who organized the event. An indoor festival at the Chicago Stadium featured a chorus of three thousand trained voices, accompanied by the Chicago Symphony, singing old Swedish hymns. This was clearly not going to be a "folk" production.

Despite the claims of organizers that the event had "no political overtones," the featured speaker was Harry Truman. The President had been formally invited to the event by a delegation of Swedish-American leaders, and he used the occasion to criticize a Republican Congress that wanted to restrict immigration to the United States by limiting the number of displaced persons that could enter the country. But the main message that Truman (and his middle-class sponsors) conveyed was that the immigrants who began arriving from Sweden a century ago were ultimately nation builders who came to a land "that needed their hardy qualities." Truman felt that these pioneers provided models for "people in slums" in the 1940s who could learn from the immigrant example that the abundance that the United States enjoyed could only be achieved through hard work.[13]

Formal civic ceremonies dominated the rest of the weekend. A banquet with speechmaking and symbolic music featured addresses by Prince Bertil, son of Sweden's crown prince, and the governor of Illinois. Both men spoke to contemporary issues in this celebration of the past. Bertil talked of the need to be "vigilant" against forces of evil in the modern world; Governor Dwight H. Green explained how the lives of the Swedish pioneers served to remind all citizens of the "openness of opportunity which is the heritage of every American." Clearly, the history of immigrant pioneers was being reinterpreted in the light of contemporary political concerns.

A church service, which closed the Chicago celebration, contributed further to the conservative and official nature of the event. Pioneer immigrants were not only contributors to a nation and models for the dispossessed but were dutiful subjects of authority, a theme that was central to much public ritual in this century. Historically, some of these immigrants had disagreed with church authorities in Sweden. But in the speech of Erling Eidem, Archbishop of Uppsala and Primate of all Sweden, no hint existed that anything in the immigrant experience suggested the desirability of dissent. Rather, he claimed that those "who moved from the old home" and their descendants made a remarkable contribution to the "creation of the American nation." He told his listeners that Swedish-Americans in the 1940s could best honor their homeland and ancestors by being "good American citizens."[14]

Prince Bertil had arrived for the centennial at the head of an official delegation that included Eidem and representatives of Sweden's labor and agricultural organizations. When the group traveled to centennial activities in other parts of the Midwest, however, they found a different tone to the events than they had experienced in Chicago. In smaller towns such as Rock Island, Moline, and Rockford the festivities were less formalistic and political in their attempt to reinforce notions of order and loyalty over dissent, and more personal and local in their explicit celebration of immigrant ancestors and pioneers.

At Rock Island in early June, a huge public pageant was presented in honor of the pioneer centennial. The ideological emphasis here was not so much tied to nation building and citizenship but to the popular images and local memories of "the history of those immigrants who came to this part of the Mississippi Valley from Sweden." Produced under the sponsorship of the Lutheran Augustana Synod, which clearly had interests of its own in revitalizing the faith of its members, the pageant nevertheless shifted attention directly to the settlement experience of ordinary immigrants. Scenes portrayed the reading of "America letters" in Sweden, the crossing of the Atlantic, the building of new homes in New Sweden, Iowa, a pioneer Christmas, pioneer religious services including a colorful procession of torch-bearing worshippers and the intrusion of national events into ethnic life such as the California Gold Rush and the Civil War. Pioneer relics were again displayed near the pageant site and not far away at Bishop Hill.[15]

During the month of June a number of other events in the Rock Island area continued to honor the first-generation pioneers. Several local residents regularly cleaned and maintained the grave markers of their Swedish ancestors. During the second week of the month a pilgrimage of seven buses and over two hundred cars traveled from Augustana College to New Sweden, Iowa. Archbishop Eiden spoke again but was forced to share the stage with the honored guest who was not a prominent figure but the daughter of the first pastor of the church at New Sweden. Prince Bertil attended the dedication of a plaque erected by the state of Illinois (which had also acquired ownership of Bishop Hill as a memorial in 1946) to honor the Swedish immigrant men and women who "broke the prairie" and built homes, schools, and churches with "honest toil." And a speaker from Sweden told a group at Augustana College that during centennials they must not only think of famous leaders but of farmers and craftsmen who carried small catechism and hymn books.[16]

At Rockford the formal banquets and speechmaking evident in Chicago gave way to a parade, a pageant, and folk festival. Citizens performed Swedish dances and dressed in costumes based on old-world patterns. A pageant reminded its audience of the "determination, ingenuity, foresight, and faith of the early immigrants from Sweden." A crowd of thirty thousand, including Bertil, reviewed the centennial parade which also featured floats depicting Swedish life and customs, aspects of pioneer life, "Indians in war paint," and Swedish women in pioneer costumes. In a speech to the crowd, Bertil, ignoring the celebration of ethnic pioneers and ordinary people around him, told his listeners that above all else he knew they were "good Americans, proud citizens of their great republic" who only wanted to pause for a moment and "take stock" of their Swedish ancestors.[17]

The symbolic thrust of ethnic festivals and commemorative ceremonies, however, was not always simply divided between national and ethnic symbols. In Lindsborg, Kansas, a center of Swedish-American settlement since the late 1860s, public memory remained insulated somewhat from nationalizing tendencies for a long period of time prior to World War II. When such celebrations did change substantially, organizers sought not so much to link ethnic pioneers and culture to a nationalist interpretation of the past but attempted to use historic symbols and interests in them for commercial purposes that would benefit their town.

Lindsborg's interest in commemorating ethnic people and culture was intensified by the existence of several strong Swedish-American institutions within the community. Both the local Bethany Swedish Evangelical Lutheran Church and Bethany College were responsible for making the town a center of Swedish-American cultural activity in central Kansas. Students and faculty from Bethany organized musical, dance, and comedic presentations for the local population in the first decade of this century, usually performing their material in the Swedish language.

It was a society at the college, interested in raising more funds for the institution, that started the Swedish "May Festival" celebration in 1912. In its earliest manifestation the event consisted mostly of customs identified with the homeland such as the winding of a maypole and a "historical pageant parade" and, like the celebrations at Bishop Hill, allowed for families and friends to restate the existence of their bonds. In a detailed description provided by folklorist Larry Danielson, the historic parade was shown to be generally devoted to the story of the immigrant pioneers of the region. Indians did walk with horses to open the parade and provide a brief but familiar baseline for Swedish immigrant entry into the history of Kansas, but the remaining seven sections of the parade were devoted to immigrant themes. People from the town dressed like immigrants and carried baggage to re-create their arrival in Lindsborg and floats carried representations of the immigrant sodhouses, churches, and schoolhouses. City officials did bring up the rear of the procession but the thematic thrust had been clearly established. Little was said of major events of American history, patriotism, or even material progress. The day belonged to local memories, values, and ancestors.[18]

In the 1920s the celebration of the immigrant pioneers in Lindsborg continued but not without the inclusion of other symbols. A small but growing middle class and a population tied increasingly to American rather than Swedish political and cultural life influenced but did not change the celebration of the immigrant experience. Scenes from the 1921 pageant included a special section devoted to the pioneers that aimed to give a "clear and historically true picture of the cultural and agricultural development of this community." One scene entitled, "The Founders" included all of the pioneers who still remained in the region. But nearly equal attention was given to the history of Kansas before the arrival of the immigrants and the achievements of professions and institutions developed since the years of first settlement. Thus, scenes depicted the Indians or "aborigines in native garb," the expedition of the Spanish under Coronado, and a "squad" of cowboys riding the plains. The history of Bethany College and the growth of mercantile enterprises in the town completed the presentation and testified to the growing influence of the professional class in the discussion over public memory. Finally, one section of the pageant revealed the influence of national patriotic campaigns of the era and the feeling such campaigns created to place ancestors into national rather than just local or ethnic history. It was at this point in the dramatization that veterans of the Civil, Spanish, and World Wars were honored for keeping the United States a "free nation."[19]

A historical parade three years later reduced the attention given to the first generation slightly more, although it still remained powerful. To the cowboys, Spaniards, and Indians of 1921 were added trappers, hunters, and early mail carriers. Local Swedish Americans were displaying a greater knowledge of American and Kansas history and placing their own past into a broader context. The pioneers and Swedish educational and religious institutions each received their due respect. But material progress was also emphasized to a greater extent with depictions of the improvement of transportation on the Great Plains, the development of farm tools, and the "contributions by the businessmen of Lindsborg."[20]

During a 1938 celebration in honor of the tercentenary of Swedish settlement on the east coast, the celebration of the immigrant pioneers in Kansas appeared to be revitalized, a pattern that resembled the heightened interest in ordinary people of the past as heroes in that decade. In Lindsborg activities revolved around a display of pioneer artifacts, publications by and about the immigrant generation, and textile designs by local Swedish-Americans. The festival concluded with the singing of Swedish songs in the native language, an event organized by the college, a smorgasbord, and a "tribute to the pioneers in the Swedish language."[21]

In 1941 civic leaders, businessmen, and officials of institutions in Lindsborg met to plan the town's contribution to the quatrocentennial commemorating Coronado's journey into Kansas. Interestingly, the meeting produced not a decision to honor the Spanish explorer, something that had been officially requested by the state governor, but the initiation of a "Swedish festival." The local planning group, influenced by the success of the tulip festival in Holland, Michigan, quickly saw an opportunity to boost local pride and the local economy by reviving "Scandinavian costumes, folklore, folk dances, customs, and history."[22]

The resulting festival, called the "Svensk Hyllnings Fest" or Swedish Festival of Tribute, was clearly meant to be both a tribute to the Swedish pioneers that settled the region around Lindsborg and a device which would boost the town itself. The decision was a ringing endorsement of the power of the pioneer symbol itself and an acknowledgment of the appeal it had to a large number of ordinary individuals; no other symbol was so well established in the local public memory and capable of generating so much approval and support.

Unlike previous celebrations of the Swedish pioneers, this tribute was concerned to a much greater extent with attracting crowds from outside Lindsborg and turning a profit. In the fall of 1941 caravans of "costumed Lindsborgians" traveled to nearby towns to publicize the smorgasbord, Swedish-American entertainment, and displays and sales of Swedish crafts that would make up the festival. Much less enthusiasm was evident here for a recitation of the historical record that was so vital to earlier celebrations. A parade was held in 1941 (although not after World War II) that included some pioneer families. But this was not a celebration for the ethnic group but a performance for others who would be attracted to the community. As such, the emphasis would be put on marketable commodities such as crafts, costumes, food, and dance, and not on historical heroes and artifacts which served as sources of personal inspiration and identity.[23]

In the rush to provide entertainment, the town officials who organized the event moved quickly to create community solidarity and standards of conduct for leisure time. Citizens were told to clean up their community and take up the art of whittling so that "authentic" wood carvings could be sold for profit. They were also urged to volunteer their time and their talents to help the celebration. A plan to hold public street dances apparently appeared undignified enough that civic leaders and church groups had it replaced by "platform dancing" by special groups. In a sense the use of commemorative festivals for boosterism and profit did not include a relaxation of the standard of civic or public conduct that had been evident in the earlier well-ordered pageants and parades.[24]

The historical representation of Swedish culture by the 1940s, moreover, was also difficult to achieve. A central part of the Lindsborg festival of tribute was the wearing of "authentic" costumes from the homeland by town citizens. Local knowledge of clothing design had been largely lost over the eight decades of settlement in Kansas, however, and festival planners were forced to rely on the research of several local people into articles on Sweden which had appeared in *National Geographic Magazine* and postcards for sale in the town that depicted "brightly clothed peasants in idyllic rural settings." The result, according to Danielson, was a predominance of costume designs and colors that emanated from a province that was not the home of most of the pioneers who had settled in the central Kansas region.[25] Memories of the homeland itself were now being manipulated to suit the needs of contemporary boosters.

By the 1950s and 1960s the festival had evolved into a biannual event "that was carefully organized by a steering committee." Danielson pointed out that entertainment at the event gradually came to be performed by national celebrities instead of local, ethnic artists. The folk dances and crafts remained, but fewer people were seen in Swedish costumes. What began early in the twentieth century as a restatement of the value of ethnic customs and institutions increasingly became a collective performance for profit and boosterism; memory served the psychological needs of members of a minority group less and the profit needs of town leaders to a greater extent.[26]

NORWEGIANS

For Norwegian-Americans, clustered primarily in the upper Middle West, commemorative activities also focused strongly on the lives of the first generation. It was not surprising that they chose to use their pioneers as a basis for discussing memory within the group. People and symbols unique or important to a minority's experience were nearly always more important in ethnic memories than heroes and messages manufactured by powerful organizations outside the group. But in no sense was the proclivity of ethnic memories to focus on the first generation solely an exercise in resistance to dominant ideologies. The first generation, after all, still made a commitment to the United States or the nation and often served as powerful symbols of traditional values despite the fact that they disrupted the continuity of their lives considerably by moving. Indeed, the act of immigration very nicely reinforced a number of messages valuable to the national effort to construct a public memory in the United States. Immigrants were symbols of change but of orderly change; they simply moved to deal with economic or political troubles but still kept many basic values and refrained, in most cases, from engaging in political movements designed to alter existing social structures. Furthermore, they cast their fortunes with the American political and economic system rather than any other once they decided to remain in this country. This was an act that could easily be construed as patriotic by subsequent interpreters interested in doing so and could very well please native-born cultural leaders who had made that same decision much less consciously and painlessly.

But Norwegian-Americans in the twentieth century were never able to fully resolve the tension between their cultures of descent and consent—between their desire to express their loyalty to their ancestors and their need to manifest loyalty to new cultures and political structures. The resulting culture of ethnicity was, consequently, neither based solely in the past or the present nor in the vernacular or the official realm. Rather it was a mediating culture grounded in present attempts to reconcile conflicting personal and political pressures. To the extent that it continually placed the memory of immigrant ancestors within the material and patriotic advance of the nation, it was ironically assimilationist.

Certainly the drive to protect and preserve vernacular culture was strong, especially before World War I. As early as 1877 teachers at Luther College in Decorah, Iowa, became interested in the preservation of objects brought to this country by the immigrant generation. Toward that end, a Norwegian-American Historical Museum was founded which acquired artifacts not only from throughout the Midwest, such as a log cabin, but obtained items from the homeland as well. By the early twentieth century the exhibit at Decorah contained hundreds of pioneer relics such as large chests, tools, and textiles. In Minnesota farm implements used by the first-generation Norwegians were acquired by St. Olaf and Concordia Colleges. The fact that most of the collections were assembled from individual gifts also suggested that the impulse to preserve something associated with the experiences of ancestors was fairly widespread.[27]

During the decade before the outbreak of World War I, Norwegian-Americans actually experienced something of a revitalization of interest in the homeland. Stimulated to a great extent by Norway's separation from Sweden in 1905, Norwegians in the upper Middle

West embarked on a campaign for Scandinavian studies in the public schools and joined ethnic organizations such as "bygdelags," associations of newcomers from the same homeland region, or the Sons of Norway in greater numbers. The latter organization was especially important in the fostering of Norwegian-American cultural interests in urban areas where it possessed its greatest strength; "bygdelags" were rooted primarily in rural centers.[28]

Perhaps the largest commemorative event for Norwegians before World War I was the celebration of the centenary of the Norwegian constitution in 1914. The constitution had ended Norway's status as a Danish province. Not surprisingly, the idea for commemorating the event in the United States appeared to originate with several Norwegian-American journalists. By the early 1900s, as historian John Jenswold has pointed out, the Norwegian population in this country was becoming more urban and, consequently, the "public-life of the 'koloni'" was falling more and more under the influence of a rising class of professionals and businessmen.[29]

The observance of the centennial initiated large celebrations in Norwegian-American settlements throughout the Middle West. Parades in colorful national costumes, ethnic music festivals, church services, and dramatic presentations, all common to ethnic commemorative activities elsewhere, formed the basis of most programs. A focal point for the entire affair was a three-day festival in Minneapolis and St. Paul. A Norwegian-American newspaper commenting on the elaborate parades, countless bygdelag reunions that often consisted of rural folk coming together in the city, "thousands of Norwegian flags waving, and a dramatic representation of the life of St. Olaf, Norway's patron saint, concluded that Constitution Day had never been celebrated as impressively in a foreign country. Loyalty to America was not forgotten as a rally was held to honor survivors of a Norwegian-speaking Civil War regiment. Symbolically, however, the 1914 celebration was overwhelmingly an unabashed and highly emotional salute to the homeland.[30]

The events of World War I, however, had a distinct impact on public commemorative activities in the Norwegian-American community. The fact that Norway had remained neutral in the struggle between the United States and Germany, meant that many Norwegian-American leaders in this country were eager to demonstrate their group's loyalty to America.[31] Indeed, the major commemorative event for Norwegians in this country after World War I was as much a demonstration of an ethnic group's loyalty to the United States as it was a continued celebration of ancestors and ethnic pride. This duality in ethnic celebration, not uncommon when groups had to communicate with "significant others" in the societies in which they lived as well as among themselves, revealed the essential tension in all rituals involving memory between the interests of dominant and subordinate structures in society.

In 1925 Norwegian-Americans and their leaders were extremely anxious to commemorate the one-hundredth anniversary of the sailing of the *Restaurationen* or "The Norse *Mayflower*." A century before the little ship sailed for New York City under the direction of Lars Larson and the first group of immigrant pioneers. Apparently the impetus for the celebration came this time from the "bygdelags" who held a keen interest in commemorating the settlement of these pioneers and ancestors who settled the rural Midwest in which most of these organizations were located and who hoped the pioneer symbol would stimulate the interest of all Norwegians born in America in ethnic culture. But the committee representing nearly all of the groups' secular and religious organizations that was established to orchestrate the celebration was not about to allow ethnic messages and themes to dominate the event alone. In the patriotically charged political climate of the twenties, created in part by the mobilization of opinion during World War I and by the antiforeign animus of the native white stock, Norwegian-American leaders could not let the celebration pass without paying proper respect to the symbols and ideals of the national state.[32]

The need to emphasize patriotism and citizenship was enunciated clearly in an article in the *American Scandinavian Review* in 1925. Rasmus B. Anderson, who had actually interviewed eight passengers from the *Restaurationen*, retold the story of the voyage for his readers and emphasized that the account was "vital in the memories of people still living." But he did not want Norwegian-Americans to concentrate on folk memories alone. He stated forcefully, in a message that was aimed at both people inside and outside the ethnic community, that the Norwegian-Americans have now become Americanized. He argued, "They acquire the English language easily and make most loyal citizens. They are by nature industrious and thrifty and pay much attention to the proper education of their children. . . . The Norwegian press is as a rule enlightened, of high ideals, and is exceedingly loyal to America and its institutions."[33]

The Norse-American Centennial celebration was dominated by a major festival in Minneapolis and St. Paul. Auto caravans of Norwegian-Americans carrying slogans, such as "The Norsemen Are Coming," traveled from rural Minnesota and the Dakotas to the "Twin Cities" for the event. Local enthusiasm and slogans of ethnic pride, however, could not alter the multivocal quality of the festival. Ethnic pride could not be expressed, in the opinion of centennial planners, in a context other than a patriotic one. Gisle Bothne, chairman of the board of directors of the centennial committee, stated that "the centennial will do for those of the *Mayflower* of the North who came in 1825 what the tercentennial celebration at Plymouth Rock [1921] did for the descendants of the original *Mayflower*." Bothne felt that by celebrating the immigrants, "the past will be clarified." In other words the complexity of public memory involving Norwegian immigrants would be rendered intelligible to thousands of citizens by centennial planners and ethnic leaders. All would now realize that these immigrants were not ordinary people but nation builders who "sacrificed that we might gain wisdom, happiness, and material comfort."[34]

The explicitly patriotic aspects of the celebration were mostly formal and organized by centennial planners rather than by the thousands of Norwegian-American citizens and groups that converged upon the Twin Cities. Indeed, the administration of the entire centennial was based on modern business principles. Ethnic leaders formed a corporation, invested managerial authority in a board of directors, and sold stock to raise capital. An official of a cultural foundation in Norway arrived to give a speech in which he urged his listeners to become "legal citizens" of the countries to which they emigrated and to "be good citizens" once the citizenship rites are over. The central patriotic event of the entire affair was a visit and address by President Calvin Coolidge. Over one hundred thousand Norwegians and other citizens gathered to hear Coolidge place the immigrant past within the framework of national history. He appealed to ethnic and personal pride when he acknowledged the heroic proportions of the immigrant deeds. He praised the Norwegian immigrant stream as having no "tinge of aristocracy" and, by implication, having contributed to the democratic ideology of the United States. He called the pioneers people of "enduring courage and high character" and proclaimed them "well worthy to follow in the wake of the Pilgrim and the Cavalier." The President, moreover, expressed thankfulness that anniversary celebrations such as the Norse Centennial "produce so much patriotism."[35]

Patriotic exhortations and flag-waving children lining Coolidge's parade route, however, could not keep much of the celebration from focusing on the memory of the pioneers and the renewal of ethnic and personal ties.[36] For several days programs at the state fairgrounds included religious services in Norwegian and rallies of church youth groups. Reunions were also held by thirty-six separate bygdelags, and members came from many states and Canada. A newspaper account of some of the gatherings indicated that people sought out old neigh-

3. Norwegian-American singers at Norse-American Centennial, St. Paul, Minnesota, June 1925. Courtesy of Minnesota Historical Society.

bors and friends with whom they had lived in various American towns and many spoke in the dialects native to their homeland regions. In some cases older men and women who had been born and reared in Norway sought news of neighbors "whose memory was almost of name alone" and "tidings of village doings" reported in letters from the homeland. Other visitors listened to choral renditions of Norwegian hymns sung by groups from Minnesota and South Dakota and joined in the singing of the Norwegian national anthem.[37]

The celebration closed with the presentation of a pageant entitled "Pageant of the Northmen." This event offered a construction of memory that clearly revealed the tension between the cultures of descent and consent. Much of the drama, which proceeded in twenty-four scenes from accounts of life in the homeland to the present in the United States, expressed themes of pride in old-world culture and the sturdiness of the pioneers. Folkloric tales from Norway were acted out as well as scenes depicting the baptism of a baby born on the American frontier, an immigrant community's encounter with cholera, and meetings between immigrants and American Indians. In an address that preceded the presentation of the pageant, a college professor of Norwegian descent made a plea to preserve ethnic culture by creating a library "somewhere in the Northwest sufficient to house all the books, pamphlets, and newspapers published on this side of the sea by men and women of Norwegian blood." But the pageant also gave substantial attention to Norwegian-American support for the antislavery crusade and the sacrifice of ethnic group members in the Civil War. In one scene Lincoln and Grant stood by the bier of a fallen Norwegian-American soldier to pay homage. Public memory for the group in the 1920s was clearly connected to the tension that existed between contradictions in the social and political structure.[38]

MENNONITES

The 1974 centennial celebration of the arrival of Mennonite immigrants in Kansas exhibited a similar complex symbolic structure. State officials, interested in boosterism and economic development, were quick to use the occasion to promote the wheat industry in the state which had benefited from Mennonite farmers, and the role Kansas wheat had played in helping feed underdeveloped nations. For local Mennonite communities in the state and Mennonite institutions, however, the centennial offered an opportunity to use the vernacular memory of the pioneer immigrants to reaffirm values that were crucial to the maintenance of ethnic institutions and communal life and to express pride in the achievements of ancestors.

In 1874 a group of Mennonite farmers left their fields in southern Russia to move to a huge plot of rolling farmland in central Kansas. The journey from the Crimea to Kansas took over two months but seemed worth the effort because of the abundant land offered by the Santa Fe Railroad. In Russia the familiar ways of the Mennonites were suddenly threatened by the actions of government officials who recinded the exemption they had enjoyed from military service and banned the use of the German language. These decrees altered privileges Mennonites had enjoyed for over a century since they had been encouraged to leave Germany by Catherine II.

Mennonites brought much with them to Kansas. They carried a rich religious tradition that dated back to the sixteenth century and which recognized no authority outside the *Bible* and "the enlightened conscience" of individuals. Their historical and religious heritage, however, while important to members of the Mennonite communities in the state, did not capture the imagination of state officials involved with the centennial celebration. For members of the Kansas Wheat

Centennial Commission the most important things that Mennonites brought with them to the state were grains of Turkey Red Wheat that were carried in two jars. It was this hardy strain of wheat, more resistant to drought and disease than other varieties used in the Great Plains, that formed the basis of the Kansas wheat industry and led to the development of additional hardy strains after World War II. Mennonites in Kansas would not hesitate to celebrate their ancestors and their ethnic and religious traditions in 1974 but, left to their own resources, they would have done so in a narrower ethnic framework and not focused so much attention on their contributions to economic growth.[39]

The state-sponsored Kansas Wheat Centennial Commission was clearly interested in promoting a "broad public relations program" that would stimulate support for the wheat industry and its products both inside and outside Kansas. In fact, late in the centennial year, one of the commission members publicly criticized the commission's priorities and charged that it wasted too much of its resources on public relations firms that ultimately contributed little in return to the celebration.[40]

The commission, however, did not stray far from its focus on the wheat industry and economic development. Mobile displays were sent throughout the state during 1974 explaining how wheat was produced, and how, through a combination of banking, scientific, and trade activity it was transformed into food products that were sent around the world. It did make some funds available in the form of small grants to communities to help them sponsor centennial projects but these were thought to be contributions to the development of tourism in Kansas.[41] Another state organization, the Kansas Wheat Centennial Foundation, announced plans to build a Wheat Center near Hutchinson that would mount exhibits explaining the production, distribution, and consumption of wheat products. The center would also serve as a place to host delegations from countries interested in buying Kansas wheat.

To a remarkable extent, however, celebrations of the centennial in local communities, Mennonite institutions, and even at the state fair did not emphasize economic development nearly as much as those orchestrated by official commissions. Pioneer immigrants, infused with strong religious values and able to work tirelessly to make the land fruitful, again emerged to dominate the symbolic content of a celebration. The Mennonite community had little difficulty in deciding what was important about this celebration and used the event to revive memories of ordinary but sturdy people who maintained their beliefs and their work traditions. In doing so they clearly contributed to the building of Kansas and, ultimately, the United States. But surprisingly little was said in 1974 in local celebrations about nation building or economic progress. For most people involved in the centennial, patriotism and development did not capture the imagination nearly as much as the history and story of the pioneers themselves.

The preoccupation with immigrant pioneers who preserved ethnic values and traditions was seen vividly in the commemorative activities in small towns. In Moundridge several Swiss Mennonite churches joined in a three-day festival to commemorate the arrival of the first Mennonites a century earlier. A monument was dedicated and pioneer activities such as hog butchering and threshing were demonstrated. A hike was also reenacted from Moundridge to a nearby town to illustrate the "travels of the pioneers 100 years ago." At Whitewater a centennial observance at the Grace Hill Mennonite Church included exhibits of clothing and "historical artifacts" used by community founders. At the small town of Grossel an enormously ambitious construction project was undertaken and completed during the centennial. A "historical complex" was dedicated by the Mennonite Immigrant Foundation of the community which consisted of three buildings. The structures included a restored community school used by Mennonite children, a second building called the "wheat palace" housed blacksmith and farm implements used by immigrant farmers, and a replica of a house in which seventeen immigrant families lived for four years before establishing several villages in the area. This latter building housed early Mennonite costumes, furnishings, and other household items.[42]

The erection of structures, monuments, and the execution of artworks formed a significant component of local Mennonite celebrations. Monuments of different shapes were usually dedicated with religious services. Speeches at such events not only discussed the wheat strain brought by the immigrants but their attachment to religious values and the shared resources they received from Mennonites in other states. Pioneer achievement and belief was further honored in the work of folk artists such as Peter Firesen. In Wichita he completed a mural over ten feet tall and forty feet long called the *Mennonite Centennial Mural.* Consisting of five panels, the mural depicted the Mennonites talking with railroad officials in New York about land; their arrival near Peabody, Kansas; immigrants standing in prayer in a Kansas field; pioneers toiling in the fields with hazards such as tornados and prairie fires in the background; and, finally, a rendering of technological progress in farm equipment from the scythe to the modern combine. Through the entire mural, pioneers prevailed over stubborn obstacles with hard work and religious devotion.[43]

Pageants were also produced in the celebration in Kansas much as they were in other places during commemorative events in the twentieth century. Those arranged by state officials and commissions tended to reconstruct a large historical framework that gave the impression of an orderly transitional flow from the time of Spanish exploration in Kansas to the emergence of the modern state. The Kansas Wheat Centennial Foundation, for instance, commissioned a pageant for presentation at the 1974 state fair. Based on the theme, "From the Great American Desert to the Breadbasket of the Nation," the pageant began with the arrival in 1541 of Francisco Vasquez de Coronado in Kansas. It traced three hundred years of occupation by the Plains Indians, the first white settlers, the introduction of soft winter wheat, the establishment of the Kansas Territory, the Civil War years, and the role the Homestead Act and the various railroad acts had in building the state. The story of the Mennonites was not ignored here. Detailed scenes in the production depicted the migration from Russia, early years of settlement, Mennonite leaders such as Cornelius Jansen and Dietrich Gaeddert, and the development of the Turkey Red strain. In this official presentation Mennonite history was placed within the context of state history and development. Displayed in conjunction with the pageant at the fair was a "tractor-drawn mock-up of the migration ship, the *City of Richmond*, complete with a smoke-spewing chimney and waving passengers." The float was built by Pretty Prairie Mennonite youth and was one of the most popular attractions at the fair.[44]

Locally produced pageants exhibited much less concern with linking Mennonite history to larger frameworks. A theatrical troupe in Hillsboro, Kansas, created a play entitled "The Anna Barkman Story: A Mennonite Migration Folk Tale," and took the production on tour throughout the summer of 1974. Anna Barkman was a member of a Mennonite family that moved from Russia to Kansas a century earlier and carried the two jars of the Red Turkey strain that were enshrined as symbols of Mennonite farsightedness and the Kansas wheat industry. In Hesston, Robert Hostetter wrote a choral drama, "Forgiveness," that dealt with social and religious issues important to Mennonites. The drama explored the necessity of Christian forgiveness to reconcile the absence of both love and justice in the world.[45]

Mennonite institutions such as Bethel College played particularly important roles in the centennial. Normally, such institutions acted to preserve values and traditions associated with an ethnic or religious group even as they provided the educational tools that could lead in some instances to a departure from the ethnic community itself. In 1974 Bethel's Fall Festival was devoted to the Mennonite pioneers and included an exhibition of relics from the past, paintings of pioneer scenes, demonstrations of pioneer crafts, and "wheat technology displays." During the weekend following the Bethel celebration three Mennonite colleges joined forces at Bethel to present a centennial musical concert and a pageant-drama. The music was essentially sacred and was performed by the combined choruses of Bethel, Tabor, and Hesston Colleges. Dramatic presentations at both weekends included an English drama about a Russian Mennonite family's decision to migrate to Kansas, readings of pioneer life in the Midwest, and a Swiss-German dialect play about the arrival of the first "Volhynian Mennonites." "We Shall Be As One" was a historically based drama tracing a Russian Mennonite family's migration to Kansas in 1874. The story was told by a young girl who draws upon her great-grandmother's diary to describe the decision to migrate, the hardships the immigrants endured, and the launching of a farm community.[46]

THE IRISH

Ethnic commemorative ceremonies always contained a complex nature. Ordinary people were intent on honoring their ancestors and relatives for the sacrifices they had made. Immigrant pioneers could serve as models of personal inspiration and satisfaction for having founded the communities and institutions in which people now lived, and preserved the values which some of them held dear. All members of the group, moreover, probably felt a need to represent themselves to the larger community as respectable and loyal citizens. Certainly they were stung by the pervasive use of ethnic stereotypes. But if the effort to promote respectability and loyalty is an indication of how strongly this need was felt, the ethnic middle and professional class appeared to be extremely sensitive to the images their brothers and sisters of similar descent presented as they moved through public space in the dress, manners, and trappings of their working-class and ethnically based lives. If commemorative ceremonies allowed ordinary people a chance to enjoy their leisure time and restate the values of their vernacular culture, the same events also afforded members of the rising middle and professional classes within ethnic groups an opportunity to fashion memory symbols that would raise the standing of the group in the eyes of the larger society and secure for the group a degree of political influence.

The pronounced views and dominance of the ethnic middle class may not have been as obvious in rural ethnic communities such as those described for Mennonites and Swedes in Kansas where communities were somewhat less stratified. They were, however, noticeable in communities that were more concentrated in urban areas where the size of the ethnic middle class was more developed. Few better examples exist of such a pattern than the Irish. Moving to America over a very long period of time throughout the nineteenth century and acquiring, at least by the end of the century, a sizable professional class, the Irish created commemorative events that were heavily influenced by the concerns of their leaders.

The preoccupation with reconciling the personal pursuit of leisure and vernacular memory with the middle-class concern over respectability and official memory was evident in the celebration of St. Patrick's Day and gave evidence that the generation of ethnic memory involved much more than the reconciliation of the cultures of consent and descent. It also involved the nature of political power within ethnic groups as well. In its earliest manifestation in this country in the eighteenth and early nineteenth centuries, before massive waves of poor Irish immigrants had created a large Irish community and a desire on the part of Irish American leaders to foster respectable images, the celebration did not include the large parades and public rowdiness that came to be associated with it. Before the 1840s these celebrations in the United States were rather small affairs held in taverns and other meeting places where men of status and rank and of Irish birth gathered to drink toasts and honor not only the land of their origin but the land in which they now lived.

The earliest American celebration of St. Patrick's Day probably took place in Boston in 1737 and was organized by Irish Protestants. The day was definitely celebrated by Irish members of the American army during the Revolution. In the half-century after the War for Independence the fact that Irish-Americans could draw upon a fairly extensive participation in the American army served as the basis for strong patriotic messages in these celebrations as well as the expected expressions of homage to the homeland.[47]

In nearly all of these celebrations, usually organized by groups such as the Friendly Sons of St. Patrick in New York City, the leadership came from a group of prominent Irish-American lawyers and merchants. Daniel McCormick who was president of the New York group for many years, came to this country poor before the Revolution but amassed a fortune in the auctioneering business in that city. The symbolic themes associated with these early gatherings of Irish leaders on St. Patrick's Day can be seen clearly in the endless toasts that they offered during their festive banquets. Guests stood and offered expressions of loyalty to the land of their birth and to the land in which they presently resided. The following list will give an illustration of the point:

> To the memory of the Saint who planted the shamrock, who instructed your forefathers how to improve.
>
> To the President of the United States.
>
> To the Land we left and the Land we live in, each consecrated to feeling and dear to our hearts.
>
> To Irish feeling, Irish friendship, Irish hospitality—may they, when transplanted to a foreign soil, preserve unimpaired that bloom and vigor so characteristic of their native growth.
>
> To Ireland and the United States of America—while we cherish, with the holiest emotions, a fond recollection of our native isle, we respect and venerate the institutions of the country of our adoption.
>
> Erin go Bragh! May the memory of her ancient renown thrill through the redress of their country's wrongs.
>
> To the memory of General George Washington, the father of our adopted country.[48]

After the 1840s, with the size of the Irish-American working class rapidly expanding, the nature of the celebration of Ireland's patron saint changed drastically. The point can readily be grasped from an excellent study on the subject by Timothy J. Meagher. His depiction of the celebration in Worcester, Massachusetts, in 1890 was of an affair that included citizens shouting in public after spending a morning drinking in taverns, people dressed from head to toe in green, and a massive parade that included bands, carriages carrying priests, and members of various Irish-American fraternal associations dressed in historical uniforms including the Knights of Father Matthew who donned steel helmets and carried battle-axes in the manner of Irish infantry that had fought the "armies of Queen Elizabeth over three hundred years before." Meagher astutely pointed out that in Ireland St. Patrick was honored without parades but in the United States there was a felt need by many Irish to symbolically proclaim to outsiders and insiders the vigor and power of the ethnic community.[49]

Meagher's study makes it very clear that from the inception of the parade in 1847 a disagreement existed in the community between more prosperous members, often from the eastern part of the homeland and "impoverished newcomers" from the Gaelic west. Over time the Irish middle class, especially through their association with respectable American temperance societies, gained more influence over the planning of the parade and the celebration of St. Patrick's Day itself. The noticeable absence of pioneer symbols in the Irish events when compared to other ethnic celebrations, moreover, raised an interesting possibility. The power of dominant institutions in the ethnic community such as the Roman Catholic Church with its doctrinal emphasis upon authority, and the urban professional class, may have been so great as to completely obliterate the celebration of ordinary immigrant pioneers from commemorative events. There is little doubt that the public displays of drinking and celebration by the Irish working class troubled the group's leadership and caused them to attempt a reform of the group's public image. But equally as strong was the resentment on the part of organizations such as the Ancient Order of Hibernians who criticized the temperance reformers as being too Americanized and lacking in [Irish] "patriotism." Meagher showed that the Hibernians were mostly recent arrivals whose "memories of Ireland were still fresh."[50]

As St. Patrick's Day parades continued in twentieth-century American cities, the distinctive ethnic nature of the event gave way to a mixture of Irish and non-Irish participants and a blend of ethnic and dominant American symbols. The public expression of culture became more complex. An eyewitness account of the parade in New York in 1985 suggested the point. Irish American ethnic marching units were certainly in abundance, although no particular class distinction was noticeable. Irish groups that dominated organizations such as the Hibernians, the United Irish Counties Associations (representing all thirty-two Irish counties), the Emerald Societies from the postal service, Consolidated Edison Company, the New York Telephone Company, and the Irish Teachers Association were prominent. But the parade was led in its first two units by civil authorities from outside the Irish group including the mayor of New York City, members of the city council, the governors of New York and Connecticut, and five divisions of the New York Police Department. The parade appeared to represent the achievement of some respectability and political power by Irish-Americans but had little to say about an immigrant or ethnic past. The bands in the line of march also offered musical selections that gave the impression of a merger of ethnic and American cultures. Almost all of the bands—Irish and American—played the same four or five Irish and American pieces: "The Battle Hymn of the Republic," "Danny Boy," "The Minstrel Boy," and "The Marine's Hymn."[51]

Interestingly, the modern parade in New York stopped for review by sacred and civil authorities, a symbolic act that reinforced the dominant power of these figures even as it allowed ordinary people to engage in leisure-time activities. The first stop was in front of St. Patrick's Cathedral where the archbishop of New York and other Catholic clergy gave a public display of approval. The archbishop had already said mass for the parade committee that morning. The second stop was the review by civic officials such as New York's mayor, senators, judges and other elected authorities, union leaders, and the heads of several Catholic universities. The entire parade was conducted in an orderly and almost "militaristic" pattern and cadence, and contrasted sharply with the carnival atmosphere of some nineteenth-century celebrations. Some contention between ethnic or vernacular interests and American and authoritarian interests did emerge in 1983 when a man, closely identified with the Irish Republican Army, was chosen as the grand marshall of the parade. The move evoked harsh criticism from the *New York Times* and many political officials who felt such an image sanctioned the violence in Northern Ireland. The year before, parade officials abandoned a practice of picking the archbishop as parade marshall and chose to give the honor posthumously to Bobby Sands, an I.R.A. leader who gained fame when he died of a hunger strike in prison the previous year. Ethnic assertiveness did not die out but clearly the dominant plot of the modern parades reaffirmed the need for order and loyalty to authority in public rituals.[52]

The middle-class offensive in commemorative events on behalf of respectability and Americanization reached a pinnacle of sorts with the activities of the American-Irish Historical Society. In the first two decades of this century this association, consisting largely of Irish-American professionals, took extreme steps to demonstrate their ethnic group's loyalty to the United States and preserve a history and memory that was centered largely on their contributions to the American Revolution. There was no room in this view of the past for the pioneer immigrants who had composed much of the Irish migration stream to this country in the first place. The group was, of course, sensitive to the anti-Catholic, anti-Irish campaigns of the nineteenth century and myths of Anglo-Saxon superiority that flourished at the time. In their own way, therefore, they were asserting Irish ethnic identity as a positive force helping to build the nation. But in so doing they were helping to create a public memory of the Irish experience in this country that had much room for patriots but almost no space for humble pioneers.[53]

Typical of the activities of the AIHS was their participation in movements to erect and dedicate monuments to men of Irish ancestry who were prominent in the Revolutionary War. In 1912, representatives from its various chapters gathered at Elmira, New York, for the unveiling of a monument to Major-General John Sullivan. Sullivan had served with Washington and had been commended for galantry at Germantown and Brandywine. Speaking at the dedication ceremonies, the Honorable Patrick McGowan proclaimed that Sullivan was an "American to the very heart's core, and I can say the same of all the members of the American-Irish Historical Society, whether their ancestors have been here for hundreds of years or not." John Murtaugh, an AIHS official in New York state and a leading figure behind the movement to get the monument erected, paid his respects to the state of New York (which financed the monument) and to the "present generation" that saw fit to remember the "sterling deeds and patriotism of their forefathers."[54]

This promotion of patriotism by an Irish-American middle class resembled the experience of Poles in American cities during the same period. Thousands of Poles gathered periodically to dedicate statues of Thaddeus Kosciuszko and Casimir Pulaski, heroic figures of the American Revolution. But campaigns to commemorate these men, which resulted in the dedication of a Kosciuszko statue in Humbolt Park in Chicago, in September 1904, and monuments to both Kosciuszko and Pulaski in Washington, D.C., in May 1910, emerged not from a simple desire to express loyalty to the United States but from a complex struggle for power within the ethnic community itself. In this case secular leaders such as John Smulski and representatives of the Polish National Alliance actually exploited the symbol of patriotism to foster support for the independence of Poland as well as for loyalty to the United States—"the second fatherland." These leaders also were locked in a duel with clerical officials for supremacy within the ethnic community and attempted to define ethnic consciousness in nationalistic rather than religious terms. Much like the Irish middle class, their unintended use of patriotism as a means to attain power was as important to them as were issues of consent and descent.[55]

MULTI-ETHNIC CELEBRATIONS

Ethnic commemorative events and, therefore, ethnic memories were not only shaped by discussions among members of the group itself or the sensitivities of its leadership class but were also heavily influenced by external agents of Americanization. Especially after the patriotic campaigns of World War I, representatives of various ethnic groups were brought together to perform in multi-ethnic celebrations that filtered out many of the personal and political symbols important to the minority group itself. Homage to the homeland as a political structure was largely eradicated and the old world was symbolized only in a narrow band of cuisine, dance, and dress in such performances. Usually presented in pageants and "folk festivals" organized by authorities outside the group, this highly selective view of the ethnic past was totally devoid of the multivocal quality of events such as the Norse-American centennial and involved a past that was neatly fitted into the larger pageant of American history. It told of an inevitable and painless transformation of diverse folk cultures into a unified American culture. This formula dominated numerous public presentations of ethnic history and culture in the twenties and thirties and kept alive the nationalistic thrust of public memory in the United States between the wars. Its triumph also suggested that the twofold structure of the Americanization movement described by previous scholars tended to have only one result. John Higham, for instance, argued that Americanization efforts beginning in the era of World War I were driven by feelings of concern for immigrant heritages and adjustment in settlement houses, and fear of foreign cultures in patriotic hereditary societies. Whatever the motive, the public presentation of immigrant culture still became more official and consensual.[56]

Numerous examples of such productions could be given for the 1920s but one in New York City in 1921 will provide an illustration. In the "America's Making Festival" an explicit attempt was made by educational officials and civic leaders to direct the commemoration of the ethnic past toward a wider audience and the need to reinforce national loyalty. Heavily influenced by the patriotic sentiments of the decade, planners organized an event in which representatives of over thirty ethnic and racial groups in the city, through exhibits, pageants, and other forms of entertainment revealed their "contributions to America." In extending an official invitation to President Warren Harding to attend the event, John Tigert, the United States Commissioner of Education informed the president that the exposition would convey the manner in which the nation was built by "men and women of all races." In response, Harding complimented the planners and the ethnic representatives in the delegation he received for looking just like "the representatives of American committees which came to the White House."[57]

The organization of the festival did not proceed without some internal dissension. Irish representatives incurred criticism from other ethnic groups when they suggested that an Irish mariner monk, St. Brendan, had traveled to North America one thousand years before Columbus and explored the continent as far west as Ohio. Representatives of the Dutch community, moreover, refused to take part in the program because they were not placed first in the order of performances and exhibitions, and they felt that their history or their early settlement in the city had given them such a distinction. Scotch and Irish representatives engaged in an intense dispute over the "lineage" of Scotch-Irish pioneers. The Irish claimed that the Scotch had no right to present Thomas McKean, one of the signers of the Declaration of Independence, and Robert Fulton, the inventor of the steamboat, as of Scotch rather than Irish descent. The *New York Times* exclaimed that however well blended the various "races" appear in the exposition of America's Making, some "merry wars" have been going on behind the scenes.[58]

Despite difficulties, the festival opened on time in late October in a New York armory. Dr. John Finley, president of the exposition, told the gathering that the "splendid festival and pageant" was convened for the purpose of "teaching" everyone the contributions of all of the elements of our citizenry to the making of America.[59] Following his remarks, people in costume marched on a large stage in an order approximating their historical arrival on the North American continent. First came the American Indians. They were followed by Leif Eriksson, Columbus, Verrazano, Cabot, and DeSoto. After the appearance of the explorers, a Liberty Bell pealed and a representation of the group of men that signed the Declaration of Independence appeared on stage. With the new nation firmly established, delegates of ethnic groups in costumes marched onto the stage in a dutiful manner to take their places within American historical time and the existing political structure. In a final scene the figure of an angel hovered over a young boy representing the United States and the words, "These shall be thy people" flashed overhead. The pageant was repeated daily for the next two weeks.[60]

During the 1930s many Americans changed their attitudes toward minorities, as Richard Weiss has persuasively argued. The racism and bigotry of nativist attacks during the 1920s gave way to a more subtle strain of Americanization in the form of programs that praised both immigrant contributions to America and immigrant heritage. The administration of Franklin D. Roosevelt, sensitive to the need to create unity in the face of the growing threat of national socialism in Europe and class conflict at home, funded radio broadcasts that stressed the "rich heritages" that had come to America from its various races and nationalities. Pluralism or the allowance of dual identity and memory started to replace an uncompromising insistence on 100 percent Americanism, although pageants and some other forms of activities had already begun this initiative in the twenties. But the movement did not represent an acknowledgment of the desirability of preserving the full ethnic past. Rather, the nonpolitical aspects of that past—folk dances and music, folk attire, and food—were stressed. A reconsideration of ethnic economic and political history had no place in this cultural construction; stories of struggling immigrant pioneers were not to be found. Immigrant contributions were cultural because the basic political and economic structure of the nation had been firmly established before most immigrants arrived and was now to be honored but not reevaluated or debated.[61]

The effort on the part of civic leaders and educational officials to direct public presentations of ethnic traditions into a nationalist framework continued in the 1930s. It was not surprising that such an effort would come in the context of large celebrations such as the Connecticut Tercentenary of 1935. In conjunction with that extensive commemoration, a "Pageant of the Races" was held and entitled "America's Making in Connecticut." Organized and produced by theatrical professionals outside the ethnic communities, the Connecticut production began with scenes depicting the colonial origins of the state and Connecticut's participation in the Revolutionary War. After the state and the nation were symbolically established, a section of the pageant presented "The Racial Groups," including French Canadians, Italians, Germans, Swedes, Lithuanians, and Poles. A selection of music and dance from each of the respective homelands was performed and, symbolically, each group was welcomed into the existing political structure never again to render loyalty to any other authority. A final epilogue entitled, "A New Soul in the Making" included representatives of numerous "racial family groups" singing "America."[62]

That the nationalist framework dominated the presentation of ethnic culture in officially sponsored celebrations comes as no surprise. But this dominance was also to be found in commemorations sponsored by nongovernmental institutions. The Catholic Church, for instance, which was administered by authorities with the same desire for control and order as secular officials, almost invariably supported the drive toward Americanization.

A vivid example of the church's concern with loyalty to both secular and church authority was evident in the ceremonies commemorating the fiftieth anniversary of the ordination to the "sacred priesthood" of William Cardinal O'Connell of Boston in 1934. Ordination anniversaries for high-ranking priests were often used as occasions not only to celebrate the achievement of an individual but to reinforce the loyalty of the faithful to their religious leaders. Thus, O'Connell was honored in three separate events. In a formal ceremony at the Cathedral of the Holy Cross in Boston, symbols of ethnic origins, political authority, and religious faith came together in a perfect fit. Inside the church a host of ecclesiastical dignitaries gathered, dressed in the black, purple, and red colors signifying the church's hierarchy, as well as the mayor and former mayor of Boston, state representatives, city councilmen, and "prominent Catholic laymen." This event was clearly for authorities themselves who had gathered to honor O'Connell, the highest ranking American prelate of his day and a symbol of social mobility since he climbed the church's hierarchy from his humble origins as a "ruddy-cheeked young American from Lowell."[63]

Outside the cathedral ceremony over fifty policemen held back a crowd of several thousand, possibly of less political and religious rank, who had gathered to catch a glimpse of the cardinal. Within the walls of the church, however, the subservience of ethnic identity to larger authority was portrayed in ritualistic fashion. Representatives of major ethnic groups in the Boston archdiocese in turn came to the altar where O'Connell was seated to offer him praise in their native languages and in English. The Right Reverend John Bolabossiere, speaking on behalf of French-speaking Catholics, praised the cardinal for treating the "various ethnical groups of your flock" with a spirit of justice. A Lithuanian-American priest thanked O'Connell for allowing the Lithuanian language to be used in the cathedral in 1931 during the celebration of the five-hundredth anniversary of the conversion of Lithuania to Christianity. The German-American spokesmen thanked O'Connell for defending the group's loyalty to the United States during World War I when others saw fit to question it. In return the Reverend Charles Gisler promised that German-Americans would be loyal to the nation, "Holy Mother Church," and "our Archbishop and Cardinal."[64] O'Connell, himself, responded to the expressions of ethnic loyalty by voicing pride in the fact that there was a "flock so varied in character" in the archdiocese that was still "united and bound to him by ties of faith and love."[65]

The day following the formal ceremonies at the cathedral O'Connell carried the celebration's message of loyalty to Catholic school children. At a Boston College athletic field some twenty-five thousand students gathered for a "children's mass." Some wore their school uniforms but others dressed as Boy Scouts and carried American flags. O'Connell urged his young listeners in explicit terms to be "true and honest and just in your citizenship—loyal Catholics and loyal Americans." He claimed that he was most proud of the role he had played in helping to shape "noble characteristics" in Catholic youth such as nurturing their devotion to "Holy Mother Church," and the "Republic" of which he felt most proud.[66]

An even larger gathering of adults took place on June 10, 1934, at Fenway Park in Boston. At this event the years of O'Connell's service were explicitly recognized as a contribution to both church and state. Indeed, a procession to a gold altar constructed in the middle of the baseball field was led not only by religious figures including Fourth Degree Knights of Columbus, but an honor guard of Boston police and government officials including the Governor of Massachusetts, Joseph Ely, and Congressman John McCormack. O'Connell again addressed the audience and invoked the theme of dual loyalty. Defending the church against critics who argued that Catholicism and Americanism were inherently antagonistic, the cardinal told his diverse audience that they were gathered together for a great ideal—"the union of hearts in God's own love and in the love of our dear America." Civic leaders such as Ely echoed O'Connell's point and used this commemoration of his years of service and devotion to articulate symbolically how much they expected average citizens to limit their individualistic inclinations and serve the public good. Ely reasoned, "The longer I live the more convinced I become that the two great bulwarks which protect our civilization are a strong national sentiment and a religion. Were these broken down a multitude of ideas would surge over the ramparts to destroy us. Then every man might set up a code of conduct to satisfy himself and justify his action."[67]

CONCLUSION

The public memory exhibited in American ethnic communities involved symbols that were selected and devised in the United States and not brought from the homeland. This is not to say that ethnic communities and their members did not discuss and think about the homeland and view it with longing and fondness. Rather, in their public rituals, whether held primarily for the group or for outsiders, they paid an inordinate amount of attention to symbols and messages that were important to individuals within and outside of the group in the United States. Members of ethnic enclaves spent much time expressing heartfelt feelings of pride in the accomplishments of ancestors and manifested a degree of ethnic assertiveness by celebrating notions of free and independent homelands. But increasingly they also worked very hard to incorporate messages and symbols into their remembered past that paid homage to the American nation-state and presented their members as legitimate American patriots. Memories of the ethnic past were grounded ultimately in the social reality of the present.

The multivocal quality of ethnic memory could be traced to a number of points of origin. Ordinary people took much pride in the achievements and struggles of their pioneer ancestors and formed a deep attachment to the communities they knew as young people. These components of ethnic memories were not simply manufactured by authorities or agents of Americanization but emanated from personal quests for understanding and emotional continuity with forebearers and from the expression of deep feelings about the social reality that they lived. Anthony D. Smith noticed such memories and claimed that they resulted from a nostalgic retrieval of a past that could be conveyed to posterity. This may have been partially the case, but the depth of these personal feelings and the degree to which they were expressed culturally in symbols such as the pioneer and the homeland were duly noted by authorities inside and outside the group. Ethnic leaders often shared some of these feelings and sought to protect them by placing them alongside expressions of loyalty and American patriotism. Other ethnic leaders sought to exploit the personal dimension of symbols important to ethnic communities by using them to revitalize loyalty to both ethnic and American institutions.[69] The point was that, especially in cities where the ethnic professional classes were larger and more influenced by their peers in the larger social structure, ethnic memory was continually generated from the tension that existed between vernacular and official culture and between those with divergent amounts of social and political power.

Although a number of interests vied for dominance in the discussion over the ethnic past, the evidence suggests that local and personal interests in symbols such as the pioneer, where it flourished, and in the homeland, persisted. These interests represented a threat to the dominant ideology of patriotism and Americanization, since they emphasized ordinary people and a vernacular culture rather than founding fathers and loyalty to national institutions. To the extent they represented a past created by younger generations that simultaneously paid homage to and fostered separation from ancestors, these interests encouraged the growth of official culture at the expense of vernacular formulations, although this implication was never entirely clear to those who constructed it. In the pioneer and in the homeland ordinary people found symbols that assisted understanding of what their own lives had been about despite the fact that such symbols served higher political agendas as well. Consequently, the celebration of the homeland and the pioneer went on for a very long time. Such celebrations, moreover, tended to mute the thrust of patriotic ideology when they diverted attention away from leaders and the American nation. In 1974 the pioneer symbol actually dominated a large celebration in Kansas a century after pioneer settlement.

Over time, however, the complex nature of ethnic memory became acceptable only if the public or patriotic stood above the personal and vernacular dimensions of the pioneer or the homeland symbols. This meant that vernacular culture came increasingly to serve political or even commercial interests outside the group. Patriotism and the reformulation of homeland symbols into bland expressions such as food or music did not come about because of some vague assimilative process but because of the determined efforts of powerful people within and outside of ethnic communities and institutions to define the celebration and presentation of ethnic heritage. This was evident in the changes that characterized St. Patrick's Day parades, the celebration by Norwegians in the Twin Cities in 1925, and the patriotic ritual of the Swedish celebration in Chicago in 1948. Outside ethnic celebrations, in performances often designed by reformers or officials external to the groups themselves, members of ethnic communities presented a standardized version of the ethnic past that revolved around dance, music, and folk costumes from some idealized place in the homeland. This political process diminished the importance of immigrant pioneers and the ethnic homeland, and removed a sense of human struggle and conflict from memories of the ethnic past. Indeed, the dominant overt political expression on the part of these groups gradually became patriotism. Where middle-class leadership was concentrated inside and outside the group, especially in cities, immigrant pioneers had a difficult time surviving as a meaningful symbol at all.

CHAPTER FOUR

Commemoration in the City: Indianapolis and Cleveland

THE COMMUNAL DISCUSSION over public memory took place not only within ethnic communities but in cities which were even more diverse in composition and interests. Urban centers clearly had large concentrations of professional classes and cultural leaders who could influence vernacular memory. Yet the subject of public memory in cities remains largely ignored by historians. Little is known of either the course of public commemoration in cities or the manner in which such activity varied from place to place. Hypothetically, powerful groups of cultural leaders may have turned all urban commemorations into celebrations of patriotism and progress. On the other hand, varied urban structures and diverse sources of political power may have forced the creation of unique forms of public memory. In comparing two American cities, Indianapolis and Cleveland, in this century, an attempt is made to look more closely at the impact of specific urban structures on communal discussions about the past.

Although both cities were located in the Midwest and contained a range of social and economic groups, they had a pronounced difference in the ethnic and racial composition of their population and, therefore, their social structure. Only about 4 to 5 percent of Indianapolis consisted of foreign-born residents in the 1920s and about 12 percent of the city's inhabitants were black. This meant that some 83 percent of the Indiana capital was of native-born, white parentage in an era when such a designation meant a great deal in the conduct of political life. In Cleveland, on the other hand, the diversity of the population was more striking. The proportion of the foreign-born population in Cleveland was nearly six times what it was in Indianapolis in 1920, or about 30 percent. When blacks and immigrant children, who represented another 30 percent of the city, are calculated, only about 35 percent of the city in the 1920s consisted of native-born whites of native-born parents.[1] It is this obvious difference in the composition of their respective social structures that make these two cities worthwhile places in which to examine the relationship between social structure and the discussion over memory. After World War I the foreign-born population would achieve increased political power in both cities. Because it was a much more significant portion of the social structure in Cleveland, however, this group would gain more political power and would play a more influential role in the cultural construction of public memory.

INDIANAPOLIS: UNCONTESTED PATRIOTISM

In the earliest years of this century before World War I commemorative activity in Indianapolis consisted of a mixture of expressions. Events such as the Fourth of July or Memorial Day were primarily devoted to demonstrations of patriotism and respect for the dead. Patriotic callings urged citizens to exhibit loyalty and service to the nation-state as dead soldiers or other patriots had done in the past. Services for the dead not only represented the fallen soldier as a model of citizen service to the nation, however, but revealed deep-seated emotions on the part of ordinary people toward friends, relatives, and ancestors, for whom they grieved. Beyond this expression of vernacular and official culture, citizens often revealed their desire to enjoy leisure-time activities during commemorative days and not direct any attention at all toward the serious matters of life.

To a great extent city officials and leaders in Indianapolis were troubled by much of what ordinary citizens did on the Fourth of July prior to 1918 but never did organize a large solemn ceremony in honor of the origins of the nation itself. Citizens often filled the streets of the city on the day, but they were not marching in an orderly fashion. Rather, they were busily going to amusement parks, picnics, or fireworks displays. One observer commented that he thought that popular interest in horse racing and betting at the state fairgrounds in the city "overshadowed any celebration of the day." A local newspaper remarked that the planning for the programs of the day had apparently been "left to a committee of 208,000," the approximate city population of the time.

The issue that was discussed most on the Fourth of July during this period was not the idea of the nation but the use of firecrackers in the streets. Many officials not only decried the potential for injury and fire by the use of these explosives but worried that they distracted citizen attention away from the patriotic significance of the day. A local editor wrote that it was "barbarous" to celebrate a national birthday by giving the "riotously inclined full liberty to make all the noise they cared to." The writer feared that the "high and holy significance of the day on which a whole people ventured life for liberty is lost in a senseless saturnalia of noise."[2]

City officials and some members of the professional classes such as ministers and businessmen did not object to large displays of fireworks that were properly organized. When they argued for a "safe and sane" celebration they specifically directed their remarks against the unregulated use of fireworks, an activity that they perceived to be the special preserve of young boys and the foreign-born. In 1910 a local writer felt that boys were missing the meaning of the day by playing with fireworks and suggested that they take part in neighborhood historical pageants that would tell the story of Bunker Hill, Paul Revere, and George Rogers Clark at Vincennes. In the same year police charged that the chief offenders of restrictions placed on the use of fireworks in the downtown "fire limit" were not young boys, however, but "Americans in the making." They cited the arrest of one immigrant, an Italian, who could not read English and did not know about the prohibitions. But the newcomer, Joseph Coppoleno, did promise that next year, "I will know what the Fourth of July is in this country."[3]

Considerably less debate took place over the proper celebration of local citizens who had died in battle. This component of memory cut close to the store of personal feelings and recollections possessed by residents of the city and, while they certainly had leisure-time activities on their minds during Memorial Day, they exhibited a seriousness of purpose that was missing on the Fourth of July. By 1910 an auto race was already attracting large crowds on Memorial Day in the city but, clearly, the commemoration of the dead was no small matter. Normal Memorial Day celebrations consisted of thousands of people walking through the streets carrying flowers to cemeteries, the strewing of flowers around public monuments to the Civil War dead and other figures from the past, and countless sermons and church services. These activities paid less attention to founding fathers and patriotic urgings (although such expressions were not absent) and more attention to ordinary people who had lived in the same locale. In 1905 an orator at Crown Hill Cemetery praised not only those who went off to war from the city but the "unlisted heroes" who stood behind the soldiers and stayed at home as a "united people." In the same year, William Reagan, a Civil War veteran, spoke at another cemetery and called for all to respect the "private" and the "common man" who did his duty. And reports from gravesite activities noted the "tears and sobs" that were evident as roll calls of the dead were read and "memories of war times" recalled.[4]

It was the commemoration of the dead and the sacrifice of ordinary people in the Civil War, at once an expression of patriotism and local and personal sorrow and pride, that served as the nucleus of the largest commemorative activity in the city's history prior to World War I. In 1902 the city erected a towering landmark to the dead in the center of town, the Soldiers and Sailors Monument. Standing over three hundred feet high, the central shaft of the monument looked down on the entire city and caused an enormous level of interest and excitement. It clearly stood for the theme of citizen sacrifice for the nation-state. But contemporary observers were quick to argue that it also honored the "private soldier" and expressed local and regional pride in what citizens of Indiana had done.

The idea for the monument had originated with Oliver P. Morton, the Civil War governor of the state, and was furthered by an association of local Union veterans which was organized in 1876. As was the norm with nineteenth-century monuments, however, patriotism and local pride were never sufficient to generate public contributions at a rapid rate. It was not until the 1880s that the Grand Army of the Republic (GAR) in Indiana was able to persuade the state legislature to appropriate $200,000 to get actual construction under way.

In its final form the monument consisted of a tall shaft surrounded by four bronze statues at each corner. The shaft was dedicated to ordinary soldiers from the state who had fought in the Civil War and contained allegorical figures on each side representing war and peace. A local writer thought the monument to be more beautiful than the "unsightly shaft" of the monuments dedicated to the battle of Bunker Hill or George Washington. At each corner of the shaft stood memorials to leading figures in the history of Indiana and the Midwest. Commemorated were George Rogers Clark and the era of the Revolution; James Whitcomb, the governor of the state during the War with Mexico; William Henry Harrison and the Battle of Tippecanoe; and Oliver P. Morton. Apparently the structure of power was such in Indianapolis that ordinary soldiers could not be commemorated without some attention to prominent leaders.[5]

At the dedication on May 14, 1902, over fifteen thousand visitors came to the city to see the structure and a parade of veterans from the Mexican, Civil, and Spanish-American Wars. Many citizens visited the monument several days before the parade because of rumors that large crowds on dedication day would prevent much of a view at all. When the veterans marched by, reporters noted "tears and sobs in the eyes" of many spectators. Several of the marchers themselves broke into tears in part, as one former soldier explained, because of the remembered deaths of "the fellows that bunked, messed, and fought with me for three years."

During the period of American involvement in World War I the wartime demands of a nation-state deflected the focus of commemo-

4. Soldiers and Sailors Monument, Indianapolis, Ind., dedicated in 1902. Photography by Bass Photo Company. Courtesy of Indiana Historical Society.

rative activity in the city. People continued to honor the dead by carrying flowers to local cemeteries on Memorial Day. Interestingly, speakers on Memorial Day, 1918, talked less about the sorrow and pride they felt for ordinary soldiers from Indiana and more about how Civil War soldiers served as "glorious incentives" for the youth who had to fight in World War I. A reading of Memorial Day orations in the city in this century suggests that the memory and example of the Civil War was used extensively during 1918, but was dramatically absent afterwards and was replaced by memories of World War I itself. But for now, as the emphasis shifted decidedly to official culture, most citizens could agree with the speaker at Butler College who exclaimed that residents could now truly appreciate as never before exactly what it meant to "preserve the union."[6]

The most dramatic change in commemorative activity during the war came about in the celebration of the Fourth of July. The day had usually been given over more to leisure and frivolity than to serious commemoration. But that would temporarily change in 1918 when the exercise of state power became so dramatic. On July 4, 1918, Indianapolis officials, at the behest of President Woodrow Wilson, organized a commemorative activity that was completely unique to the city and discussed issues that had previously been absent from commemorations. The event was the Americanization Day parade of July 4, 1918. As a public exhibition of unity and loyalty, the parade included many diverse sectors of the social organization of the community but featured primarily immigrant newcomers who had seldom been heard before in civic discourse. The one ethnic group that had been visible in public, the Germans who celebrated German Day each October, was now unable to assert ethnic identity during the war and marched in the parade not as an ethnic unit but as the "Friends of German Democracy" and carried only an American flag. Other ethnic aggregations carried flags from both their homelands and the United States to tell the rest of the city that ethnic identity and background were not incompatible with the ability to manifest loyalty to the American nation-state.

The parade was organized by the Marion County Council of Defense. It was these officials who allocated space in the line of march and called upon "all loyal citizens, no matter of what extraction, to show their Americanism and patriotism." The line of march, organized by governmental authorities, symbolically placed the immigrants within the structure of American patriotism that had already been important to public discourse in Indianapolis. Following units of city police, military bands, Boy Scouts, and the Daughters of the American Revolution carrying American flags, immigrants marched in native costumes and rode on floats as they presented themselves to the dominant society.

Immigrants characteristically expressed a mixture of ethnic and American interests. Thus, the Italian-American floats featured a caricature of the "queen of Italy" and groups of Italian-American school children carrying American flags. Slovenians, numbering over 350 in the line of march, presented a truck carrying Slovene-American children and farmers pledging loyalty and a second truck filled with women in folk costumes. The group carried a banner that read, "Slovenians: We Are For America First, Last, and All the Time." Romanians created a float that depicted a man dressed as Uncle Sam "triumphing" over another figure that represented "autocracy." At the end of the parade each ethnic group carried its homeland flag to a stage dominated by a large American flag in the middle. Wymond Beckett, an attorney active in planning local defense activities, addressed the group and apologized to the foreign-born on behalf of the rest of the city's and nation's prominent classes. He admitted that in the past in the United States the newcomer was treated "as a mere economic unit, to be used, worn out, and cast aside." He promised that this would end, however, and insisted that the foreign-born were needed to maintain the foundations of the republic.[7]

Once the tribulations of wartime had ended, however, city leaders and officials quickly eliminated immigrant voices from public discourse and reverted to the energetic quest to link local and personal feeling for the dead with the promotion of patriotism and even the progress of the city itself. Veterans, both living and dead, became a dominant object of commemoration because, like all symbols, they mediated several of the most powerful interests in the city. Ordinary people felt a strong need to understand what wartime sacrifices were all about and express sorrow and grief. City leaders and boosters were anxious to stimulate civic pride as a basis for continued prosperity and growth and submit to the powerful currents of patriotism that had been reinforced by the federal government during and after the war. Although there was a clear exercise of power on the part of dominant political and civic leaders in the city, there was a democratic thrust to the commemoration of patriotic veterans; veterans came from all social classes, ethnic and religious groups, and races.

This democratic component of the memory system and culture actually helped to contain the spread of a more intolerant strain of nationalism that was manifested by the rise of the Ku Klux Klan in Indiana. Indianapolis, in fact, actually became a Klan stronghold by 1925 when the organization mounted a successful campaign to elect a mayor and an entire slate of schoolboard candidates. But despite the fact that the Klan became a truly powerful force in the city, it was continually opposed by all of the local newspapers, which were run by local elites, and Catholic, Jewish, and Protestant bodies who had all participated actively in the winning and commemoration of the war. It was not uncommon, for instance, at commemorative events during the height of the Klan's power in the city to have representatives from all three faiths speak at services and ceremonies, a symbolic demonstration of opposition to the Klan's anti-Catholic and anti-Jewish biases.[8]

But the symbol of patriotic veterans was not only democratic and linked somewhat to the needs of ordinary people but was intolerant and hegemonic as well. It aggressively sought to use memories of past wars and historical actors to stimulate loyalty to existing institutions and, therefore, institutional leaders who tended to reside in the professional classes. To this extent patriotism was fostered in such an uncompromising manner that it really nurtured the power of large governmental and economic structures in the city, the state, and the nation. It was the vested interest that city leaders shared with state and national leaders in maintaining existing structures that partially explained their attempts to foster the commemoration of soldiers rather than pioneer or immigrant settlers in the 1920s.

After the war, veterans were commemorated not only on one day but two. Memorial Day celebrations continued with their orations, the placement of flowers at gravesites and monuments, and increased attendance at the speedway. Orations were always given by members of the professional classes, especially ministers, military officers, and lawyers. And the past continued to be a device that served to educate citizens in the present. At the Soldiers and Sailors Monument in 1929 the Rev. Warren Wiant told his listeners that the "glory of our history is that when the testing day came, our fathers were not afraid to sacrifice." He asserted that the same spirit of sacrifice for the nation must be manifested again in the future if "our priceless heritage is to be preserved."[9]

The major celebration of the veteran, however, in the decades after World War I was Armistice Day. For years after the termination of the war on Nov. 11, 1918, citizens who experienced the jubilation and sense of relief of the ending held that day in high regard. People did not normally parade on the Fourth of July or Memorial Day but they always did so, between the wars in Indianapolis, on November 11th. Although the Ku Klux Klan parades in the 1920s in the city consisted largely of middle- and lower middle-class, white Protestants, the Armistice Day parade affirmed the equality of all religious groups and consisted of clergy, veterans, and Gold Star mothers of all faiths. Parades of five thousand were not uncommon, American Legion dances were inaugurated, and speakers used the occasion not only to "revive cherished memories" but to sustain the ideal of continued service to the nation.[10]

But patriotism became the dominant ideal of commemorative activities in the 1920s in Indianapolis not only because of the memories of the dead and wartime sacrifices but also because of the active efforts of the city's business and professional classes. In their classic investigations of the 1920s in Muncie, Indiana, the sociologists Robert and Helen Lynd argued (somewhat narrowly) that patriotism and civic pride were fostered together by the business class to promote an orderly society that would assist leaders in their efforts to attract new business. The Lynds failed to realize that the expression of honor for the sacrifices of soldiers offered a place for the agency of ordinary people within the construction of public memory. At the same time they were correct in seeing that the willingness of city boosters to commit large amounts of resources and energy to the building of patriotic sentiments and landmarks represented a central force in the construction of patriotism.

In 1919 the Indianapolis delegation to the American Legion convention in Minneapolis, with the help of the Indianapolis Chamber of Commerce, was able to secure the selection of their city as the site of the legion's national headquarters. Indianapolis triumphed over Washington, D.C., by arguing that the headquarters should be located near the center of population in the nation and near the "center of the flag." Supporters for Indianapolis also argued that the legion offices should be located where the "poorest man in the country can come to the headquarters" and that in Washington the legion would be overshadowed by federal institutions. Just six days after the convention decision a joint group of representatives from the chamber of commerce, the city's real estate board, the board of trade, and the legion in the state met to discuss the need to build a facility for the headquarters. Fearing that other cities would still lure the legion away, city leaders pressed for the building of a $10 million memorial building and plaza that would house the legion and honor the war dead at the same time. Some former soldiers protested that the money would be better spent on veteran bonuses, and residents near the downtown where the plaza was to be built opposed the loss of their homes and the use of public funds for the project. But the initiative of economic and political leaders could not be repressed. In Marion County local leaders, along with local legion posts, conducted a massive publicity campaign to "educate" the voters.[11]

5. Parade to honor General John J. Pershing and dedicate Indiana War Memorial, Indianapolis, July 4, 1927. Photography by Bass Photo Company. Courtesy of Indiana Historical Society.

On July 4, 1927, a huge plaza which stretched for over half a mile just north of the downtown with an Indiana World War Memorial which rose two hundred feet above its base was dedicated. In what was probably the greatest patriotic ceremony in twentieth-century Indianapolis, General John J. Pershing came to the city to lead a parade of citizens. The *Star* commented that thousands of young men whom Pershing led to France, old warriors who kept the Union intact in the "early sixties," and veterans of other wars passed through the streets proclaiming that Indianapolis did not forget its heroes. Only patriots marched behind Pershing in 1927. Immigrants who were visible in the Americanization parade or "pioneers" who were noticeable in the city's centennial parade in 1920 were not to be found. The message here was that the city was united and that patriotism radiated from all of its people and was not the private preserve of any segment. If Indianapolis could not be the capital of the nation, it could still be the capital of national sentiment.[12]

At ceremonies following the parade, interests that served both high emotional patriotism and local and personal feeling and pride were served and united. Pershing spoke for the patriots and stressed the familiar association between visions of the past and the need for unity and loyalty in the present:

> This is an experience of a lifetime. It is an inspiration of a degree never exceeded in my experience. The thrill of seeing the people of Indiana and particularly of Indianapolis rise as one to celebrate this day . . . and honor the memory of their sons. These men of Indiana fought to sustain the eternal principles of liberty upon which our government is founded. . . . Like that of our forefathers their valor and their sacrifices have become the heritages of the ages.[13]

When Pershing placed a wreath on a staff of a gold star flag and spread mortar for the cornerstone the crowd became extremely quiet and, according to one reporter, appeared to be "under a spell." All acknowledged at this moment how complete the triumph of patriotic interests had become.[14]

Local pride and personal memories of the living and the dead were not by any means eliminated from the celebration which only appeared to be devoted exclusively to the ideal of loyalty to the nation. We cannot tell what thoughts and feelings filled the consciousness of those in attendance, but we do know that much that was important to local citizens and their memories of friends and relatives who fought and died in the war went into the cornerstone of the new memorial. Included were the names of 140,000 Indiana World War veterans, a Gold Star honor roll of Indiana, a report on American Red Cross service in the state during the war, a list of the state's officers and members of the American Legion, a history of the "colored men's" branch of the YMCA during the war, and a report of the Jewish Welfare Board's wartime activities.[15]

The intensity of the celebration of the war dead did wane somewhat by the late 1930s. As the memories of the wartime experience receded and the attention of city leaders was diverted from boosterism to rectifying economic problems, the organized celebration of patriotism diminished. Armistice Day became devoted less to the serious patriotism and the commemoration of the dead and more to leisure and enjoyment. In 1937 the *Star* indicated that the downtown parade was larger than in the past but also that "gaiety was peculiarly more predominant." A news reporter described a military band that curiously played "Indiana, Our Indiana," and a high school band that played a variation of "Jingle Bells." The reporter noted that the drum major went through "capers revealing that they had no memory of the first Armistice Day and its surging emotions." The paper even described a group of legionnaires, pausing for a temporary delay in the parade, dancing a jig and shouting at onlookers. The Butler University band actually played a "quick-step version of the Butler war song." However, deep emotions and seriousness of purpose still existed to be sure in 1937. One observer revealed that "tears were brushed away" in a caravan of automobiles carrying a group of war mothers, and "aging veterans stood grim faced" during ceremonies. But both the *Star* and the local American legion noted on the day that the "bright edges of what they believed were unforgettable memories" seemed "remote" to a new generation raised since the war. In fact, based on that perception, the legion mounted a display of posters from the era of World War I in the city so young people could read about how citizens sacrificed by going to war, purchasing Liberty bonds, serving in the Red Cross, and conserving fuel.[16]

The emphasis on patriotism was predictably rejuvenated in commemorative activities during World War II. Commemorative days during the war such as July Fourth and Armistice Day were used to engender citizen support for the national mobilization and for the "fighting men." Speakers on these days praised Hoosier farmers for feeding the soldiers and workers in war industries and civil defense agencies. Service to the nation rather than forms of entertainment were emphasized and citizens were told by military spokesmen that "we are all in this together."[17]

Once the war had ended, however, the public promotion of patriotism appeared to wane much more quickly than it did in the 1920s. People in the city still paraded on Armistice Day and placed flowers on graves on Memorial Day. But leisure interests predominated on these occasions as never before and the effort to place memory in the service of the nation was considerably weaker than after World War I. Parades honoring veterans were smaller, and Memorial Day increasingly became associated with the Indianapolis 500 auto race. In 1952 a pageant was held on the Fourth of July that was devoted to a theme that had been neglected during the patriotic celebrations of the dead—"Pioneer Days." A local editor observed after World War II that the "Fourth was not as grand and glorious."[18]

An effort to revive the emphasis on patriotism and civic loyalty in commemorative activities did manifest itself in the late 1960s and early 1970s when the nation-state was attacked again, this time by dissidents within the country. In response to urban unrest and antiwar demonstrations in the nation at large and to incidents of "rowdy behavior" by youth during several public events in the city, attempts were made to use commemorative days to instill sentiments of patriotism and civic responsibility. On July 4, 1969, the *Star* featured on its front page a plan by which Indianapolis could celebrate the upcoming observance of its sesquicentennial and the nation's bicentennial. Conceived by Edward Pierce, a leading architect in the city, the proposal consisted of several specific projects designed to rejuvenate a sense of civic and patriotic obligation. Pierce called for frequent decorations of the Monument Circle to promote a "community spirit," renewed attention to the creation of radial avenues emanating from downtown (as well as additional parking spaces) that would facilitate access to the area, and the development of an Indiana Lincoln Memorial Center. Pierce argued specifically that historic landmarks could serve as an "inspiration for future generations." Although all of Pierce's ideas were not developed, the promotion of his plan did indicate that members of the city's professional classes sensed that public symbols and monuments could contribute to a feeling of community and civic loyalty. In part, their desire for reinvigorating what was perceived to be an increasingly divided city, both racially and geographically, was incorporated in the development of Unigov, a plan that allowed Indianapolis to expand its boundaries in 1971 to incorporate a good deal of surrounding Marion County. The city's mayor at the time, Richard Lugar, claimed the annexation would "heal" the divisions between the suburbs and the city and make the city more livable.[19]

In 1970 some effort was even made to restore the patriotic component of Fourth of July celebrations in the city, although the stimulus came from outside Indianapolis. Entertainer Bob Hope was prominent in an effort to hold an "Honor America Day" celebration in Washington, D.C., on July Fourth of that year to tell the world, which had watched protests by American citizens against its government and political structure, that "the love of America by Americans is as real and vital as it ever was." This movement stirred some local organizations into action. The *Star* offered readers inexpensive lapel pins in the shape of the American flag and completely sold its initial order of forty thousand out in just a few days. It also cited reports that claimed that the sale of American flags had risen dramatically along with the sudden use of flag decals on automobile windshields. Although Fourth of July parades were seldom significant events in this century in the city, four were held on "Honor America Day" in various parts of the city. They all ended together in the parking lot of a shopping center, however, instead of near a monument for a patriotic ceremony.[20]

This organized attempt to stimulate patriotic expressions did not become as long lasting as it did after 1918. By the late 1960s even Memorial Day was devoted less to the veterans and the dead patriots and much more to entertainment and leisure. A parade was now held several days before the "Indy 500" race and emphasized not commemoration but fantasy and escape rather than the serious matters of life. The commemoration of the dead on Memorial Day, in fact, was done in a very unorganized way. Most of the attention of civic leaders and officials was devoted to the organization of the "500 Festival Parade," while the commemoration of the dead was left largely to individuals and small patriotic or veteran organizations. Unlike the 1920s, when the commemoration of the dead was a joint effort of city leaders and ordinary citizens, the public was left to express its commemorative sentiments in its own way. Consequently, the commemoration revealed less of an expression of national loyalty and more of an expression of sorrow and loss. Small ceremonies and personal visits still took place at cemeteries but no organized parades were evident and no monuments were dedicated. Newspapers now carried personal statements from individuals who had lost loved ones both in wartime and peacetime. In a sense the public revelation of personal feelings was more widespread than it had been in the past during public commemorative events. At the same time, this expression of feeling would be, in part, diminished by the enormous scale of the festival celebration and parade that was attended by several hundred thousand people each year just before Memorial Day.

Although they may have drawn less public attention, published Memorial Day expressions were poignant. Not all involved the articulation of grief for military dead. In fact, any deceased friend or relative was likely to be remembered. But the veterans constituted a very large portion of the approximately one thousand messages that were printed each Memorial Day and the sorrowful component of private memories was evident. The family of a man killed in Vietnam in 1966 exclaimed:

> When the evening shades are falling
> And we are sitting all alone
> In our hearts there comes a longing
> If he only could come home.

The friends of Lance Corporal Larry James Pierson wrote:

> Died in the service of his country in
> Vietnam, Hill 512, Quang-tri Province, May 26, 1969.
> You gave us a wonderful memory of a friendship so dear.
> Our hearts ache with loneliness to hunt and fish with you near.
> But God chose to call you home to everlasting peace.
> And someday we will join you friend, to a life that will not cease.

And finally, the family of a veteran killed in Korea in 1953 expressed their longing. They lamented:

> Nothing can ever take away
> The love a heart holds dear.
> Fond memories linger every day
> Remembrances keep him near.[21]

These expressions of personal grief and memory contrasted sharply with the celebration of the festival parade and the automobile race itself, events which dominated the Memorial Day weekend in the city. The parade each year in the late sixties and early seventies was devoted to entertainment and eschewed the serious themes of loyalty, Americanization, progress, and the triumph of the pioneers that had punctuated marches held in the city and the region before World War II. As such, they reduced the level of serious public discourse that had characterized the prewar era and suggested that commercialized entertainment now threatened to end the public discussions of the "things that mattered." In 1969 the parade's major theme was that of an international fiesta. The grand marshall at the head of the line of march was a governmental official in charge of tourism from Spain who was accompanied by riders on horseback in "traditional" Spanish dress. Floats were the central ingredient in the parade and treated the history of aviation, deep sea fishing, a "good-guy cowboy preparing to lasso a steer," and "Polynesian Surfing." Although most floats were sponsored and produced by local companies and corporations, they in no way reflected local civic themes. Rather the energy of the professional classes was now directed to the promotion of the city, not through patriotism but through pure forms of entertainment. The same year, 1969, that several hundred thousand citizens came to see "Polynesian Surfing," a small ceremony was held at the Soldiers and Sailors Monument and the flags in the city were flown at half-mast at the request of President Nixon as a "mark of respect" for Americans who had died in Vietnam. But most people expressed sorrow in their own personal way or attended the "fiesta parade" or the race. In 1971 the *Star* found the parade so entertaining that it claimed that thousands cheered for bands, celebrities, and floats and "for awhile last night Vietnam and the dollar did not seem nearly so important."[22]

During the Bicentennial celebration of 1976, the "500 Parade" temporarily returned to patriotic themes. But the approach was clearly from the viewpoint of entertainment, and the didacticism and civic instruction of the past were missing. Award-winning floats in 1976 included one honoring the nation and was sponsored by the Indiana National Bank called "You've Come a Long Way Baby," which featured an infant with an Uncle Sam hat and a birthday cake. Another float called "Marching Along Together" carried a colonial soldier playing a flute and a bear strumming a guitar.[23]

CLEVELAND: THE CHALLENGE OF ETHNIC DIVERSITY

The discussion over public memory in Cleveland in the quarter century before World War I was similar to the one in Indianapolis. Several interests were expressed but the dominant voices belonged to patriotism, which was aggressively promoted by local veterans, and local feelings of pride and sorrow for the sacrifices of friends and ancestors. Other interests existed to be sure in the Ohio city. During the celebration of Cleveland's centennial in 1896, which was orchestrated by prominent entrepreneurs and the local chamber of commerce, the symbolic emphasis was predictably on material progress. A log cabin was built on the public square to honor the pioneers, but it was strategically placed across the street from a modern bank building in order to emphasize the progress the city had made from "poverty to wealth." A marching pageant viewed by thousands of citizens began with a scene depicting "Cleveland of 1796," showing Indians and pioneers, and ended with depictions of the commerce, art, and industry of the city in 1896.[24] But no commemorative event was a more important expression of the interests that dominated memory in the city at the turn of the century than the construction of a monument to honor the soldiers and sailors from the Cleveland area that had fought in the Civil War.

Despite the obvious support that existed for the idea to memorialize local citizens who had helped save the nation, the effort to build the monument, which was led by a delegation of veterans who were also prominent citizens, encountered difficulties. Some of the problems, such as the matter of raising funds, were normal for such efforts. Others were somewhat unique. Overall, the entire project dramatically revealed not only what was important to the city's public memory but how serious matters of commemoration could become.

Few people dissented with the idea of honoring individuals who had served in the Union army from Cuyahoga County when the idea was first proposed by William Gleason, a leader among local veterans, in 1879. The state legislature readily approved a temporary tax to help fund the endeavor. Legislators were apparently moved by arguments that the monument should be placed in the center of the city where people would pass it every day and be reminded of "love of country" and the duty that each citizen had to his native land.[25]

The road to completing the Soldiers and Sailors Monument, however, was soon filled with obstacles. Cleveland veterans disagreed on the type of memorial that should be built. Some wanted a simple shaft rising toward the sky and others felt a memorial hall should be built where veterans could gather for various occasions. In the end the memorial actually incorporated both of these ideas.

But a more serious difference would not be resolved with any degree of compromise. The city had organized a monument commission consisting of leaders of the veteran's organization to administer the project. The commission, however, had decided not only that they wanted their memorial to stand in the most prominent spot in the city—Public Square—but that they did not want any other structure to overshadow the one they would build. Few citizens took issue with the idea that the new memorial should stand in the square. But a great many Clevelanders were unprepared to accept the proposal of the commission to replace the most important monument in the city—the memorial to Oliver Hazard Perry and his victory over the British in the Battle of Lake Erie in 1812 which was erected in 1860—with a new one.[26]

The plan to replace the Perry Memorial provoked genuine opposition and badly divided the city when it was formulated in the early 1890s. When the city park commission recommended that the veterans use a section of the one hundred acres of Public Square other than the spot where the Perry Memorial stood, the new monument commission became militant. They actually "took possession" of the spot that they wanted and erected a fence around it. A crowd of citizens that wanted to retain the traditional symbol of Perry's victory, which by now was really a symbol of local memory and part of the existing environment as well, angrily retaliated by tearing down the fence in 1890 and making speeches against the planned structure. It took an Ohio Supreme Court ruling in favor of the monument commission for the Perry memorial eventually to be destroyed on September 12, 1892, the anniversary date of the first news of Perry's battle. When a crowd gathered on the square that day, the *Cleveland Plain Dealer* astutely observed that they came not only to honor Perry but to protest the removal of a memorial that had been part of their memories for over three decades.[27]

The dedication of the Soldiers and Sailors Monument on July 4, 1894, represented the major public commemorative event for the city between 1865 and 1918. The monument itself effectively integrated the sense of pride and loss that the community felt for its veterans, along with a strong desire to demonstrate patriotism and civic duty that had traditionally been stressed by both political, business, and veteran leaders. The sense of personal loss and pride was conveyed by carving into the interior walls of the monument the nine thousand names of Cuyahoga County residents who had served in the Civil War. This listing was the result of a tremendous effort by local volunteers who distributed over ten thousand copies of a list of veterans for revisions and additions and handled over five thousand pieces of correspondence with area families. But the nation and prominent people had to be acknowledged as well. Images of Ohio war governors and generals were cast in bronze inside the monument. On top of the shaft a statue of the "Goddess of Liberty" was placed as an emblem of loyalty to the nation.[28]

The dedication ceremonies were very elaborate. Held on the Fourth of July in 1894, they included the expression of numerous interests: patriotism, entertainment, civic order and antiradicalism, and local pride. Lanterns were strung across downtown streets and the square was decorated to look like "a magnificent temple." The railroads sold special excursion tickets to the city and "thousands upon thousands" of citizens came to see displays of Civil War battle flags, parades, speeches, and the monument itself. Governor William McKinley, who personally recalled hearing George Bancroft speak at the dedication of the Perry memorial and viewing the body of Lincoln on the square, asked the crowd in his speech if they knew what the new monument represented. He quickly provided an answer. McKinley felt that the unity of the republic was secure as long as "we continue to honor the memory of the men who died by the tens of thousands to preserve it." A long parade followed with veterans, military units, and civic and ethnic organizations including the Irish, Czechs, and Poles. The fact that a carriage in the march carried the Catholic bishop of Cleveland reinforced the point that Catholics and the foreign-born held some influence within the overall social structure. And both McKinley and the local press alluded to the fact that the sense of civic order and duty represented in the celebration contrasted favorably with the disorder and protests mounted on the same day in Washington, D.C., by unemployed men.[29]

Although the discussion over the past in Cleveland prior to World War I appeared to involve more controversy and interests than for the same period in Indianapolis, in both cities public commemoration was dominated by the memory of the Civil War and personal, local, and national concerns that were incorporated in that aspect of the past. In the period between the world wars, however, public memory in Cleveland would assume a focus that differed from the pattern in the Indiana capital city. Both communities quickly took note of their foreign-born citizenry and their "heritage" in 1918. But expression of ethnic interests and heritages was essentially dropped from public commemoration in Indianapolis once the war was over. In Cleveland such an omission would have been unthinkable after 1918. Immigrants were simply too numerous and, therefore, powerful in the Ohio city. Already in 1921 the city's mayor had ordered local police to "supress" the Ku Klux Klan, a demonstration that Catholic and probably Jewish interests exerted influence in city politics. The need to accommodate ethnic interests was further increased by the legacy of the widespread Americanization campaigns that had pervaded the city since the era of World War I and the memories of a tumultuous May Day riot in 1919 that raised a false specter of the foreign-born as potentially threatening to civic order and national unity. Civic leaders now concluded that immigrants needed to be incorporated into public commemoration rather than excluded from it.

The period from 1918 to 1921 provided ample evidence as it did not in Indianapolis that forces existed in the city that could threaten not only civic order but the traditional political and economic power of businessmen and middle-class professionals. Ethnic power was manifested in events such as the Americanization parade of the Fourth of July, 1918, when some seventy-five thousand immigrants and their children marched through the downtown streets. Obviously the ethnic communities made a point of demonstrating their loyalty to America in a parade organized by the mayor's Americanization committee, a group of prominent, native-born civic leaders. The marchers carried American flags and mounted floats that expressed patriotic messages. Emigrants from Germany and Hungary, always suspect during 1918, wore red, white, and blue sashes in the parade that carried the inscription, "America First." But the foreign-born were also insistent on proclaiming their own pride in their memories of homelands and backgrounds, and this is what made them appear especially threatening to civic order. Numerous groups marched in native costumes or built floats that depicted a past that was dominated by memories of European villages. Lithuanians, for instance, presented a "crude cart constructed of rough boughs and branches of trees" that was drawn by a horse.[30]

Socialist power and the implied threat it carried to the dominant economic and political structures as they existed in the city and the nation at the time was manifested in a dramatic manner in the commemoration of May Day in Cleveland in 1919. In a graphic reversal of the orderly marches of immigrants in 1918, a parade of Socialists in the city turned into a full-scale riot. The Socialists were led by Charles Ruthenberg, a Cleveland native who was preparing a run for the mayor's office; a number of veterans; and included "Ukrainian Socialists," who carried the "largest red flag" in the line of march. Marchers carried banners that did not proclaim loyalty but, instead, demanded rights: the release of Eugene Debs, a Socialist leader, from jail and help for the unemployed. Family members and friends of the marchers stood on the sidewalks, wore red ribbons, and applauded, but many other citizens jeered. The jeers soon turned to beatings and assaults when scattered groups of veterans, youths, and apparently some police attacked marchers and destroyed the Socialists' headquarters. The ensuing riot, which resulted in one death and scores of injuries, necessitated the use of army tanks to "crash through the maddening crowds."

In the aftermath of the riot Ruthenberg was arrested, outdoor meetings of Socialists were banned, the red flag was prohibited from any more parades, and the Cleveland police placed an order for several more tanks. Some evidence exists to suggest that the local business community, which had usually celebrated progress and patriotism in public commemorations, actually armed some citizens with clubs in anticipation of the Socialist march, but most of the restrictions implemented after the riot were directed against the victims and not any alleged perpetrators. The events of the war era, however, had certainly reinforced the desire of city officials (and probably many immigrant leaders) to reinforce notions of loyalty to civic institutions and authorities. In Indianapolis this celebration of patriotism and civic loyalty could proceed in an unrestricted fashion. In Cleveland, however, the commemoration of the past would be distorted significantly by the power of ethnic interests.[31]

By no means did the commemoration of the war dead and patriotism disappear from Cleveland after World War I. The celebration of Armistice Day in 1919 witnessed a mammoth gathering of forty thousand people on the square where city clergymen asked the crowd to remember the dead and denounced "radical agitation in America." Catholic power was evident after the ceremony when many from the crowd marched down Superior Avenue for services at the Roman Catholic cathedral. During the celebration of the city's 125th anniversary in 1921 a special day was devoted to veterans and a "War Memorial Day" parade was held. But an "All American Day" was given over to a "Festival of Nations" pageant that included the performances of Ukrainian folk dancers, German gymnasts, and Italian singers.

The real strength of ethnic diversity, however, was manifested in the creation of the Cleveland Cultural Gardens, the city's major commemorative activity in the three decades after 1920. Unlike Indianapolis, public memory in Cleveland would contain not only patriotic expressions in celebrations such as Memorial Day and Veterans Day, but would also include a concentrated effort by both the native-born and foreign-born middle class to recognize a version of ethnic heritages.[32]

Ethnic interests and civic interests reached a form of accommodation in the creation of the cultural gardens. The middle-class desire to regulate the thought and behavior of all citizens through commemorative activity found a creative outlet in the building of a system of monuments and gardens that stretched for over a mile on the east side of the city. Today visitors to the cultural gardens would notice dozens of busts, statues, and ornate columns in a parklike setting that were defaced with graffiti. But for a generation that lived in the city after World War I, the gardens offered a place for the symbolic expression and exchange of ideals and viewpoints that were of the utmost importance.

The cultural gardens were created by members of the professional classes inside and outside ethnic communities in Cleveland who favored notions of pluralism and tolerance over the aggressive Americanism that proved powerful in the 1920s. These leaders were not in the least opposed to Americanization; they generally saw it as inevitable and were themselves models of upwardly mobile professionals who had thrived in new urban structures. But many were also dependent upon urban ethnic communities for their status, for their clientele, and sometimes for their votes. Those from ethnic backgrounds also shared many memories with others of similar origins. Furthermore, the ethnic leaders prominent in the cultural gardens movement easily found common ground with the native-born middle class in the city which had long sought to foster Americanization more directly through calls for patriotism, dutiful citizenship, and even the celebration of ethnic cultures which were cleansed of any ideals that could in the least way be construed as politically oppositional.

Leo Weidenthal, the editor of a Jewish-American newspaper in the city, first conceived the idea of the cultural gardens to commemorate what he felt was the "earliest memory" of mankind. This idealist felt that at some point in the past before the onset of mass warfare, tribal and racial feuds, and rampant individualism and competition ruled by the "jungle law of the survival of the fittest," all men shared a common cultural heritage. His vision was one of a "common cultural memory" in which everyone held a love for peace, harmony, and cultural expression in the arts. By celebrating the attainment of high culture in the past on the part of various groups in the city, Weidenthal and those who shared his dream hoped not only to encourage ethnic harmony and, therefore, civic order in Cleveland, but also to promote efforts toward international peace and brotherhood.[33]

By 1926 civic reformers, political officials, and representatives of the city's major ethnic groups had coalesced into the Cultural Gardens League with Charles Wolfram, a leader in the city's German-American community, as president. The goals of this organization were not as lofty as Weidenthal's. They simply wished to encourage friendly intercourse, beautify city parks, memorialize cultural heroes, and "inculcate appreciation of our cultures." The emphasis on culture and cultural heroes was not accidental. It not only represented part of Weidenthal's original vision to move beyond political and economic conflict, something that had dominated the era of World War I, but was used as a standard by which potential monuments for the gardens were judged. Thus, when ethnic organizations proposed to honor local political leaders on several occasions they were turned down; the attempt here would be to reconstruct a public memory devoid of controversial statements. The Cultural Gardens board claimed that it "zealously" guarded against placing anything of a political or military nature in the gardens in order to avoid any "controversy of feelings."[34]

The responsibility for selecting commemorative symbols in the gardens was centralized from the very beginning. In the early 1930s the Cultural Gardens Federation organized a group of ethnic representatives who were to convey plans and suggestions from their respective groups to the federation's board of trustees. These representatives were all prominent members of their ethnic communities. Louis Petrash, for instance, was a Hungarian-American lawyer; Dr. Ignatius Jarzynski was a Polish-American physician; Anton Grdina, a Slovene-American, and Philip Garbo, an Italian-American, were businessmen. Once the board had approved an ethnic plan, it was the responsibility of the ethnic group to raise the necessary funds, usually through community dances, dinners, and other social activities. Contributions of labor were also made to the projects by the city and, during the 1930s, by the Works Projects Administration.[35]

A survey of the "cultural heroes" eventually commemorated in the various gardens reveals that the attempt to commemorate individuals who were culturally but not politically significant was only partially successful. In reality a number of political messages and heroes were given prominent places within these gardens. Moreover, the tolerance that Cleveland officials showed for ethnic distinctiveness resulted in a celebration of individuals who, while not always American heroes, were often patriots in their own right—a symbol that had always appealed to the middle class. Indeed, it was neither ethnic diversity nor American heroes that were missing in the gardens. Ordinary people—immigrant pioneers—who had forged the great migration streams to America in the first place and who had lived and toiled in Cleveland's ethnic neighborhoods were nowhere to be found.

Before World War II, ethnic communities raised funds largely to commemorate heroes who defended above all else the ideal of an ethnic homeland. These individuals were usually acceptable to trustees because they tended to be cultural figures such as poets, composers, and writers. But more often than not these figures were also political activists whose cultural expressions helped to maintain the fight for national autonomy in Europe. Ethnic leaders, in other words, did not move inevitably toward the celebration of America's founding fathers when given some freedom of choice or the commemoration of ordinary people from their own ranks. Rather, they moved toward a cultural middle ground that used the homeland symbol to please both their peers in the larger American society who were interested in the ideal of patriotism and national loyalty and their cohabitants in ethnic enclaves who still felt the emotional pull of homeland images. Again an attempt had to be made to reconcile official and vernacular cultures.

The Italian and German organizations were among the first to organize in the 1930s and select their "cultural heroes." The former group erected a bronze tablet with the names of one hundred famous Italians and medallions to "six great Italians whose genius has enriched the world," including Michelangelo and Leonardo da Vinci. Germans decided to erect two bronze statues at the center of their garden to honor two poet-philosophers: Johann Wolfgang Goethe and Friedrich von Schiller, both of whom represented nationalistic as well as cultural themes.[36]

Groups from eastern Europe, an extremely influential segment of the Cleveland community, continued to honor cultural heroes who were also sources of nationalistic and ethnic pride in both the homeland and in the United States. In 1937 Polish-Americans planted trees in Cleveland that were taken from the garden of Frederich Chopin in Poland as "symbols of the cultural contributions of the city's largest cultural group." Ten years later busts of Ignace Jan Paderewski and Chopin were unveiled at the site. At the dedication ceremonies Judge Frank Piekarski of Pittsburgh attempted to appease the larger society when he declared that there was no desire on the part of Poles in establishing the gardens to "impose" the Polish culture on America.

6. Dedication of Italian Gardens, Cleveland Cultural Gardens, 1930. Courtesy of Western Reserve Historical Society.

The goal here, he asserted, was to better acquaint the American people with the quality of Polish culture.[37]

Other eastern European groups continued to mix culture and politics. Slovaks unveiled two busts in their garden in 1934. From their past they selected two religious leaders, an indication of the power of such figures in their ethnic communities, who were also advocates of ethnic culture and homeland nationalism. The fact that one came from the large group of Slovak Catholics and the other from the Slovak Lutherans in the city probably represented something of a political compromise among two religious strains in the Cleveland Slovak population. The Reverend Stefan Furdek, who had emigrated to the United States in 1882, served as a Slovak and Catholic leader in Cleveland for over thirty years, founded a number of Slovak fraternal unions, and published a series of books for immigrant school children on subjects that included the homeland and Slovak language instruction. Jan Kollar, a Lutheran minister who was also honored, had fought "fearlessly" for educational and language rights for all Slovaks, regardless of religion, in the homeland under Hungarian rule. Furdek was an especially important historical symbol for the larger Catholic majority who continued to celebrate him as an "outstanding man among American Slovaks," and someone who stood "For God and Nation" for years afterward.[38] He embodied what most of these ethnic symbols did: loyalty to religious and political structures. At the same time, his memory sustained an interest in ethnic identity in a form that was not threatening to the host society.

Exceptional men who were also religious leaders were honored by the Slovenes and Serbs as well. The former group dedicated a bust of Bishop Frederick Baraga who came to the United States in 1830, well before the mass immigration of Slovenes, and who worked as a missionary among the Chippewa Indians and became a "hero of the Northwest Territory." Serbs celebrated Petar Njegosh, a "Prince-Bishop" who wrote poetry and who obtained recognition for Montenegro as an independent state. Slovenes erected additional busts to Simon Gregoric, a priest-poet of the homeland and Ivan Cankar, "the immortal poet of the Slovenian people."[39]

Rusins in Cleveland, whose origins can be traced to eastern Europe, also decided to honor a priest active in cultural and patriotic activities. The Reverend Alexander B. Duchnovich achieved fame because he defended the Rusin language in the face of Hungarian rule and authored the Rusin national anthem and national march. He was arrested for such activities in 1849 but praised by ethnic leaders ninety years later in Cleveland who asserted both pride in the homeland and the need to be loyal to their adopted nation. The Reverend Joseph

Hanulya told a crowd of about one thousand that the Rusin garden "will become a spot of our homeland here in this country." But Bishop Basil Takach reminded his listeners that they must not let their interest in the culture of their ancestors preclude loyalty "to this our adopted country.[40]

Despite all the emphasis on ethnic homelands and cultures in the gardens, they were never allowed to stand completely devoid of messages that explicitly celebrated the American nation. Thus, a part of the cultural gardens was continually turned over to patriotic subjects. In 1935 a section of the park was dedicated as the future site of the "American Gardens" by the Cleveland Council of the Parent Teachers Association who sought to teach not only understanding among diverse groups but respect for American culture and its heroes. Mark Twain was the "first American" to be commemorated in the American section. In 1939 a bust of John Hay, the American Secretary of State from 1898 to 1905 and a former Cleveland resident, was unveiled near Twain's. The onset of World War II further stimulated the effort to honor figures from an American rather than an ethnic past. Five days after the Japanese attack on Pearl Harbor in 1941 the federation's board of trustees adopted a resolution stating that it would concentrate all of its activities "upon the development of the All-American Garden, which is the keystone of the chain of cultural gardens and is emblematic of our love of country and patriotism." The tolerance for ethnic symbols of any kind was abruptly suspended. Although some members of the board expressed concern that the public would interpret such a resolution as an "apology for a lack of unity and patriotism," the federation leaders thought that it was crucial to use the war as an opportunity to show that "nationality groups" had an even greater right to be known as "100 percent Americans" because they had come here to escape "obnoxious things in foreign governments," a statement that badly obscured the true social and economic origins of their migration streams, and had "adopted American ideals."[41]

Activities at the gardens turned decidedly patriotic during the war and remained that way to a large extent after 1945. Ethnic communities were encouraged directly to demonstrate their loyalty. In 1942 a series of festivals were held at the gardens commemorating the principles that were enunciated in the Atlantic Charter, such as the right of people to resist territorial aggrandizement by outsiders, a point that was especially close to ethnic groups interested in preserving the integrity of their European homelands. These festivals usually consisted of dramatic presentations at various cultural gardens that spoke of ethnic contributions to the building of America rather than of heroes who contributed to the maintenance of the particular group or the homeland. Thus, Italians presented a play on the discovery of America by Columbus. Unlike prewar gatherings that were orchestrated by the ethnic groups themselves, these depictions of history were based on professionally written scripts that were given to the respective communities. One Cleveland newspaper even called upon ethnic groups to use their traditional folk stories to assist the cause of American patriotism. Slovaks were told, for instance, to use their folk hero, Janosik, and tell their children that he was the "Ethan Allen of the Slovaks" and that they could serve their nation as well.[42]

Cleveland's ethnic communities fell quickly into this patriotic march. In the Hungarian gardens a forty-foot steel flagpole and an American flag were erected next to the bust of Franz Liszt. The Slovak Cultural Gardens Association transferred all of its activity to War Bond solicitation and to "patriotic unity programs."[43]

Ethnic harmony in Cleveland rather than any particular homeland or hero dominated the messages relating to ethnic groups in the Cleveland sesquicentennial celebration in 1946. A seven-mile parade from the city's downtown eastward to the cultural gardens was a highlight of the event and celebrated the themes of "One World" both at home and on the international level. This time ethnic interests, while not abandoned, were presented more forcefully within the larger structure of the city's history; ethnic contributions to America formed a more important theme than the cause of independent homelands. The parade was led by political officials and members of the Early Settlers Association "who were cheered all along the line" for their depiction of the founding of the city in 1796 by Moses Cleveland. Pioneer symbols followed with a Conestoga wagon and a depiction of a hayride. The ethnic groups came next, reduced in significance and entrenched within a larger framework of American history. And their themes were pointed more directly toward messages that were designed to please the dominant host society rather than assert interests of their own. Thus, Greek-Americans featured a float with a replica of the Parthenon which symbolized the idea of democracy. Hungarians presented a float representing an idyllic "village scene" from the homeland with ethnic costumes and music. But it was not meant to celebrate the homeland, the audience was told, but to show the "transplanting of the color, music, and national vitality of Hungary to America's shore." Hungarians did not let their depictions of contributions to the nation stop there. They constructed two additional floats. One portrayed ordinary working people to illustrate the fact that Hungarians had toiled in American fields and factories. Another showed Hungarian-Americans in the professions and was meant to affirm the idea of rapid assimilation and mobility on the part of these newcomers into American society.[44]

7. Hungarian-American float representing idyllic homeland village, Cleveland Sesquicentennial Parade, 1946. Courtesy of Western Reserve Historical Society.

8. Float depicting Hungarian-American pioneer workers' contributions to America, Cleveland Sesquicentennial Parade, 1946. Courtesy of Western Reserve Historical Society.

By the 1950s the assertion of ethnic interests in the homeland or ethnic heroes was less frequent than it had been before World War II. More common in events at the cultural gardens was the theme of "One World" in which harmony between ethnic groups was stressed over distinctive ethnic cultures, or the contributions theme by which groups recalled a past that spoke of their participation in building the American nation. The only homelands that were recalled were those under Communist domination. Interest in captive homelands usually served to reinforce the ideology of the American nation and its Cold War interests, however, rather than ethnic pride in a land that it had left. Thus, the 1953 Ohio sesquicentennial celebration, One World Day, which was celebrated continuously after 1946, involved speeches and a pageant at the gardens. Curtis Lee Smith, president of the Cleveland Chamber of Commerce, told the audience that Cleveland's creation of its own "One World" of nationality groups should serve as an example to men and women in other parts of the country and the world of unity and cooperation. The pageant that year symbolized the contributions of ethnic groups to the building of the city, the state, and the nation. Indians and Moses Cleveland were depicted in early scenes. But later parts reenacted the arrival of Irish, German, Jewish, Czech, Hungarian, Polish, Slovak, Italian, Slovene, Lithuanian, Russian, Ukrainian, Greek, and Finnish settlers. And the pageant concluded with the presentation of a young woman dressed as the Statue of Liberty; a complex ethnic past now fell neatly into place as a component in the process of nation building.

Other events at the gardens in the 1950s continued to stress the ethnic past mainly as it related to the rise of the nation-state. The chief celebration of Irish-Americans at the gardens, for instance, became "Barry Day" in honor of an Irish-American immigrant who had fought in the American navy during the Revolutionary War. And the cultural gardens federation sustained its patriotic agenda by dedicating a bust of Abraham Lincoln.[45]

Although the expression of patriotism became monolithic and less multivocal after World War II, the intensity of patriotic commemorations declined on an overall basis just as much in Cleveland as in Indianapolis in the postwar period. Patriotism dominated commemorations during World War II, especially the huge Festival of Freedom at Cleveland Stadium that was held every July Fourth and at which images of military heroes such as Douglas MacArthur were cheered.[46] Patriotic celebrations contained some vigor just after the war in the late 1940s. It seemed that traditional commemorative days such as Memorial Day, Veterans Day, and the Fourth of July, however, were invested with less discussion and exchange and more concerned with leisure time by the 1950s. Certainly leisure activities were important during such events even before World War II, but now both the interest of ordinary people in expressing sorrow or ethnic pride and the aggressive attempt to promote patriotism all had given way to rather bland expressions of leisure pursuits. Picnics and fireworks had always dominated the Fourth of July in both cities in all but a few exceptional years. Cleveland did not quite have anything like the auto race for Memorial Day, but it did have a deep interest in its major league baseball team on that day and others.

If there was a revival of the determined assertion of interests during commemorative events in the Ohio city it was during the era of the Vietnam War. Public discourse became somewhat heated again as it had in Indianapolis. Memories of sorrow and grief over war dead were revived and images of public disorder similar to 1919 also returned with the outbreak of a race riot on the city's east side in July of 1968. Memorial and Veteran's Day celebrations downtown were larger than they had been for awhile in 1968 and 1969. Speakers, always from the military, told crowds of about ten thousand on the square that they must defeat "subversion" and "aggression" wherever it existed. On Memorial Day in 1969 local high school students formed a human cross to commemorate the deaths of Cleveland area residents who died in Vietnam, and the local press printed a list of the dead. In fact, the vernacular dimension of patriotism, particularly sorrow for the dead, appeared to be the dominant expression of interest in 1969. As in Indianapolis, a local newspaper began to print personal expressions of grief and sorrow for all who had died regardless of whether they had served in the military or not. Again a sense of personal loss dominated public expressions of memory rather than service to the nation. Those who had fallen in Vietnam were remembered with "loving memory." The deceased were recalled not as patriots generally but as brothers, sisters, and parents.[47]

During the 1970s entertainment and leisure dominated commemorative events more than ever before. The program for the celebration of the city's 175th anniversary in that year revolved around entertainment by national celebrities and a modest reenactment of Moses Cleveland's landing. Pioneers, immigrant heritages, and even patriots were hardly mentioned at all. For the bicentennial celebration of July 4, 1976, a religious oriented service called, "One Nation Under God" was held on the square, a log cabin was dedicated by a local women's club, and baseball, picnics, and fireworks predominated. As in Indianapolis, the tendency for commemorative activities to promote civic discourse or instruction appeared to be giving way to the pursuit of entertainment and leisure.[48]

CONCLUSION

Social structure and the nature of political power clearly influenced the nature of cultural expression and, therefore, public commemoration in cities. In the period between World Wars I and II, Indianapolis and Cleveland focused their discussion over the past in divergent directions. The former city was heavily influenced by business and civic leaders who promoted loyalty to the American nation as a means of incorporating personal experiences of sorrow, grief, and association with the military into a larger movement for civic unity and the pursuit of economic progress. City leaders in Cleveland were interested in similar goals but their power was contested by the presence of a very large population of first- and second-generation immigrants. These newcomers had an alternative cultural agenda that included loyalties to their ethnic ancestors and homeland. The ethnic middle class itself, extremely anxious to give consent to American political and economic authorities and still tied to their culture of descent, invented a cultural compromise or an ethnic heritage that stressed patriotism and consent but in distinctly ethnic terms. They were able to celebrate ethnic patriots and heroes until the power and the demands of the nation-state became irresistable in 1941.

In New York City the situation regarding public commemoration may have actually revealed another variant. Numerous plans were advanced over how to commemorate World War I. Prior to the conflict, much public sculpture reflected the attempts of influential classes and artists themselves to teach lessons of proper civic conduct and celebrate progress and the nation. After the war a greater diversity of interests proved capable of asserting their commemorative interests in the discussion over a possible monument, including women and city planners, and resisting the commemorative initiatives of "Americans of old stock ancestry." The result was a failure to erect any permanent memorial.[49]

The ability of ethnic leaders in Cleveland to mediate the calls for American patriotism and loyalty in the 1920s and 1930s, however, does not suggest that ethnic diversity inevitably leads to ethnic influence in the discourse over memory. Blacks were present in both cities in substantial numbers and were largely neglected in public commemoration. The point here is that disparate sources of political power not the mere existence of diversity were prerequisites for creating meaningful cultural exchanges.

Finally, the experience of these two cities suggested that the power of national political ideals not only penetrated the discussion over commemoration on a communal basis but that they were strongly supported by a variety of cultural leaders in these locales. The tendency of the middle class—government officials, businessmen, and professionals—to organize and define the scope of public commemoration was clearly powerful in cities and ethnic groups. Their interest in promoting numerous forms of loyalty and civic order as a means of reducing conflict and disunity was pervasive. Even the overall campaign to Americanize immigrants—whether it was conducted through American or ethnic variants of patriotism—emanated not only from the needs of the nation but from the needs of influential people in the nation. By the 1960s and the 1970s some evidence existed to suggest that commercial forms of entertainment were replacing patriotism as a means of fostering unity but this effort too was connected to the attitudes and interests of individuals of some prominence.

Part Three

A REGIONAL FORUM

Our pride of local birth has an origin which antedates
both cabin and cradle. We inherit a pride derived from
ancestors born in the pavilion of liberty and rocked
in the cradle of the Revolution. Well founded state pride
intensifies national patriotism. A patriot may think first
of the Union or the flag but his heart quickly recalls
a favorite state.
—*Ohio Archaeological and Historical Publications 6, 1898*

They [pioneers] became real to me.
They had broken the prairie. . . . As a boy
I saw some of these old-timers in their seventies
and eighties, hard-bitten, grizzled and fading. . . .
These old-timers became part of my mind
and memory. . . . They were segments of history.
—*Carl Sandburg, Always the Young Strangers*

CHAPTER FIVE

Memory in the Midwest before World War II

THE ATTEMPTS to mediate local or vernacular versions of the past with those that were increasingly nationalistic was made not only in smaller ethnic enclaves and cities but in much larger regions as well. Linked by elements of a shared past and participation in similar economic activity, geographic areas such as the Midwest were the scene of widespread commemorations that were infused with a multivocal quality. Cultural leaders such as professionals, businessmen, and government officials eagerly sought to use patriotism to foster citizen unity and loyalty to existing structures of power. Ordinary people continued to use symbols such as pioneers as a defense of local and personal concerns and frequently viewed commemorative activities as opportunities for simple entertainment and leisure.

The nationalization of midwestern culture, which had already begun in the nineteenth century, was intensified after the 1890s. This could be seen most clearly in the rising influence of the patriot symbol. During the nineteenth century the region's culture had been dominated by a native, Protestant middle class that celebrated self-reliant, small-scale capitalists as model citizens. This cultural construction reflected the belief of middle-class leaders that they had been responsible for the region's growth and an attempt by them to reform the behavior of thousands of immigrants whom they felt did not share their commitment to self-improvement and progress.[1] These leaders and the communities in which they lived were certainly proud of the patriotism of their ancestors, but they saw all that they had built grounded ultimately in the rugged individualism which they believed they and their pioneer ancestors had exhibited.

Urban growth, ethnic and religious diversity, and the spread of large corporations destroyed the reality of Protestant, middle-class power in the region and the ability of their ideology and the pioneer symbol to remain uncontested. The region's leadership class came to include Catholics as well as Protestants, corporate leaders, professionals, and small producers. This new and expanded leadership group now articulated patriotic symbolism and ideology to a greater extent, although pioneers were not forgotten by any means. Patriots now became the basis for much public commemoration and a dominant model for citizen behavior.

The rise of the patriot symbol was facilitated greatly by the expanding power of government. The expansion of state and federal government structures to deal with the problems of a growing national economy and the mobilization of people and culture for patriotic purposes during periods of war advanced the movement toward the nationalization of culture and memory. Governments in the region assumed pivotal roles in the celebration of state centennials in the twentieth century and helped to further mediate the diverse interests of immigrants, natives, businessmen, professionals, and all citizens. States in the Midwest willingly complied with wartime mobilization and the dissemination of patriotic ideology; some governmental bodies in the region even passed a series of loyalty oaths. Although the Midwest was a much larger entity than any ethnic or urban structure, it was no less susceptible to the type of cultural exchanges that discussed and distorted the nature of a past for the present.

Prior to World War II the discussion over public memory in the Midwest, therefore, was dominated by a contest between ordinary people who drew upon local and personal memories to interpret massive social change and cultural leaders who sought to eliminate social divisions and accommodate pluralism and change by integrating regional and local cultures with a national one. This contest was not waged with weapons but with symbols and messages. It was dominated, in fact, by the symbolic images of pioneers and patriots which pervaded the interpretation of memory in the region. Both symbols attracted considerable public interest and support, but by the end of the 1930s it appeared that the power of the patriot symbol was slowly altering public declarations of what pioneers were to represent.

These developments could be seen clearly in large state centennial celebrations that occurred in states such as Indiana and Illinois. Government itself, especially state legislatures, assumed a more vigorous role in the sponsorship and coordination of activities designed to shape and promulgate versions of the past for mass consumption and in the fostering of specific interpretations of powerful historical symbols. Today the influence of special government commissions, state historical agencies, and even a certain amount of federal sponsorship of commemorative activities is taken for granted. But much remains to be learned about how such bodies functioned in the past and in various locales over time. In this case the Midwest is only a laboratory that can illuminate a much larger process of cultural exchange that characterized modern American society.

PIONEERS AND PATRIOTS

Two massive commemorative celebrations that engulfed entire states provide an introduction to the study of the uses of state power in the shaping of public memory. In Indiana in 1916 and in Illinois two years later, statehood centennials caused citizens to consider their past and discuss the nature of their collective memory. In the latter celebration a greater concentrated effort was made to use the event to stimulate patriotism due to World War I and look at the past in patriotic terms. In both states, however, definite similarities existed in the ideology that was promoted.

The government of Indiana initiated its centennial celebration in 1915 by creating a commission to publish historical materials and arrange a historical and educational celebration for the following year. In a pattern that would become important in twentieth-century commemorative activities, the commission coordinating the event consisted almost entirely of middle-class professionals and government officials. This alliance of government and the middle class created a broader support group for the idea of civic education through commemorative activities than the class of elite merchants who had influenced such activities in the previous century. In Indiana the commission distributed bulletins explaining how local celebrations should be conducted and sent appeals to public school officials to bring the student population into the celebration. An Indiana college professor, active in the state commission, expressed the hope that the celebration would be one of the "greatest educational agencies for revealing the past life of a people to itself ever attempted by any American commonwealth."[2]

Most of the activity during the centennial took place on a local basis. In this way communities could focus on a history that was especially relevant to their interests. At the same time, however, they were expected to relate that past to the development of a larger political structure. Ultimately, such an arrangement led to the celebration of symbols that served the needs of both small places and larger structures. But in 1916 such considerations were not in the minds of local planners who enthusiastically went about the business of describing and disseminating versions of the past. In Bartholomew County a pageant was held, for instance, consisting of five scenes. The dramatic presentations opened with a depiction of "Indiana and Fur Traders" around 1818. This was meant to draw a symbolic baseline from which future material progress and county development would take place. A second scene depicted early county officials in the process of naming the town of Columbus, the county seat. Two scenes that followed dealt with representations of "pioneer life," including a schoolroom, corn husking, and the Civil War, with actual sounds of bugles, fifes, and drums. The final scene presented a modern school, a sign of local progress and the advance of civilization over the wilderness, and a flag salute by "old settlers." Elements of patriotism stood out in the entire portrayal but clearly the dominant symbols were local and essentially progressive with pioneers, embodiments of ordinary people, playing a central role.

In Boone County, the editor of the *Lebanon Pioneer*, Ben McKey, assumed the role as chief organizer of the celebration and took his responsibility as a "sacred trust." He centered activities on the annual homecoming celebration in September and stressed that the commemoration was not to be a carnival. Festivities stretched over several days with each day devoted to a different theme, although pride and interest in local pioneers appeared to be the strongest sentiments expressed. A play in which students acted out phases of county history was held and included scenes about the "First White Settlers," "An Old Time Church Service," and "The Quilting Bee." By any measure the past that appeared most worthy of commemoration during decades of widespread economic and industrial expansion in the region was one populated by sturdy and presumably self-sufficient pioneers.[3]

In other towns local bankers, educators, lawyers, and professionals in general spearheaded the organization of commemorative ceremonies. A local attorney in Dekalb County arranged events around Old Settler's Day that included parades by fraternal organizations and a "processional pageant" portraying events of local history. In Madison County people brought thousands of items of pioneer relics to a display that included silverware, hay forks, firearms, and coins.

Despite the fact that over 250,000 citizens saw at least one community pageant in Indiana, the celebration did not take place on the local level alone. The state sponsored several major events to celebrate itself. A huge pageant at Indianapolis was held in October that included over three thousand performers. It covered familiar ground including portrayals of early French explorers in Indiana; battles that led to the conquest of the Northwest Territory of which the state was a part; scenes of pioneer transportation in the 1830s; the building of canals; the Civil War, a topic not dealt with as extensively in local dramas; and examples of industrial progress, a theme that appeared more explicitly in urban than small town and rural celebrations.[4]

The attachment to the pioneer past could not be ignored, however, even in statewide celebrations. At Corydon, the first state capital, women on horseback representing America and the states of the Northwest Territory, and school children doing "symbolic " and "folk" dances led a pilgrimage to the spot where the first state constitution was drafted. The assembled sang a song entitled "Indiana," and Governor Samuel Ralston gave a revealing address. Ralston reaffirmed the value of pride in locale. "Enshrined in the hearts of every people is some place, some loved or sacred spot, to which they journey for inspiration, courage, and renewed faith," he asserted. As Jews make pilgrimages to Jerusalem and Americans return to Mt. Vernon, he reasoned that Hoosiers should come to Corydon to recall the sacrifices of "Pioneer Fathers" and strengthen their love for the principles of free government enunciated in the state's first constitution of 1816. Ralston eschewed any attempt to speak about commercial or industrial progress but astutely reached for citizen loyalty by tapping into the realm of vernacular culture and personal feeling and memory in the Midwest. His words were pointed: "If I were asked to single out the dominant thought of 1916 in Hoosierdom, I would not hesitate to say that it is home building and home life. The people's best efforts and highest aspirations are put forth to make the home more secure in its purity and its comforts." Ralston stressed that the centennial was as much a celebration of the "farm and the factory" as it was of progress and "Wall Street." He felt that it was only "common sense" that the great majority of mankind will always remain hewers of wood and drawers of water. It was important, in an age of growing cultural change and class discord, to celebrate "little Davids" with their flocks against "those thirsting for power." Finally, Ralston, having made his attempt to reinforce the pride in geographic and social place of ordinary people, paid his respects to the growing power of the national state by correctly explaining how state pride could serve as a basis for national patriotism. In a brilliant move to link local memories and sentiments to an expanding state and national political structure, he asserted that behind the love of nations and patriotism stood "families, homes, and the institutions of a free people."[5]

In 1918 Illinois reached the centennial of its admission into the union. Its celebration would be equally as extensive, although the theme of patriotism would play a much more prominent role. Again the cultural leadership in the celebration was seized by public officials and members of the growing professional classes in towns and cities. The state appointed an Illinois Centennial Commission consisting of fifteen members including state legislators, professors from the University of Illinois, and officials of the state historical society. In towns and counties judges, teachers, county commissioners, and editors played prominent roles in organizing local activities and following the advice of the state commission to "work through official channels."

Interestingly, Illinois officials expressed concerns that had been heard in Indiana two years earlier. In both states a degree of public indifference to centennial celebrations had to be overcome. Ultimate public participation and enthusiasm for these events was widespread, but it was never entirely clear if they would have reached the proportions that they did without concentrated efforts on the part of dedicated professionals and officials who expanded the symbolic content of commemorative events beyond local concerns. The Illinois commission was particularly upset that the state was unable to generate sufficient support to erect a permanent memorial to Lincoln during the centennial of his birth in 1909. They did not want to let this centennial effort encounter similar failures. They also reasoned that most people were too busy working and, therefore, they needed organizations such as the commission to carry out their "ideals" and "plan their memorials and arrange for the observance of their historical anniversaries, to be in a sense keepers of their historical consciousness."[6]

Some concern over the need for a centennial celebration in the state in the first place stemmed from the fact that the United States was engaged in a world war and a feeling that nothing should be done to intrude upon that effort or distract people from patriotic thoughts and obligations. But few public officials in the state appeared willing to forgo an opportunity to revive a public discussion on historical consciousness and civic values. Their solution was to launch a celebration that would integrate the interest and sentiment in local pasts with the powerful patriotic ideology that was then emanating from the Wilson administration in Washington. In an address on the eve of the centennial celebration, Illinois governor Frank Lowden declared that he did not agree with those who felt the centennial celebration was not fitting during a time of war. He acknowledged the burden of fighting a war but claimed that "Our fathers before us too bore heavy burdens" and still "triumphed over danger and difficulty." According to Lowden the history of Illinois was rich in deeds of "patriotism and heroic endeavor" and a celebration would enable citizens of the state to fulfill their patriotic duty more "heroically."[7]

The symbol of the pioneer persisted in the Illinois celebration but it was placed within a higher structure of patriotism. The official centennial poster presented a pioneer holding a rifle in one hand, bowed down on one knee, and clutching an American flag. The centennial commission continued Lowden's theme and attempted to impose a framework of national loyalty and contributions to the union upon the local historical record. Lincoln, of course, was the well-established symbol of sacrifice for the union for both the state and the nation. But now even "founders of schools, priests, pioneer preachers, the circuit riders . . . the Indian fighters . . ." were spoken of as individuals who had only one transcendent meaning: they had contributed to the building of a nation.[8]

As in Indiana, the state centennial directors of Illinois attempted to offer guidelines for local celebrations. They also went further in formulating an agenda for statewide activity that was more extensive than similar events in the Hoosier state. Local organizers were told that the two important considerations to be kept in mind were the history of the state and the need to keep things "decidedly patriotic in character." Thus, in street parades members of the Grand Army of the Republic were to be given a place of honor because they answered the call of their nation.

A pageant in Chicago in October indicated the social and political needs commemorative rituals had to serve in 1918. The drama presented scenes of the arrival of French missionaries and the early white settlers. But less time was spent on pioneers and much more devoted to themes of a triumphant political structure such as the state's admission into the union, the Civil War, the "call to arms in World War I," and a symbolic roll call of nationalities to promote unity.[9]

Statewide celebrations continued to place a heavy emphasis on patriotism and some commemoration of the local past. Lincoln was continually invoked, of course, as a symbol of pioneer pride and national loyalty. Two mass meetings held in Springfield on Lincoln's birthday in 1918, under the auspices of the state centennial commission and the Lincoln Centennial Association, were well attended. These events included a chorus of twelve hundred Springfield school children singing patriotic songs and a call by the governor for an intensified observance of Lincoln. "The Lincoln spirit still walks the earth," he declared, "his life remains the greatest resource to the forces fighting for freedom and righteousness throughout the world."[10]

Finally, in October, a massive gathering at the state capital paid homage in symbol and ritual to state heroes and national unity. Statues were dedicated to Lincoln and Stephen Douglas in the statehouse yard. Veterans of the Civil War spoke on the occasion, told of their own battles to save the union, and one declared that "today boys in khaki are paving the way for liberty by their acts on foreign soil." Secretary of the Navy Josephus Daniels told the gathering that the statue of Lincoln would instill "the great example of unselfish patriotism in others." Two days later Catholics gathered from throughout

Illinois to hold a large field mass. A parade preceded the event in which various Catholic organizations such as the Knights of Columbus, the Ancient Order of Hibernians, and "national Slavic societies in uniform" marched in a display of unity and loyalty over diversity. At the mass itself a church official from Chicago asserted the teachings of the church were in no way at variance with "sound Christian morality or the demand of exalted patriotism. Catholics refuse to have their patriotism impugned."[11]

Government-sponsored commemorative activities in Indiana and Illinois clearly focused much attention on the dominant symbols of pioneers and patriots. Only a brief retrospective look at commemoration in the region, however, can suggest whether this focus represented a continuation or a departure from previous practice.

EARLY MEMORIES IN THE MIDWEST

By the closing decades of the nineteenth century towns throughout the Middle West were certainly tied to national cultural traditions and values such as patriotism. In Iowa, Memorial Day was added to the list of official holidays in 1880 and Lincoln's Birthday was recognized in 1909. The pervasive effort in Illinois to memorialize Lincoln was well underway before the nineteenth century had been completed. Fourth of July celebrations were widespread and frequently boisterous and extensive. A Fourth of July celebration in many towns included the firing of cannon, long parades, and large crowds from the surrounding countryside.[12] The celebration of the fourth in Galena, Illinois, during the 1876 centennial of the nation produced the largest procession ever to pass through the streets of the town up to that point. Five bands, groups of voluntary associations and ethnic organizations, and individuals dressed symbolically to represent national themes including "The Godess of Liberty" and "Thirty-Seven States of 1876" marched.[13]

However, the patriotic fervor of the Civil War and the centennial celebration never eradicated popular interest in vernacular memory. Instigated by an elusive but genuine realization that the agricultural and small-town character of their region was slowly changing, residents began to commemorate their ancestors and the people who built their communities more and the Union a little less. They in no sense forgot their patriotism or the contributions their ancestors had also made in the Civil War. But in facing the prospect of economic dislocation and urbanization at the turn of the century, they reached to other portions of their segmented memories and generated historical knowledge that put personal lives into perspective, reduced some of their anxiety, and helped them grasp a massive reality that could not be totally understood.

The heroes of their cultural construction were not signers of the Declaration of Independence but ordinary people. They were the "pioneers" who first settled the prairie in the early nineteenth century and initiated white civilization in the region. As early as 1874 the *Galena Gazette* hinted at the theme when it argued that citizens have a "moral duty" to honor the "pioneers" who settled the town. "Their memories should not fade," the paper cried, "We, their successors, ought to revere the good of their example and teach our children to honor them."[14]

The desire to honor and draw inspiration from local people, often of similar bloodlines and social station, instead of Founding Fathers, gathered momentum as the pace of social and economic change quickened by the late nineteenth century. Old Settler Associations were established throughout the region and pioneer picnics were held annually in many areas. At such activities a long oration would detail the history of local settlements and glorify the achievements of relatives, ancestors, and loved ones. At one such gathering in Kalamazoo County, Michigan, in 1883, the speaker celebrated pioneer gatherings as events where one could catch "the spirit of the olden time" and the feeling that once made this "entire community a band of brothers." In a direct rebuttal of the growing emphasis of a national culture on economic gain and expansion, the speaker told his listeners to keep the spirit of brotherhood alive, "especially in these times when the love of money-getting withdraws men from all social relations and narrows life down to a mere business channel."[15]

By the earliest decades of the twentieth century the celebration of local people in Midwest history had expanded into a fascination with the region itself. The natural landscape of prairies, woodlands, cornfields, and small towns—the places of the pioneers—came to dominate much cultural expression in the region as it was threatened by industrialization. In a sense this expression, usually outside the control of government institutions, became an artistic version of the traditional folk consciousness and middle-class ideology of the region, and elevated it to a higher level of abstraction and articulation. The setting or the "physical structure" conquered and created by the pioneers now became as celebrated as the pioneers themselves. Ironically, the nationalization of political and economic life promoted expressions of vernacular culture such as regional pride and local consciousness much as it had done in New England and the South.[16]

Perhaps the drift into a mythic Midwest, originating in the reassertion of familial and communal values in pioneer celebrations, reached its apex in the creative outpourings of Carl Sandburg. Born on a "cornhusk mattress," Sandburg was deeply affected by the urbanization of the prairie and by the pioneers who were his ancestors. In his autobiography he recalled seeing "pioneers and old-timers" on Main Street in his hometown of Galesburg, Illinois, and at Old Settlers' picnics. Drawing upon his own private memory, he wrote:

> They became real to me. They had broken the prairie, laid the first roads and streets, built the first school and churches, colored the traditions of town and country where I was born and raised. . . . As a boy I saw some of these old-timers in their seventies and eighties, hard-bitten, grizzled and fading. . . . These old-timers became part of my mind and memory. . . . They were segments of history.[17]

Sandburg also described Old Settlers' picnics he attended as a boy. He recalled old men talking about virgin prairie grass six feet high. And he expressed amazement that some of these men had actually cut a field of grain with a hand sickle and threshed it by horse feet tramping out the wheat. He fervently wished for a photograph of a pioneer breaking the prairie with his plow. Pride in place and pride in ancestry filled Sandburg and, as is well known, he used that inspiration to write poetry and prose about the region. Not surprisingly, when he published his monumental account of another midwesterner, *Abraham Lincoln: The Prairie Years* in 1926, he dedicated it to "August and Clara Sandburg, Workers on the Illinois Prairie," an indication that private memories helped to shape public expressions of culture.[18]

Orators at pioneer picnics and Carl Sandburg were clearly not alone in reflecting upon the past and the present in the Midwest of the early twentieth century. Sherwood Anderson and others wrote about the region in novels and poetry and reflected upon the changing patterns of life. Anderson's collection of poetry published in 1918, *Mid-American Chants*, spoke directly to the intellectual currents and private memories of ordinary folk in the region. The book's forward contained a lament about the "terrible engine" of industrialism and many of the poems expressed regret about the passing of a village culture in which he himself was raised. In "Song of Industrial America" he recalled old men he knew as a boy in "my village here in the West" and how they made wagons, harnesses, and plows themselves. "Then a change came," he noted. For Anderson that change was the expansion of cities "where people could not breathe" and the difficulty in finding anymore "memory haunted places."[19]

There can be little doubt that the pioneer symbol and the pioneer habitat became important in the region by the end of the nineteenth century. Its popularity was such that John Mack Faragher, in his study of a nineteenth-century Illinois community, found aspiring leaders directing pioneer celebrations in an attempt to "wrap themselves in the homespun mantle of the founding generation" as a means of legitimating their own social positions.[20] The cultural power of the symbol, moreover, was derived from a number of sources. It stood as a metaphor for a closely knit community that was now perceived to be threatened by urbanization and the rural exodus in the region. And, as always, it represented the ongoing reality of ordinary people continually overcoming various kinds of difficulties.

A PATRIOT FOR ALL: GEORGE ROGERS CLARK

The challenge to uses of the past that focused on communal values and ancestors evident in the Illinois centennial and the patriotic propaganda of World War I was sustained throughout the 1920s. Campaigns to promote patriotic history and sentiment were widespread in the Midwest as they were in other regions and were led by veteran organizations, middle-class leaders, and government officials. This effort to fashion public memory was particularly striking in the movement to build a monument to George Rogers Clark, a Revolutionary War hero who helped conquer the Old Northwest for the new American nation. On the eve of the sesquicentennial celebration of Clark's capture of Fort Sackville, a British outpost at Vincennes, Indiana, a number of prominent citizens in that state began to organize an elaborate commemoration. Ewing Emison, a Vincennes lawyer interested in the history of the Old Northwest, used political contacts to get the Republican State Committee in 1926 to adopt a plank in their platform calling for the memorialization of the capture of Vincennes by Clark in 1779 that had "resulted in the addition of seven great states to the Union and made possible its extension across the continent." At the local high school in Vincennes that year a mass meeting attended by over five hundred citizens met to consider how local interests could promote the entire effort. And during the later years of the 1920s, it was hard to read local newspapers without reading accounts of Clark, his campaign, and his band of men.[21]

Spreading outward from its local base the movement to honor Clark and the capture of the Old Northwest moved in many directions. Local committees acquired the land on which Fort Sackville was located, planned a pageant for 1929, and formulated a strategy for obtaining state and federal funding for a monument. A local state senator from the Vincennes area presented a speech in the Indiana legislature calling for support for a levy on taxable property in 1928 and 1929 that would help finance the project and the acquisition of more land. The speech of Curtis Shake was actually interrupted in the state legislature by loud cheers when he exclaimed that the achievements of Clark were responsible for making the Midwest part of American territory. To Shake, Clark deserved to stand alongside Washington as an exemplary patriot.[22]

Indiana officials approached the federal government for funds necessary to complete a proposed monument to Clark. But careful political tactics and not mere sentiment were needed to generate enthusiasm in Washington for a historic monument in a small town in Indiana. By a convenient stroke of good fortune, Ewing Emison had managed Calvin Coolidge's primary campaign in Indiana. He convinced the president to mention the memorial favorably in his message to Congress in 1927. Additionally, Frank Culbertson, a Vincennes attorney, received financial support from the local chamber of commerce to stay in Washington and lobby for the memorial. Kentucky lent support to the movement in Washington because it wanted Indiana to help it secure federal funds for a Clark memorial of its own; Clark had organized his campaign in the state and was credited with the founding of Louisville.[23]

Congressional hearings on the question of financial support for a memorial and government participation in the sesquicentennial celebration of the conquest of the Northwest Territory were held by the Joint Committee of the Library in 1927. The committee chair, Senator Simeon D. Fess of Ohio, a staunch supporter of midwestern historical commemorations at the time, overcame some initial reluctance to support the Clark memorial and used the hearings to allow a whole host of supporters to air their views on the project. The resolution under consideration stated that the capture of Fort Sackville "was the most important military engagement in the Revolutionary War west of the Allegheny Mountains and was one of the most important events in American history, contributing largely to the present greatness of the Republic.[24]

Vincennes celebrated loudly on February 25, 1928, the 149th anniversary of the fall of Fort Sackville, when the Senate approved 1.74 million dollars for the monument and a historical and educational celebration for the town in 1929. Church bells rang, factory whistles blew, and fireworks lit up the sky in celebration. "Lobbyist Culbertson" was cheered upon his return by several thousand local residents. He called on "all classes of people" to work harmoniously on the celebration and heard a local minister declare that Vincennes would become the "patriotic capital of America." Coolidge proceeded to appoint a federal George Rogers Clark Sesquicentennial Commission that included Ewing Emison; Simeon Fess; and Luther Ely Smith, a St. Louis businessman who promoted a memorial to Thomas Jefferson and the pioneers who moved westward from the St. Louis waterfront several years later.[25]

The centennial of Clark's victory in 1879 passed quietly in Vincennes. A small item in the local press noted that it did not seem possible that a century had passed since Clark "took this place." A few miles away at Washington, Indiana, children from the fourth grade sang "America" for an assembly of citizens, and a local teacher criticized historians for paying insufficient attention to Clark. Also censured were town residents who failed to come to the assembly and brave the February cold as Clark had done. Fifty years later, however, the situation had drastically changed. The Clark sesquicentennial was an enormous community celebration with visiting dignitaries, college bands, historic pageants, and parades. Packed buses arrived in Vincennes with Boy Scouts and Girl Scouts, and visitors filled local hotels. Over five thousand individuals listened to Governor Harry Leslie of Indiana declare that Clark's victory extended the boundary line of the United States and that citizens should "rededicate" themselves to the same standard of "fearless patriotism and service." A pageant re-created the events of the Clark expedition. Scenes dramatized Clark's appearance before Patrick Henry and Thomas Jefferson in Virginia seeking approval for his strike in the West, and his capture of Fort Sackville in the dead of winter. Crowds were so large at each performance that single men and women were eventually asked to stay away so that every schoolchild in the town could see the production.[26]

The actual monument dedicated in 1936 was a stately "Doric Temple," circular in shape, encasing a rotunda that was dominated by a heroic bronze figure of Clark and embellished with historical murals that extended the theme carved in stone on the monument's exterior: "Conquest of the West." The murals pictured Clark entering Kentucky on a white horse; negotiating with the Indians at Cahokia, Illinois; marching across Illinois; surrounding Fort Sackville; the surrender of the fort; the proclamation of the territorial government for the Northwest Territory at Marietta, Ohio; and the raising of the American flag at St. Louis in celebration of the Louisiana Purchase. In form and symbolic meaning the Clark memorial celebrated the Midwest only as it contributed to the larger nation. This left something behind for those interested in regional pride but very little imagery and meaning for those whose ties stretched back to ancestors, pioneers, and specific places.[27]

THE 1930s AND THE PERSISTENT PIONEER

The social conditions of the 1930s contributed somewhat to a revival of interest in the fate and, therefore, past, of ordinary people. This revival was rooted in the public discussion of people struggling with hard times and unemployment, the protests of the workers, and the rhetoric of government leaders who sought to reassure citizens and address some of their concerns. In some of the discourse in the Midwest less was made about patriotism and more about pioneers who had always been representations of ordinary people who faced difficult times. This transformation was by no means complete. That is to say that the promotion of patriotism by cultural leaders remained alive and government continued to support commemorative activities that infused the pioneer symbol with patriotic messages. The major memory debate for the decade in the region, however, was whether the revived emphasis on pioneers would in any way threaten the dominance of patriotic instruction that had emerged after World War I.

Certainly the possibility of altering the power of the patriot symbol did not appear likely in the decade after World War I. Crusades to Americanize the immigrant and demonstrate the highest form of loyalty to the state were as strong in the Midwest as in any other part of the nation. But the 1930s offered another type of political atmosphere. Public discourse and political exchange became more heated and possibly more democratic. Various interests argued vehemently over the role and size of government rather than simply loyalty to it. On a personal level individuals looked for cultural symbols and messages that offered hope in the face of hard times.

This search was manifested in commemorative activities and gave evidence that the patriotic offensive of the previous decade did not eradicate the attachment and meaning given to pioneers by localities and ordinary people. Not untypical was the scene on a remote bluff overlooking the Au Sable River in Michigan in 1932 where four thousand people gathered. The crowd was diverse and consisted of "old-time river drivers," "shanty bosses," descendants of timber barons, government conservationists, state officials, and even "Indians in garb." Nearby a "lumberjack feeding camp" was set up by people from nearby towns that had once been "roaring lumber settlements" near Lake Huron. The group had come together to dedicate a statue of Michigan's lumbermen of a century before. Engraved on the side of the monument's granite base were words that collectively expressed the sentiments of most in attendance: "Erected to perpetuate the memory of the pioneer lumbermen of Michigan through whose labors made possible the development of the prairie states." In an emotional move filled with strains of democratic feeling, ancestor worship, and pride, ninety-one names of old-time lumbermen were inscribed on three sides of the granite base. The dedication ceremonies themselves consisted of speeches by the governor and William B. Mershon of Saginaw who had been largely responsible for leading a fund drive that raised $50,000 for the erection of the monument itself. Mershon explained how he and members of "old-time lumbering families" planned the monument in 1929. The memorial itself, according to the account of a reporter at the event, made an impressive sight. Consisting of three sturdy figures in bronze "silhouetted against the sky," the statue turned ordinary people into heroes. The reporter observed: "The riverman with his hand gripping a peavy, the landlooker consulting his charts, the woodsman with his axe and crosscut saw; those three staunch figures, the virile strength of bodies seeming to show through their rough clothes appeared almost alive."[28]

History occupied the minds of Americans to a remarkable extent during the 1930s. Economic decline and social unrest had brought into question some of the most fundamental values promoted in the twentieth century. The notion of the inevitability of material progress, a prominent theme since the nineteenth century, was cast in some doubt. The future appeared more uncertain than ever but a past still existed that promised to reaffirm the fact that difficult times had been overcome before. It was this past that drew the attention of midwesterners and other Americans to an ever increasing extent.

The return to the past during the depression decade moved on a straight line into the realm of local and regional events. In this way people, disillusioned with some prospects and promises associated with an industrial economy and large political structures, turned to what was familiar and personal. Artists, for instance, who were sensitive to the popular mood, were able to capture that tone in their creations and expand tremendously the impact of their work upon the public imagination and memory. It was in just such a way that Grant Wood attempted to celebrate the rural Midwest in his paintings. Wood resented the fact that some critics called him a "flag-waver" for the Midwest. He argued that his celebration of midwestern farmers and life was justified because the farmer was central to the region's culture and a "rugged individualist who was in constant struggle with nature." The image of surviving during a period of crisis was important to many at the time.[29]

In a similar vein artists employed by the federal government to paint post office murals during the depression often listened closely to public opinion and memory before executing their creations. Consequently, murals depicting scenes of local history were very popular. One scholar who has studied the mural program concluded that these works of art provided local populations with a view of the past that was reassuring. Murals were generally nonpolitical and often portrayed a sense that history moved in distinct stages and slowly, thus calming fears of "imminent catastrophe" or rapid social change. Karal Marling described the effort of artist Wendell Jones who talked to people in a town about their past and attempted to execute a painting that melded the interests of the "people and the painter." In Granville, Ohio, this process led to a depiction of the arrival of the first Presbyterian pioneers in lush forests in the area because the memory of that event was so fixed in the minds of the people whom Jones interviewed.[30]

The most significant expression of the popular meaning of the pioneer symbol in the region throughout the 1930s took place during the celebration of the sesquicentennial of the first white settlement in the Northwest Territory at Marietta, Ohio, in 1788. This event was organized by members of the professional classes and government officials who were quite conscious of the need to reaffirm patriotic messages. But in the charged atmosphere of the Great Depression they made concessions to popular interest that would have been rare in the 1920s and encountered a depth of interest in the pioneers that they probably had not expected.

As in Indiana, local boosters partially interested in Marietta's future and members of the professional classes initiated the commemorative celebration. But the desire to push the local economy could not explain the extensive amount of popular interest in the celebration that eventually took place throughout the Midwest. In 1934 Marietta officials contacted their elected representatives in Columbus and Washington to explore the possibility of staging a celebration. The state of Ohio went about the business of trying to attract some modest funding from other states of the old Northwest and the federal government approved the formation of another body, The Northwest Territory Celebration Commission.[31]

It was not unusual to celebrate the first settlement at Marietta. One year after the founding in 1789 an orator paid tribute to the "firm band" that settled this "far distant region." Nearly every year afterward, April 7th was held in "sacred reverence" until the population became so large and diverse that the interest in the event diminished somewhat. But on the fiftieth anniversary in 1838 "a general and enthusiastic meeting" was held, and in 1841 a Marietta Historical Association was organized to establish a "library cabinet and repository worthy of the oldest settlement in Ohio." During the centennial celebration in 1888 the cornerstone was laid for a monument to the first settlers.[32]

From the beginning state and local officials who planned the tribute had a clear vision. Unlike the Clark memorial which stood majestically on the banks of a river waiting for citizens to come to it for inspiration and education, the Northwest Territory Celebration was consciously designed to reach out to a large number of towns and citizens over a wide area. A news release from the celebration commission stated bluntly that it planned to take the event "to the people." The idea was that any sentiments and attitudes nurtured by the program would be intensified by the greater personal involvement of the public. Complaining about "school histories that emphasize heroes, battles, and victories of war," the commission asserted that all too little has been said of the collective thoughts and emotions of the common man.[33]

The central device to be used in reaching the public was the staging of a reenactment of the trek of the first settlers who moved from Massachusetts to Marietta, Ohio, in 1778. This "pioneer caravan" was in reality a moving pageant that would retrace the exact path of the eighteenth-century travelers in as precise a fashion as possible. It was elaborate and certainly expensive but the commission grasped the possibility that the caravan would "come closely in contact with the Northeast quarter of the United States, containing almost half . . . of the nation's population." It also had the benefit of attracting much free publicity and lasting over a long enough period of time "to afford the advantages of repetition and what advertising men called 'soaking in.'"[34]

The plan for the caravan was extensive. College boys would be recruited to walk with an ox-drawn Conestoga wagon some eight hundred miles from Ipswich, Massachusetts, to Marietta. Because the original trip started in December, the mountains of Pennsylvania would have to be crossed on foot in the middle of winter and 150 miles of river navigated in the spring. The caravan would even be required to spend several weeks in West Newton, Pennsylvania, building a boat as the original pioneers had done to take them down the Ohio River to Marietta. Diaries would also be kept by individual marchers to record their impressions. Radio, magazines, and newsreel coverage would bring reports of the caravan's progress to a public eager to look to the past.

The fondest expectations of the caravan planners were ultimately exceeded. At nearly every stop along the way large portions of the local population turned out to greet the boys and the wagon, often with patriotic parades, meals, and local hospitality. As the caravan pulled into the mountain community of Everett, Pennsylvania, in bitter cold, for instance, on January 13, 1938, hundreds of inhabitants lined the streets. In another town the next day a huge banner welcomed the party, a man dressed as "Uncle Sam" appeared, and automobiles draped with American flags drove by. A marcher recorded in his diary that he found a "sturdy people possessing a sincerity and deep sense of appreciation. Here exists a love of country and a deep respect for the historical heritage that is theirs. Of such clay was moulded their forefathers; men that made possible this empire that is ours."[35] It is not startling to learn that such diary notations were designed to be broadcast over radio stations by the celebration planners.

At Steubenville, Ohio, the local celebration surprised even the people who had planned it. The mayor had started to organize a proper welcome two months before the caravan was scheduled to arrive at the city's riverbank. Planners felt a crowd of twenty-five thousand would appear but three times that number actually came out on April 4, 1938, in what the local press called the "greatest celebration in the history of the upper Ohio valley." The "pioneers" were welcomed by an "endless parade" of floats, bands, musicians, horses, automobiles, and organizations. "Tumultuous applause" and "showers of confetti" greeted the marchers, with the loudest cheers reserved for those who walked with the wagon from New England. Symbolically, the parade not only represented folk enthusiasm for the pioneer symbol but was an organized affirmation of unity in a society that was diverse and segmented. Floats representing different towns in the area, religious groups, voluntary organizations, and companies filled the line of march. But the themes of loyalty and patriotism were again expressed in floats such as one sponsored by the Wierton Steel Company that carried a banner proclaiming: "Live American and Support the Ideals Our Forefathers Fought For."[36]

Marietta's reception for the caravan was multifarious and revealed further the cultural discourse that was sweeping the Midwest in 1938. Several days before the landing, a pageant, "Wagons West," opened nightly performances at a local stadium. Consisting of a cast of one thousand, the dramatization told mostly of the "pioneer days" in Marietta, including "The Landing of the Pioneers," "The First Sermon," and "The First Wedding." At the end of the production the entire cast formed "a living flag," an event that a local reporter called a "Grand Finale Spectacle." On the eve of the arrival of the caravan the national celebration commission held a dinner at which pioneers were praised for their contributions to the present generation. Charles Fogle, the chairman of the Ohio advisory commission for the celebration, expressed a need to preserve "our cherished democratic forms of gov-

9. Landing of Pioneer Caravan at Marietta, Ohio, April 1938. Courtesy of Ohio Historical Society.

10. Pioneer Caravan on parade, Marietta, Ohio, April 1938. Courtesy of Ohio Historical Society.

ernment" against internal threats of government expansion as seen in the New Deal. Several days later the president of Marietta College, in a speech to the local pioneer association, warned of the need to be faithful to the government of the founders of the nation and resist fascism, communism, and "radicalism in American institutions."[37] The celebration of the pioneers could serve many interests at once.

On April 7, despite inclement weather, over seventy thousand people filled the town and riverbank before noon. Stores were closed and the local papers printed a special edition, actions that contributed to the sense that what was about to take place was extraordinary. A "bomb explosion" signaled the arrival of the flotilla and residents ran down the muddy bank to welcome the arrivals. A "Pioneer Parade" followed with floats and bands from the surrounding region, and the crowd again "cheered loudest for the pioneers in the coonskin caps." The *Marietta Daily Times* remarked that it all bore mute testimony to the immense appeal of the Northwest Territory Centennial Celebration to the populace far and near.[38]

The caravan encountered enthusiastic receptions again as it continued to move throughout the Midwest for six additional months after it landed in Marietta. The celebration commission in Minnesota felt the caravan surpassed any public observance or demonstration of its type in the history of the state. Minnesota officials actually advised all towns hosting the "pioneers" to have their citizens wear "pioneer costumes" and have their businesses erect window displays of historic objects. Additional reports sent to the Marietta headquarters reflected amazement at the public's reaction. Toronto, Ohio, claimed that the caravan was responsible for the "largest patriotic gathering" ever held in the eastern part of the state. At Dayton, in what was probably the largest reception for the caravan anywhere, almost two hundred thousand people witnessed a giant parade that included thousands of school children carrying flags. Over a dozen "foreign organizations" joined a crowd of one hundred thousand at Youngstown. The directors of the celebration in Indiana reported unexpectedly large and enthusiastic crowds of twenty thousand at Plymouth, ten thousand at Valparaiso, and twenty-five thousand in Lafayette. Crowds in excess of sixty thousand each gathered at Bloomington and Rockford in Illinois. The federal commission estimated that over two million people saw the caravan in Ohio and several million more watched it throughout the rest of the region.[39]

The parade welcoming the caravan in Bloomington, Illinois, was exceptionally revealing in its thematic content. Stretching for over six miles, the line of march consisted of several divisions that were devoted respectively to themes of national and local, official and vernacular, history. The complex character of this ritual was clear. The parade's first division consisted mostly of people and floats representing national history and citizen devotion to it. In sequence came the "Discovery of America in 1492," "Miles Standish (in full uniform)," "William Penn and the Conestoga Indians," "Puritans," "Patrick Henry," the "Spirit of 1776," and many other representations.

Local history and pride were manifested in later divisions which portrayed Abraham Lincoln in Illinois, old farm equipment, a pioneer wagon train, and a country school. "Historic McClean County" sent thirty-one horse-drawn covered wagons to the parade, representing each township in the county. Concerns about ethnic unity were secondary in the parade but nonetheless real. One particular float, presented by the local Americanization school, carried people from ten different nationalities who were shown taking the oath of allegiance to the United States.

The parade closed with a patriotic finale. "An All-American Episode" was enacted on the reviewing stand. There stood individuals dressed as George Washington, Abraham Lincoln, Ulysses S. Grant, and Judge David Davis of the United States Supreme Court, a local native. "Washington" delivered excerpts from his farewell address to the Continental Army in 1796 and "Judge Davis," portrayed by his great grandson, introduced "his friend" Lincoln who delivered his Gettysburg Address. After the parade festivities closed the caravan marchers presented a pageant of their own in front of the local "Soldier's Monument."[40]

"Freedom on the March," was the title of the pageant the caravan presented at each of its stops. The image of an ox-drawn wagon and young men dressed as pioneers attracted much interest among American citizens, but celebration planners were not interested in celebrating pioneers alone. Instead, they were anxious to use the pageant as a central project to achieve the "essential purpose" of the Northwest Territory observance. They described their goal in clear terms: "To recall to the minds and thoughts of all Americans the humble heroism and constructive determinism of the plain American citizens who first determined the type of government under which they willed to live and pushed that government westward across a continent and to eminence among the nations of earth."[41]

The pageant was a project funded by the federal government to provide "inspiration for Americans today who, though facing newer conditions, still have the opportunity and the responsibility for carrying the nation forward." In eight dramatic scenes focusing entirely on the period prior to the settlement at Marietta and celebrating the process of nation building, the caravan "pioneers" gave their message. In an opening scene or "milestone" the Albany Convention of 1754 was explained. The convention's plan was portrayed as an early attempt to unite the colonies and, thus, create a united nation. Unity in an age of growing social tensions and nation building were further emphasized in the second "milestone" which dramatized the capture of Fort Sackville by George Rogers Clark. After re-creating an encampment of the American revolutionary Army, a fourth scene discussed the Treaty of Fort McIntosh of 1785 in which four Indian nations turned over the land that became a portion of southeastern Ohio. Next came the formation of The Ohio Company in Massachusetts in 1786 for the purpose of settling the new region. In a scene depicting the Continental Congress in 1787, the Ohio Company asked Congress for guarantees of both property and human rights. In the penultimate episode called the "Trek Westward," twenty-one men assembled in Ipswich on December 3, 1787, to make final preparations for the trip to Ohio. And in the final scene a reenactment took place of ceremonies that were held in 1788 to mark the first steps by which the new nation extended civil government west of the original colonies.[42]

The Northwest Territory Centennial Celebration was enormously popular because it was able to combine its promotion of civic loyalty and antiradicalism with the popular language and images associated with pioneers and local history. It mediated diverse interests including those of the nation-state, cultural leaders, and ordinary people. In an age of growing social tension it preached unity and loyalty; in response to heightened fears for the future it offered images from the past of survival; in its celebration of local and regional history and citizen independence, it also expressed concerns about the growing centralization of national power. In its restatement of social reality it inevitably blended divergent political and social positions and thus softened those differences. But such blending did not occur without domination. For ultimately the celebration was a form of ideological promotion, although it was in a more subtle form than was the memorial to Clark. The ability of pioneers to overcome hard times and resume the forward march of civilization and material progress provided an appealing symbol to the masses of ordinary folk looking for hope in a period of uncertainty. But pioneers were also turned into patriots who were devoted to the founding principles and institutions of the nation rather than to any alternative or subversive ideological system. Ordinary people could get something of what they wanted in the celebration's mythical representations, but overall the twentieth-century alliance of government and the professional middle class that had come to dominate the discussion over public memory remained intact at the decade's end in the Midwest.

CONCLUSION

In the Midwest in the first four decades of this century the dominant symbols of public memory—pioneers and patriots—certainly performed some of the functions that Clifford Geertz claimed they could. That is, they mediated somewhat the conflicting interests inherent in the discourse over the past. Thus, the pioneer symbol served the needs of several groups and because it did it became widely used and powerful. The meaning of pioneers was diverse enough that as a symbol it was able to simultaneously soothe the personal needs of ordinary people and the political needs of professionals and officials. It allowed ordinary people to celebrate local ancestors and seek inspiration in the present by making their counterparts in the past seem almost heroic. For cultural leaders, probably as interested in place and ancestry as well, pioneers could be used as a metaphor for people who endorsed the prevailing system of political power that supported the status they enjoyed.

This particular construction of collective memory represented, moreover, a definite break with the ideology that had governed the region in the middle decades of the last century. In the nineteenth century the ideology and politics of the Midwest were dominated by a powerful Protestant, middle class of businessmen and professionals in towns and cities that spread the ideal of self-improvement and progress. This group had come to prominence by the 1860s in a period of commercial capitalism where individual initiative was frequently rewarded. They saw pioneers as progenitors who laid the foundation for the prosperity that they now enjoyed. In a new century, however, a broader set of cultural leaders and political interests had to be served. Pioneers became nation builders, conservators of tradition, and models of survival during difficult times. At the same time the power of middle-class businessmen in the region to retain a "hold on midwestern minds" remained but was diluted.[43]

Cultural leaders in the region relied more heavily on a mixture of pioneer and patriot symbols after World War I, in part because government itself now exercised a stronger influence in cultural activities and political discourse. The greater reliance on patriotism suggested that these leaders felt that the pioneer symbols and the ideology of self-improvement were insufficient to reshape the attitudes of the masses. Patriots were not so much self-reliant strivers as they were self-sacrificing citizens who would place the common good over individual interests. Patriots better served the pluralistic and contested political structure of the region now than did pioneers, although the first settlers were not forgotten.

The thirties were particularly interesting because they appeared to involve a discussion over public memory that was more contentious than the one that took place in the twenties. Labor militancy increased dramatically in industrial cities in the region. Cultural leaders intensified their efforts to preserve unity and loyalty through patriotic symbolism and the transformation of the pioneer into a patriot as well, especially in the commemoration of the founding of the Old Northwest. Their actions may have been based on a perception that increasing civil disorder and protest on the part of ordinary people would have led to a decline in order and loyalty. Ordinary people came to large celebrations and parades in 1938, however, because they were fiercely asserting their traditional interest in the pioneer symbol and caught up in the ritual and entertainment arranged for them by officials. The pioneer symbol was very well received by the public, and it was able to reclaim some of the symbolic space it lost in the 1920s.

Scholars such as Warren Sussman have noted this "debate over the nature of culture" in the 1930s and have argued that the American middle class exhibited a fascination with folk culture in an attempt to find order and meaning in a "mythic America." But if the experience of the Midwest is any indication, the interest of the middle class in folk and local culture was more than an intellectual and psychological search for understanding. Members of the professional classes and government officials acted as "disciplining authorities" as well who sought to inculcate civic obedience and loyalty in an era when discontent was widespread, and transform the meaning of vernacular symbols. They attempted to shape discourse over the past in an effort to remain influential in the present.[44]

CHAPTER SIX

Memory in the Midwest after World War II

JUST AS public memory, growing out of public discourse, responded to official and vernacular political interests in the period prior to World War II, it would fulfill similar functions in the postwar era. The structure of ideas, metaphors, and representations that constituted its ideological framework in the region after 1918 had been influenced tremendously by the patriotic fervor unleashed by World War I and the expansion of the power of the nation-state itself. Themes such as material progress, which were powerful in the nineteenth century, remained but receded in importance as government officials and other professionals became more important than businessmen in shaping the symbolic content of discourse over memory.

World War II and the subsequent Cold War did little to diminish the powerful position of the national government in American society. State governments, eager participants in the war effort, also continued to expand the scope of their activities. It comes as no surprise to learn that they remained extremely active in staging large centennial celebrations throughout the Midwest once the war had ended and continued to stress the need for patriotism, which by implication meant loyalty to individual states as well as to the nation, and for honoring the founders of the system of local, state, and national government.

But the ideological content of public memory was always susceptible to alteration and multiple interests, and the period from the late 1940s through the 1960s would reaffirm this point. State governments sponsored enormous historical celebrations that featured pioneers and patriots. But the symbolic content of the communication over a past for the present that took place during the Cold War and the turbulent era of the 1960s expanded beyond the sharp focus on patriotism and pioneers that dominated much commemorative activity in the region in the 1930s. Themes such as the celebration of ethnic cultures and material progress were reinvigorated. As government officials and other cultural leaders sought to counter the perceived challenges of world communism to the idea of the American nation and its political apparatus from abroad and of discontent at home, public memory came to accommodate more interests. A more determined effort was made to mediate vernacular and official interests and preserve the structure of pluralism by reviving the celebration of ethnic contributions and material progress in the region and by devoting more attention to the contributions of women. Ethnic contributions as a symbol could transform ethnic pride into national pride and acknowledge the growing political power of second- and third-generation immigrants in the region. Material progress, of course, always a staple of the public memory bank, could now serve to generate political consensus by discrediting the relatively backward economies now under Communist domination. Praising the role of women in the past tended to reinforce the notion of family stability and, therefore, social stability. Together they helped to construct a narrative that effectively blended vernacular and official versions of the past.

When the American state and economic system again came under severe criticism at home in the 1960s over its foreign policy in Southeast Asia and the unequal distribution of resources to minorities, centennial planners in Illinois attempted to restate a case that had been recounted hundreds of times before by organizing an incredibly large celebration in honor of the sesquicentennial of Illinois statehood. Either the mass of ordinary people had not been listening throughout the twentieth century or state officials were not sure they had made their points. Because, by 1968, Illinois began to make the case for loyalty all over again.

WISCONSIN IN 1948

Public memory quickly became a subject for discussion in postwar Wisconsin. In 1945 the state legislature decided that "it was in the best interest of the people" to commemorate the state's centennial three years hence. Wisconsin had been as active as many parts of the Midwest during the 1930s in holding huge commemorative celebrations. Madison was the site of a large event in honor of the George Washington bicentennial in 1932, and the southern part of the state observed the centennial of the Black Hawk War, marking the end of the Indian "menace" on the Wisconsin frontier, in the same year. The "greatest historical spectacle" ever held in the state occurred at Green Bay with the tercentennial of the landing of the French explorer Jean Nicolet in 1934. That experience was now put to use in the organization of an elaborate centennial celebration to be administered by a centennial planning committee consisting of twenty representatives from various parts of the state and numerous subcommittees. Some scholars have suggested that such activity after World War II on a local basis stemmed in part from a newfound desire on the part of Americans to celebrate their "heritage" including their values and the extent of the country's achievements in the face of the "political menace" of the Soviet Union. To an extent this was true, but it was also true that the struggle over "heritage," what it was and how it would be understood, had certainly preceded the Cold War.[1]

The idea to celebrate the centennial of Wisconsin's admission to the union on a grand scale received an immediate endorsement from the influential state historical society. In addition to seeking increased public support, the society responded affirmatively to the high goals articulated by the planning committee. Both society and state officials agreed that the celebration should be "dignified" and "primarily educational" and would attempt to teach as many citizens as possible by looking for ways to reach into every geographical area of the state. The lessons of the Washington bicentennial had not been forgotten nor had the need to maintain the continual effort at civic education.

The state historical society submitted its own plan of action to the state centennial committee in 1946. In an ambitious and rather elaborate agenda that mirrored many of the goals of the state committee itself, the society proposed that it implement six major projects. Focusing mainly on the theme of material progress over time, the society suggested a "central display" on the development of Wisconsin to be presented on the state fairgrounds. Visitors to the fair could acquire an overall picture of the growth of agriculture, industry, banking, culture, and the professions in the state before they entered specialized exhibits on these activities which they could then view with greater appreciation and historical perspective. The society also proposed to establish chapters of its organization in local schools so that a "more lasting appreciation of the significance of Wisconsin's heritage among our future citizens" could be created. The society had already obtained the support of the state's department of public instruction for the project before bringing it to state centennial planners for approval and possible financial support. In addition to plans for greater support for publication and research programs at the society, a "travelling show" was also proposed that would tour over fifty cities in the state and "dramatize the heritage of Wisconsin."[2]

The actual centennial celebration not only included many of the society's proposals but consisted of an almost innumerable list of programs and activities. In many ways it surpassed in scope the state celebrations that were held in Indiana and Illinois in the era of World War I and set an elaborate model that would be copied by other states in the region in the postwar era. Civic celebrations at the state capital and in towns throughout Wisconsin, a giant exposition, and new forms of communication and entertainment were all used to push the level of discourse over the past to new levels of sophistication and complexity.

The state historical society in particular took a lead in promoting civic instruction through new forms of technology. A series of radio scripts were presented throughout the centennial year stressing the manner in which the state's history could be used to learn valuable lessons for citizen behavior in the present. Although the technology was relatively new for use in commemorative activities, however, the messages were mostly familiar. Pioneers and patriots dominated the stories that were told over the airways. They were now joined, however, by a greater stress on the value of political freedom that was enjoyed in the United States; Cold War concerns now comingled with the traditional emphasis on service to the state and heroic deeds of ancestors.

The radio scripts appear rather formulaic and trite when read in our own times. But centennial officials of 1948 were very earnest when they announced before each show that the programs were designed to acquaint the listener with the "rich and colorful inheritance that belongs to you." Thus, Wisconsin residents listened to the story of Jackson Kemper, an early explorer and the first missionary "Bishop of the West." Kemper represented another tale of pioneer endurance and triumph over adversity. He survived fever and the Black Hawk War and, through it all, managed to keep his religious faith and help spread Christianity throughout the region. Patriotism was recalled in the story of Bernard Cigrand. Living as a simple Wisconsin school teacher, Cigrand started a campaign to honor the American flag and continually urged his contemporaries to show respect for the country. His efforts ultimately culminated in the proclamation by Woodrow Wilson establishing a national flag day in 1916. Several stories told of the experiences of immigrants who came to Wisconsin to find freedom from tyranny and "class distinction." Agoston Haraszthy, born in Hungary in 1812, was typical of the type commemorated. He brought his entire family to Wisconsin, operated a general store, saloon, and brickyard, and became rather successful. He was meant to represent most newcomers to the state in the level of his achievement and in the sentiment he expressed in explaining why he came. "I want a land that is free," he reportedly had exclaimed, "where people work hard from morning to night and are proud of being citizens with the right to vote . . . and free to choose their own occupation."[3]

To reach every community and settlement in the state with the messages and the spirit of the historical commemoration, the state planning committee relied on an elaborate system of subcommittees. It was these organizations that mobilized the people of the state along the lines of their normal work activities or personal interests. In a very real way the committee took the activities of everyday life and directed them toward civic or public rather than simply personal objectives. Of particular importance to the Wisconsin celebration were the subcommittees on agriculture, conservation, recreation, education, government, music, drama, art, pageantry, families, and women.

In an attempt to celebrate the contributions of a large segment of the state's population to the progress and development of the state itself, the subcommittee on agriculture focused most of its attention on the creation of appropriate exhibits at the state fair held each August near Milwaukee. Rather than simply earning a living, endeavors of rural people were represented as part of a larger collective effort aimed at the attainment of material progress. Turning the mundane into the sacred, officials created an agricultural exhibit that included two model farms, one from 1848 and another from 1948. The 1848 farm "authentically duplicated" the average farm of the period, complete with an explanation of pioneer tools and methods. In striking contrast, a contemporary farm was designed to display a modern farm home, buildings, and machinery. In what was perhaps one of the most popular displays at the fair, agricultural officials built a paean to the state's dairy industry called "Alice in Dairyland." "A fantasy in form and color," the exhibit "depicted the greatness" of Wisconsin's dairy products. The dominant figure in the entire display, which attracted over 1.25 million visitors, was "Alice," a mechanized figure that was able to stand, sit, gesture with her hands, and move her head. By means of clever technology, Alice told the story of the state's dairy industry. She was surrounded by individual product displays that were illuminated by special lighting that was designed "to delight and please."[4]

The subcommittee on conservation and recreation attempted to both celebrate the Wisconsin landscape and the men who first settled it. It did so not only by constructing exhibits, in a sense temporary landmarks or monuments, but also by inserting its theme of natural beauty and pride in place into "recreational" activities such as parades during the centennial year. At the state fair the subcommittee created a two and one-half acre display representing Wisconsin in its natural setting, complete with waterfalls, streams, a beaver pond, fire tower, wildlife, and a park and forest setting. Floats were also manufactured for use in parades. They expressed such themes as the need to protect Wisconsin forests and the attractiveness of the state's wilderness as a vacation destination.[5]

Educational interests were served during the centennial through the preparation of historical publications that were distributed to schools and, again, the mounting of a special exhibit at the state fair. Planners in this area expressed the notion that young people must be made to appreciate Wisconsin's past and "democratic way of life" so that they will strive to preserve such legacies in the future and, by implication, resist any dramatic forms of social change. Booklets distributed for instructional purposes detailed the history of schools and libraries in the state and, as in many early pageants in the Midwest, celebrated the triumph of educational institutions, another ingredient in the formula that led to the achievement of material progress. Instructions on how to integrate centennial activities into the curriculum and twenty-one display booths at the state fair were devoted to educational topics such as the rise of the University of Wisconsin, the growth of Catholic and Lutheran schools, vocational schools, and the role of the Wisconsin Congress of Parents and Teachers.

A sizable effort was expended in the centennial to celebrate the achievements and demonstrate the worthiness of state government. This was an important theme in the Midwest in this century and a direct appeal for loyalty and obedience to existing political structures. In this case the chief emphasis was placed on motion picture and radio presentations. Over $50,000 was spent on films such as "Your Government in Action" and "Wisconsin Makes Its Laws." These presentations portrayed the "democratic process" by depicting the sequence of events that went into the making and implementation of laws by state government. In the form presented to the public the political system met social needs precisely; no need ever existed to alter it. Because some rural towns and schools did not have projection equipment, filmstrip versions of this material were also developed and distributed. The historical dimension of government was further celebrated through twelve radio programs describing such events as the making of the Wisconsin constitution, the "fight" for statehood, and the passage of legislation to improve working conditions.[6]

Artistic activities, which became a central feature of large commemorative celebrations after World War II, constituted a significant way in which the Wisconsin centennial attempted to link personal interests to public ideals. Hundreds of music festivals featuring Wisconsin folk, ethnic, and historical music were held in towns and cities. Most of the music clubs in the state built their entire year's program around Centennial music or the study of music that was germane to the state's history. Wisconsin music and teacher associations turned their annual conventions into festivals featuring songs prominent in Wisconsin's past. Ethnic and folk groups performed music and dance at state festivals and expositions, and churches offered presentations of religious scores. A spectacular All-State Centennial Music Festival built around Wisconsin music and composers was given at the state fair and included a chorus of a thousand voices, an All-Star High School Band, and two hundred "spectacular" folk dances. Playwriting contests and drama festivals all featuring Wisconsin themes rounded out the extensive artistic program that managed to increase citizen participation in the civic celebration considerably.

Pageants were not neglected in the postwar commemorative ceremony, although they no longer held the central role that they once had in such events. An incredibly diverse array of methods and techniques were now used to deliver messages and encourage citizen participation in commemorative activity. Nevertheless, two pageants were designed and produced for adoption throughout the state. "A Century of Progress, Cavalcade of Wisconsin," portrayed highlights of Wisconsin's history during the past century and was designed so that it could be adopted for a performance in any community. Thirty-five towns eventually used this production of staged authenticity with its prefabricated blueprints, music, and dialogue. "Children of Old-World Wisconsin" was a pageant written mainly for production by grade school children and was presented in over fifty schools throughout 1948.[7]

In many ways "A Century of Progress," written by Ethel Rockwell of Madison, captured the symbolic thrust of the entire celebration. The performance was organized around six major thematic stages. Unity was celebrated in the opening scene which recited immigrant contributions to the "varied life" of Wisconsin and had all participants in the production join hands in a show of "brotherhood." Civic loyalty and patriotism were encouraged in scenes which called for continued attention to commerce and education. In a finale the cast exclaimed, "Forward, All!"[8]

Other events reached even further into the organizational basis of everyday life and sought to focus consciousness on the meaning and the events of the centennial. Several hundred thousand people attended centennial sporting events and tournaments. A project organized by the subcommittee on pioneer families accumulated historical records pertaining to families who first settled Wisconsin and their descendants. In a sense this continued the old celebration of the pioneer. But now even that emphasis was diluted a bit by "counter-celebrations" that marked the contributions and folk styles of more recent arrivals. Nevertheless, a program that awarded certificates to a family that had continuously owned a farm for at least one hundred years was very popular.

More indicative of the need to diversify the content of commemorative activity after the war was the existence of a subcommittee on Wisconsin women. Composed of one hundred women of "every race, creed, and variety of activity," the group developed an elaborate agenda that included an attempt to have the over five thousand women's organizations in the state "bring the centennial observance down to every community and, in turn, to every family in the state." With some exceptions the presentation of women from the past in this celebration and in many others throughout the Midwest reinforced traditional notions of women as keepers of domestic realms. Domesticity was one way in which women had properly met their civic duty in the past and could continue to do so in the present. One of the radio broadcasts sponsored by the state historical society did tell the story of a female German immigrant who had worked for women's suffrage in nineteenth-century Wisconsin, although such a story carried messages of civic duty as much as it did of female liberation. This story was balanced, however, by a program on a pioneer woman, Juliette Kinzie, who gladly followed her husband to Wisconsin and somehow thought her small living quarters at Fort Winnebago looked "like a mansion." The subcommittee on women also chose to sponsor an exhibit on home life in Wisconsin at the centennial exposition that focused on women's domestic roles and dress since the last century.[9]

Two pivotal statewide events marked the year-long celebration in addition to the thousands of local activities. The Centennial Exposition held in conjunction with the state fair in West Allis attracted over 1.5 million people, comingling historical and civic ceremony with carnival-type entertainment. In its form and substance this event recognized the existence of powerful forces pushing the creation of a public historical consciousness for the purposes of inculcating messages of civic loyalty and respect for the existing order of society and the refusal of ordinary people to completely relinquish the desire for forms of entertainment of their own choosing, completely free from the incessant calls of civic obligation. In a second instance, the entire state focused its attention on the capital at Madison in May of 1948 in the celebration of "Statehood Day." The existence of entertainment was real on this day but the entire event was much more an explicit exposition of civic messages through history and pageantry.

The Centennial Exposition celebrated the exploits of pioneers and patriots as expected but, above all, the diversity of the existing population and collective achievement of material progress for which all segments of society—labor, industry, agriculture, education, and government—were responsible. The agricultural exhibit mentioned previously invested a good deal of attention in pioneers. Components

11. Pioneer symbols at the Wisconsin Statehood Day Parade, Madison, 1948. Courtesy of State Historical Society of Wisconsin.

of the overall exhibit told of "Pioneer Life of Yesterday," how pioneers "Bravely Conquered a Wilderness," and how "From These Cabins Came Great Men and Women." Patriotism received a resounding endorsement in a "gigantic" celebration at the fairgrounds that included a competitive parade by veterans' bands, drum and bugle corps and drill teams, appearances by nationally known military figures, and demonstration flights by squadrons of Army and Air Force planes. But a typical day also included carnival rides, circus acts, and performances from groups that represented the components of a diverse society all coming together symbolically to celebrate their common past and present achievements. Thus, one could attend in a given day performances by the Milwaukee Ballet, the Log Cabin Square Dancers, the Urban League Chorus, or the Croatian Folk Dance Troupe. Pianists and vocalists competed with fireworks and poultry shows. The message, in other words, was not in the particular performances or displays as much as it was in the representation of the triumph of unity over diversity and of the collective nature of progress. Every citizen had a role to perform. None was valued more than the other on the level of culture, although material rewards distributed in the actual social structure failed to reflect this idea. Pioneers, immigrants, and patriots in the past had already demonstrated how individual roles could be fulfilled in the society. In this idealized world everyone was in their debt and expected to continue contributing regardless of cultural background or social position; no need existed for looking for alternative ways of arranging social and political affairs.[10]

Over 125,000 people descended upon Madison on May 29, 1948, to observe and participate in a celebration of pioneers, patriots, ethnic diversity, and place. The melange of symbolism that had come to characterize the Wisconsin centennial was all in evidence. In one event-filled day new voters were sworn in from each county to emphasize the high regard for citizen participation in the political system, and Admiral William D. Leahy, chief of staff of the armed forces, told the people of Wisconsin that they lived in one of the leading commonwealths in "industry, equitable distribution of wealth, education, and individual freedom and the ideals of Americanism." But prevailing over all other events was an astonishingly large parade or "twelve-mile cavalcade" that moved through the streets of the capital city. It was the biggest parade in the state's history and, in its composition, again reinforced the ideal of unity over diversity, a symbol of growing importance as both local and national leaders sought to build a consensus in the face of a perceived Communist threat at home and abroad and to use the public sphere for the integration of diverse interests.[11]

Descriptions of the impressive review of citizens caught the enormous complexity of both the event and of the society that observed it. In a march that represented a century of state history were veterans who defended the state, "costumed delegations" from the nationalities that composed Wisconsin, Indians in war paint, uniformed members of fraternal orders, and "bands, bands, bands."

The parade was organized much like the centennial committee had organized the entire celebration. Marchers and floats were placed into specific sections in order to underscore the themes of patriotism, progress, and unity. Thus, specific divisions of the order of march were devoted to the military and veterans, agriculture, transportation, nationality groups, and fraternal clubs. In such a manner were individual identities linked to those of larger structures. Floats usually reinforced the presentation of themes. The float of the new voters came first and were followed by those of veterans, including one that depicted the raising of the American flag on Iwo Jima. A float sponsored by the Knights of Columbus honored Catholic nuns who came to teach in pioneer Wisconsin. Ethnic groups such as the Swiss paraded behind both the American flag and the banners of their homelands. Girls from New Glarus wore quaint costumes of various Swiss cantons with "embroidered aprons and odd shaped caps." Another float carried a Swiss chalet with a yodeler loudly at work. Italians, like many groups, felt the need to explain their history in terms of citizen contributions (rather, than, for instance, the continual quest for family survival) and presented three floats showing laborers, singers, and athletes. Norwegians presented a giant replica of a Viking ship which brought new immigrants to America.[12]

The climax to Statehood Day came at the University of Wisconsin stadium. In the evening over thirty-five thousand citizens assembled again to witness a festival of music, dance, and pageantry. Much of the program centered on the ethnically diverse nature of music in the state. Oscar Rennebohm, the governor, had already proclaimed earlier in the day that "our forefathers were of many bloods but we have become fused together as one people. Out of this melting pot has come a hardy, courageous, progressive race of men." Entertainment continued the symbolic message of unity over diversity. Selected marching bands from across the state formed a large "W" and a "100" on the football field. Then ethnic musical groups took turns performing. First came the Germans. The Wisconsin Saenger or "Circle of Song" sang "Springtime on the Rhine" and Wagner's "Pilgrim's Chorus." Greek Orthodox religious music, Dutch "Klompen" dancers, Italian singers, and Swiss yodelers came next. The *Wisconsin State*

12. Symbols of civic loyalty at Wisconsin Statehood Day Parade, Madison, 1948. Courtesy of State Historical Society of Wisconsin.

Journal was moved to report that "men and women of all faiths, of many ancestries were there to show their compatriots the wealth of their fatherland's culture and to recall the striving days of Wisconsin's history."[13]

OHIO IN 1953

Although the state-sponsored celebration of the sesquicentennial of Ohio's admission into the union did not take place until 1953, it too was planned and conceived in the political atmosphere of the late 1940s. Inevitably it reflected some of the same themes and concerns that had appeared in Wisconsin. As always on such occasions, moreover, a compromise was struck between the felt need to educate the population about a heritage that was appropriate for perpetuation and the need to allow for the entertainment that the ordinary people demanded. Patriotism and respect for the pioneers was still in evidence, but again a more determined effort was made to recognize ethnic diversity and expand the definition of heritage to include the millions who entered Ohio society after the pioneer waves had cleared the forests and the fields. It is possible that this thrust, as in Wisconsin, was the result of the greater political influence that the representatives of later arriving nationality groups now had after 1945. But it is also evident that the desire to expand the definition of heritage to include greater ethnic diversity in the region was stimulated by the felt need of many to join the national consensus to fight the Cold War.

The attempt to incorporate diversity into the celebration began with the organization of a planning committee in 1949. Appointed by the state governor, who inevitably had to consider political alliances and factions, the sesquicentennial commission included representatives of business, labor, religion, ethnic and racial groups, women, and elected officials. Business and government leaders dominated the appointments with Harvey S. Firestone, Chairman of the Board of the Firestone Tire and Rubber Company, acting as head of the state commission. But the planning group did include the publisher of a Hungarian-American newspaper, and the president of the Ohio Federation of Women's Clubs. In their diversity the planning groups that administered commemorative celebrations after 1945 appeared to be quite different from similar groups operating prior to the war.[14]

The composite nature of the planning group was apparent several years later in a booklet that it produced for statewide distribution. Designed to help state citizens find ways to celebrate the 150th anniversary of Ohio, the publication made the usual suggestions for parades, pageants, exhibitions, civic ceremonies, and festivals, and even permanent construction projects such as parks, museums, and the restoration of local historic sites. But the booklet also made a strong plea for reconciliation between old-stock citizens, whose ancestors had settled rural Ohio and much of the rest of the Midwest, and citizens of more recent ancestry whose relatives had come to fill industrial jobs in towns and cities. Planners explicitly told citizens to "overcome the divide" between "old settlers" and the "hundreds who were pouring in during the period of industrial expansion." A specific recommendation was made for projects or pageants that would have "old-timers" making "formal gestures of welcome to their juniors" and demonstrate to them how both groups now share in the evolution of Ohio society. Newcomers were told they could then respond by mounting exhibits showing their contributions to their "new community" and also their different backgrounds. Parades and folk festivals such as those in Cleveland in 1953 and 1954 would follow some of this advice.[15]

As in Wisconsin, a great deal of stress was placed on the educational functions of an anniversary celebration. Planners saw clearly that another opportunity existed to imprint civic messages on the minds of ordinary people. In nearly every classroom in the state attention was devoted to the celebration. Students built model canal boats and studied local history. Often hundreds of students would participate in pageants with "pioneer life in Ohio" being the favorite theme. In the primary grades much of the emphasis was placed upon the local community. One third grade class made cardboard models of the places in which their fathers worked and other youngsters built models of the first statehouse or Indian tepees.

Educational efforts were marked by a close cooperation between the sesquicentennial commission and the state department of education. The state educational officials sent letters to every school in 1952 with suggestions of how to observe the sesquicentennial and study Ohio history. The letters carried a message that claimed that "today's children" neither appreciate the "advantages of life" or progress that has been made since "pioneer days" and "know too little about Ohio writers, industrialists, and women of achievement." State education officials argued that there was "an urgent need for each child to see how he can contribute to a better community life" and they hoped by celebrating material and individual progress they would encourage students to express loyalty and commitment to the political and economic system that made all of it possible.[16]

A dramatic tribute to education in the service of civic responsibility and the maintenance of public memory was given in Ohio by President Dwight Eisenhower. In October of the sesquicentennial year Eisenhower made a well-publicized trip to Defiance College to lay the cornerstone for the Anthony Wayne Library of American Studies.

Over seventy-five thousand citizens came to hear and see the man who had known the college's president, Kevin McCann, when he had served on Eisenhower's staff at the Pentagon from 1946 to 1948. The President used the event to sustain the celebration of education for civic good that was an important aspect of the Ohio celebration. Eisenhower declared an "ultimate faith in education as a hope of the world." The president knew well the core of public memory in the Midwest and saluted the "explorers, trappers, missionaries, traders, and farmers" that built Ohio. They left for all citizens, Eisenhower claimed, a "heritage" that was more important than public prestige or social position. And the "chief bulwark of our heritage against any such decay or loss," he felt, was the American school system, "from the one-room, red-brick building at a country crossroad to the largest of our universities." For Eisenhower citizen loyalty and, therefore, unity were impossible without the educational system. He reasoned that the "job of being an American citizen is more complex than ever before," and only through the schools could citizens gain the knowledge and understanding needed to maintain a concern for community and national welfare.[17]

Not all activities were so formal, however, and entertainment again was strategically integrated with civic ceremony. In Toledo a large celebration extended over twenty-four days and attracted over 250,000 people. A stage show told the familiar story of pioneer settlement and canal building and the progress made in transportation from the use of mules to the coming of the first locomotive west of the Allegheny Mountains and north of the Ohio River. A pioneer village was erected nearby for visitors to gain a further appreciation of the efforts of ancestors and the distance traveled in terms of material advancement. Patriotism was vivified in special Flag Day ceremonies that attracted over thirty thousand people and the main speaker, Kevin McCann, told the crowd to support a strong military defense until "Communist economies crack under the weight of sterile military machines." The entire audience then recited the "Pledge of Allegiance" and a local Elks lodge traced the history of the American flag. Finally, model citizen behavior and local pride were celebrated in a special show honoring the late entertainer and native-son Danny Thomas. The audience lit matches in the night and sang along with Thomas who was praised by local officials for being a "fine, clean, honorable man," qualities that were worthy of emulation by all citizens.[18]

The culmination of the Ohio celebration was the staging of a group of sesquicentennial events at the Ohio State Fair in Columbus. The fair in the words of one state official "offered material proof of Buckeye greatness achieved in 150 years." Over half a million visitors witnessed historical pageants, farm and factory exhibits demonstrating progress, parading bands, and military displays. The need for youth to participate actively in the institutions and activities handed over to them by their parents was again emphasized in a special "Youth Day" celebration attended by over sixty thousand students. Young people marched around the race course at the fairgrounds and the Future Farmers of America were selected for a special tribute for completing twenty-five years of activities in the state. Industrial progress received special attention when for the first time in the history of the state the "massed might of Ohio's industries" was displayed under one roof in a newly constructed Merchants and Manufacturing Building. The familiar story of progress through improved means of transportation was retold by an exhibition of old and new railroad equipment sponsored by fourteen railroads operating in the state.

"The 17th Star," a pageant and "symphonic drama" by playwright Paul Green captured the most attention throughout the days of the fair with performances given every night for twelve days. The production was presented on a landscaped stage almost three hundred feet long and eighty feet wide with a sophisticated sound system that carried performers' voices to the farthest point of the grandstands. With the exception of a few professionals, all members of the cast were Ohioans who volunteered their services. Opening night for the pageant attracted not only considerable publicity but all of the notable officials and planners that had been behind the execution of the sesquicentennial itself. The governor, Frank Lausche, and the chairman of the sesquicentennial commission, Harvey Firestone, wore period costumes from 1803 Ohio. At the end of the opening night performance, according to the local press, ten thousand people rose to their feet and roared a loud approval.[19]

In typical fashion the pageant's presentation of history was progressive. Scenes moved inexorably from depictions of prehistoric Ohio mound builders, to Indians fighting white settlers, to pioneers plowing the land, to the formation of state government, to "people of all nationalities" finding homes in Ohio, to the Civil War, to the creation of industry and the birth of the atomic age. The past was portrayed in terms that made it appear understandable, and the progressive evolution of modern Ohio and the United States was made to appear inevitable. In a telling moment near the end of the entire production the "shadow" of an Ohio pioneer spoke to a "1953 youth" and urged him to keep faith in the same political and economic system that had ostensibly produced the progressive transformation portrayed in the pageant itself. The "pioneer" exclaimed:

> There's a wilderness to conquer—hate and suspicion and fear! And work and faith will do the job. All that's gone before has prepared for this. If you work as hard to solve these human problems as we worked to give you these tools and machines, then it will be done. Have faith, boy, it can be done. It will be done! These machines and mass production will help you do it.[20]

MINNESOTA IN 1958

The ritual of commemorating the admission of states in the Old Northwest into the union continued in Minnesota. State political organizations again took the lead in formulating plans for a celebration of the 100th anniversary of Minnesota statehood in 1958. The central planning committee for the event consisted more of state officials and somewhat less of business, religious, and ethnic leaders than in Ohio, but an extensive system of local and county representatives brought people from all sections of the state's society into the planning and implementation of the affair. And minor differences in the planning structure failed to alter significantly the symbolic content and historical messages selected for public discussion and veneration.

Although all state centennial efforts paid a good deal of attention to encouraging and shaping local participation, Minnesota seemed to go farthest in instigating and directing activity in every county and community. As early as 1956 the state centennial commission concluded that the success of any community activity would be measured by the "extent of active, dedicated participation of its people." The commission was vitally concerned that the celebration "mean something personal to each Minnesotan" and, in its quest to link private worlds and public values, sought to dramatize local history and stimulate pride in community and county as a means to building pride in the state itself. During 1956 a list was compiled of key individuals in each county, an approach that was similar to one used by the national George Washington Bicentennial Commission in the 1930s. Those individuals selected from preliminary surveys were brought together by the centennial commission for instruction in how to foster local participation. Over six thousand county representatives received a monthly bulletin throughout the next few years suggesting all sorts of approaches for conducting local observances of the event.

The results of this extensive effort were obvious. A tremendous expression of local pride in place and ancestry was very evident in the Minnesota centennial. This is not to suggest that such sentiment was manufactured. The local outpouring of emotion and interest was too pervasive to be attributed solely to the efforts of state planners.

Rather, as in numerous celebrations before, planners carefully nurtured personal sentiments of local pride that they already knew existed and attempted to direct those feelings of ordinary folk toward public and civic ends. At times, the expression of local and personal pride in the Minnesota celebrations actually appeared to overwhelm and obscure the messages of patriotism and social unity that were so important to planning officials at state and national levels.

Local celebrations were dominated by an interest in pioneers. In Anoka County pioneers were honored by the presentation of certificates attesting to their historic status. In Cottonwood County twenty thousand people visited an exhibit of pioneer relics gathered from a "treasure hunt for historical artifacts," and a project was begun to preserve a one-room pioneer schoolhouse. Pioneer graves were cleaned up and marked in the cemetery at Old Crow and in Lac Qui Parle a sod hut, "the type used by pioneers," was built inside the 4-H building at the county fairgrounds. An ox-cart trek that included a man who wore pioneer clothing and used authentic tools and utensils attracted significant attention in Marshall County, which also restored an old grist mill used by early settlers. Where ethnic diversity was more pronounced, such as on the iron ranges of St. Louis County, the boundaries of local history had to be expanded to include not only pioneers but later arriving immigrants from southern and eastern Europe that had come to work in the mining operations. Thus, while a Museum of Pioneers was established in the county, an All Nations Food Fair and a Finnish-American festival were also held.[21]

At the state level the symbolic messages were more numerous and the historical content wider as officials sought to accommodate many "positions" and interests and still reinvigorate devotion to the ideals of loyalty and unity. The state committee, therefore, made several grants to help produce a film showing how agriculture contributed to progress in Minnesota and supported organizations that mounted exhibits pertaining to rural life. One popular display described the progress in farm machinery following the early use of oxen. Another effort to support traveling exhibits in the arts received considerable backing. A committee on the arts arranged for exhibitions of watercolor portraits of famous historical structures in the state and works by Minnesota artists. Pride in the state was also fostered by the commissioning of a "Minnesota Symphony," a competition for state playwrights, a Folk and Square Dance Festival at the state fair, and the publication of pamphlets on the history of music and drama in the state.[22]

The state commission also spent some of its funds on education and historic preservation. Over one hundred radio programs were produced to help citizens realize "a better understanding" of Minnesota.

Topics included Minnesota's participation in American wars and events in the state that "changed" national history. A booklet for schools briefly described the lives and contributions of the state's most distinquished citizens and famous people. And historic restoration efforts were initiated at Fort Snelling, a U.S. Army outpost established in 1819 to encourage the first settlement of white people in the region.[23]

Sports was also an important means of expanding citizen participation in the centennial observance. Again planners attempted to merge popular attitudes and leisure-time activities with public rituals in an attempt to link vernacular with public concerns. Without such an effort it was never certain that ordinary people would turn enthusiastically to civic programs. Government had to compete for the attention and consciousness of the public just as advertising, religion, or any other institution. In Minnesota all kinds of sporting events were held in conjunction with the centennial, although it was never clear how precisely ordinary people made the connection between their participation in such events and the symbolic messages of unity, patriotism, and local pride that were so important to planners. In 1958, nevertheless, over two hundred thousand people took part in centennial sports programs. Over half this number wore a special centennial sports patch on their uniforms to signify their participation and as a "salute to Minnesota sports down through the years." Sporting events attached to the centennial included the national and state speed skating championships, boxing, tennis, basketball, swimming, and even a "Land-O-Lakes Regional Centennial Sports Car Rally."[24]

Special efforts were made to insure the participation of women in the centennial celebration, something that was not so easily found in such Midwestern activities prior to World War II. A women's division was added to the centennial planning committee and chairwomen were selected for each county. Again the cultural presentation of a female past privileged messages of women's domestic roles over their independence from such responsibilities. Women's work at home was displayed as a contribution to the overall material progress of the state. An exhibit at the state fair that "excited more interest than anyone had anticipated" drew a contrast between an "authentic" pioneer kitchen and a modern, "streamlined" kitchen of 1958. The women's division produced a cookbook with recipies from all eighty-seven counties and a display of bridal gowns. The division even distributed a "Minnesota Women's Centennial Prayer" that was recited "thousands of times" during the year by all faiths in the state which asked "Our Gracious Heavenly Father" for strength "to guard our heritage so that their [pioneer women] trials and sacrifices will not have been

13. Symbols of pioneer men and women, Minnesota State Fairground, 1958. Courtesy of Minnesota Historical Society.

in vain." The statue of a strong "pioneer mother" at the state fairground was only one of many such structures that were erected in the Midwest throughout the first half of this century.[25]

A Minnesota Centennial Train that toured most of the state was the single most dynamic project undertaken by the centennial commission. Believing that "the story of Minnesota" should be taken to the people of the state, the train carried exhibits to eighty-six of the state's eighty-seven counties and attracted over 630,000 visitors. The exhibits like the centennial itself were designed to "increase awareness of Minnesota's heritage, to instill greater pride in the state, and to stimulate enthusiasm for the state's future." In many of the smaller counties the visit of the centennial train provided a stimulus to build a community centennial celebration with parades, entertainment, special sales by merchants, pageants, and band concerts. The heritage of the pioneers, pride in place, and bright prospects for continued material prosperity were again the thematic cornerstones of the exhibits. Paintings and charts revealed how pioneers settled the land, how large the state's agriculture and industry had become, and the "spectacular advancements" that had taken place since the nineteenth century. At several small towns with populations of only a few hundred, thousands of visitors to the train congregated from surrounding areas to see the displays.[26]

ILLINOIS IN 1968: ANOTHER SIDE OF THE SIXTIES

The full-blown nature of commemorative activities in the postwar era became evident in Illinois in 1968. With nearly twenty years of experience since the Wisconsin celebration, planners now had a good idea of the range of values they wanted to promote, the diversity of interests they needed to accommodate, and the techniques that would allow them to make the most effective presentation in the discussion over public memory that periodically engulfed the midwestern states. As the social and political system became more complex, more groups demanded attention and benefits from the expenditure of public funds and energies. Tourist promoters, minority groups, civic and patriotic organizations, religious bodies, political parties, and business interests all wanted to see their concerns addressed. Communication paths became crowded and public discourse more complex than perhaps they were prior to World War II. This resulted in celebrations that appeared unwieldy and confusing in their goals and meaning. But above all of the complexity, frenetic activity, and competition for attention, certain basic continuities persisted. In a fashion reminiscent of the Midwest in the 1930s, the Illinois celebration was closely tied to the political controversy and discussion of the 1960s itself. But it was also a product of a long tradition that continued to assert itself even in the face of extreme discontent directed toward the social and political system. Beyond the desire to attract tourists, entertain, and satisfy the wishes of numerous constituents within the state, it was ultimately a civic ceremony that emphasized solemnity over entertainment, continuity over change, and loyalty over dissidence.

The Illinois Sesquicentennial Commission was typical in its composition. Political leaders, prominent individuals, and representatives of the major components of the social order all came together to initiate a massive discussion and celebration about the past, present, and future of the state. Members included the president of the Illinois Bell Telephone Corporation; the head of a Chicago advertising firm; Allen Nevins, a prominent American historian and a native of Illinois; and a Democratic ward official from Chicago. The entire body was chaired by the indefatigable Ralph D. Newman, a Chicago civic and business leader who pursued American history with a passion. Newman was an authority on historical documents, past president of the Illinois State Historical Society, and had served on the U. S. Grant Association and the federal Civil War Centennial Commission advisory board. Newman's expertise in business and history was supplemented by Ver Lynn Sprague who brought several years of experience as a consultant on tourism to his position as director of the sesquicentennial staff.[27]

Early in the planning process Newman let it be known that the sesquicentennial celebration, while ostensibly about the past, would also serve political and economic needs in the present. This tendency had certainly been evident in the celebrations in Wisconsin, Ohio, and Minnesota. It was now more central and explicit. The need to make the past and its interpretations serve the goals of powerful political and economic interests as well as psychological needs became acute once more as currents of protest over social inequality and the national government's foreign policy threatened to frustrate the achievement of unity and material progress. Newman had already shown Illinois officials how effective he could be in impressing the public with historical imagery. At the New York World's Fair in 1964–1965 he was responsible for installing an electronic Lincoln at the Illinois pavilion that spoke to visitors and caused a great sensation. He now promised to again "recount the drama of the early days of Illinois, the beauties, the advantages, the opportunities of present-day Illinois, and the magnificent promise of a future Illinois." By 1966 he was able to articulate the goals of the celebration which included industrial expansion, an increase in exports, the promotion of tourism, the modernization of the transportation system, and even the support of cultural activities. This was a considerable expansion over the thrust of the state centennial celebration in 1918 that focused so much attention simply on patriotism. But Newman was quite aware of contemporary political issues as well. He told a planning conference at the University of Illinois in 1966 that their gathering together was unusual because "it's not a protest meeting." "No one here is 'agin' anything; we're all 'fer' something!" he exclaimed, "and that something is the welfare, prosperity and education of the State and all of its citizens."[28]

Despite the range and contemporaneous nature of Newman's objectives, the Illinois celebration continued to make substantial use of the traditional symbols of midwestern public memory. If it took patriots and pioneers to build Illinois and the nation, it would require people with the same sort of attributes to defend it from its critics in the 1960s. This message, in the minds of state officials and leaders, needed retelling to both the mass of the citizenry and to the activists and the protestors of the 1960s who, in the eyes of many cultural and political leaders, had forgotten what public memory had told them for decades.

The commission's message, for instance, was made emphatically in a special Memorial Day celebration it sponsored in the southern part of the state at Carbondale. The event and its patriotic imagery, which was a central event of the state commission, was held in the city because of its ties to John Allen. Lamenting the fact that American flags that draped the caskets of servicemen were seldom flown, Allen, "a local historian," organized a National Flag Bank. If the owners of such flags sent them to Allen, he would return them with a certificate indicating that he had flown them. A "Gold Book" was kept at the local city hall listing the names and the service histories of veterans for whom flags were flown. Consequently, Carbondale felt that it had a legitimate claim to host a somber and serious ceremony on Memorial Day.

The affair in Carbondale in 1968, a year of widespread protest in the United States over civil rights and the war effort in Vietnam, was an elaborate patriotic ritual. In its symbolism and in its messages it constituted another side of the 1960s usually ignored by historians of the decade. It articulated a conservative position in the discourse of the decade that was infused with so much discontent. Carbondale continued the powerful association between patriotism and memory when it launched its celebration by honoring servicemen at the cemetery where the flags of deceased veterans had been flying for the flag bank program. An address was given at the site by the Chief of Chaplains of the United States Navy, J. W. Kelly, and the town held a large parade viewed by over twelve thousand citizens along with a pageant celebrating Illinois, entitled "Make Her Wilderness Like Eden."

In addition to military and patriotic units, the parade featured the Illinois Sesquicentennial float that proclaimed the theme of progress with symbols of covered wagons, industrial smokestacks, and the state capitol building. In the evening presentation of the pageant, vignettes of state history including scenes depicting Lincoln, George Rogers Clark, and U. S. Grant, by now familiar symbols of patriotism, were performed to underscore the theme that in Illinois individuals in the past had rallied to the defense of the national state in times of political crisis.[29]

The Carbondale celebration was quite conscious of how starkly its brand of patriotism contrasted with the protest and civil disobedience that existed elsewhere. The local newspaper noted that while groups of people riot, kill, and destroy property, other groups "all over the nation" are quietly preparing ceremonies to honor the war dead. It especially welcomed the keynote speaker for the affair in Carbondale, entertainer Arthur Godfrey. It was Godfrey's visit and speech to the town that actually attracted the most public attention and crystallized some of the patriotic sentiment that pervaded civic ritual even in the sixties.

Godfrey's message was not only a ringing endorsement of patriotism but a denunciation of extremism of any kind. He relied on his own personal memory to tell of a Memorial Day he recalled as a youth in New Jersey where he marched as a Boy Scout, and almost every home along the parade route displayed a service star "proudly." He claimed that patriotism during his youth was simple and eloquent. "It was the Fourth of July and there were fireworks and flags and bunting," he explained. But in 1968 he saw the situation differently. He noted extreme measures around him to desecrate America and defend it. He wished to discredit both and still retain the basic message of patriotic loyalty that dominated public memory:

> There are among us, those who think patriotism in any form is embarrassing. Well I am embarrassed for them, nitwits who burn the American flag or fly the colors of the Viet Cong from a window on the campus and other such neurotic nonsense. And I am just as embarrassed by those who would clap these characters in irons or otherwise banish them. My faith in our country is such that I figure there's room for all kinds of nuts of every persuasion.[30]

The call for patriotism at another state-sponsored celebration in Salem in June was less moderate and restrained but carried much of the same thematic thrust. Sesquicentennial officials took advantage of the annual Soldiers and Sailors Reunion which had been held continuously since it was started by the Grand Army of the Republic in 1884 to devote special days not only to old settlers and Illinois history but to a local casualty of the Vietnam War. A memorial ceremony was held in honor of Jerry P. Hawkins, a graduate of Salem Community High School, who lost his life while serving with the U.S. Air Force. The main speaker, William Doyle, a candidate for the office of national commander of the American Legion at the time, called for a military victory in Vietnam. "We who support America's policies in Vietnam, and we are in the majority," Doyle claimed, "can take heart in the fact that America is not alone in seeking the freedom of the South Vietnamese people. We have supporters throughout the world."[31]

Pioneers were not forgotten in official statewide activities. Although Illinois did not devote the attention to ethnic diversity that other midwestern states had done in the 1940s and 1950s when attempts were made to solidify a Cold War consensus at home, it did maintain the symbolic emphasis on the earliest white settlers. A major promotional event was the reenactment of the travels of early explorers of Illinois territory. In this instance, the voyage by canoes of the explorers Marquette and Jolliet from Canada to Illinois in 1673 was reversed. An "armada of canoes" left Kaskaskia in June for the sixteen-hundred-mile trip to Expo '67 in Montreal. Sesquicentennial planners wanted to honor the men for bringing "their philosophy and their religion" to the territory and for opening trade routes and even produced a film of the trip, with support from a corporate sponsor, so that students could "visualize the hardships" of the early explorers.[32]

Pioneers also figured prominently in a number of other statewide activities. A traveling exhibit of miniature rooms and local scenes sponsored in part by a Chicago department store contained displays of a tavern from 1831, "a gathering spot for pioneers," a farm kitchen of the 1850s, and Lincoln's Law Office. A Sesquicentennial Medallion commissioned by the state planning committee symbolized progress again with a representation of a covered wagon drawn by oxen, and a supersonic jet plane. In an expensive and elaborate celebration of state government, a powerful symbol of pioneer times, the old state capitol building, built by early settlers, was taken apart and faithfully reconstructed.[33]

In its zeal to expand the number of citizens who participated in the sesquicentennial, Illinois went further than other states in promoting the use of artistic events. Tapping the deep interest of all kinds of community groups and individuals in various types of artistic endeavors, nearly every form of artistic expression practiced in the state was linked in some way to the sesquicentennial observance. Again an attempt was made by officials administering a civic event to direct the interests of ordinary people toward public rather than purely personal ends. The commission established a special arts committee and developed relevant programs in architecture, painting and crafts, music, theater, writing, and "special events."

Art exhibitions were developed largely around themes of Illinois history, although other subjects were treated. The Chicago Historical Society mounted an exhibit that dealt with themes such as "Illinois Enters the Union: 1818" and "Chicago State, 1849–1859." The Field Museum of Natural History told the story of Illinois prehistory "before the coming of the white man." Touring exhibitions presented work by Illinois artists, and the Illinois Bell Telephone company commissioned twelve oil paintings commemorating great events in Illinois history for statewide display. A special "folk life and crafts" festival took place during October near Springfield with expert craftsmen re-creating "the life of early Illinois" and "many things of a homespun age." Special ceremonies were also held in October in Chicago to honor Richard Hunt, a distinquished black sculptor and his work in metal of John Jones, the first black official elected to the Cook County Board of Supervisors; the ceremony was one of several that made a very modest effort to include some black history into the larger celebration.[34]

It was always in the study of purely local activities in such celebrations, however, that evidence was found to suggest that the concerns of authorities for a progressive history, patriotism, and economic development were not completely shared in the smaller scale of the locale and the community. On the large scale of state centennial celebrations, officials had a large and full agenda. But in the smaller confines of neighborhoods and towns, ordinary people sometimes appeared to be primarily interested in their local past and place and in socializing with friends. They could approve of and share sentiments for remaining loyal to the state and sustaining the drive for material prosperity, but when left to their own resources, they usually marked anniversaries with social gatherings or activities centering on the exploits of local ancestors.

In a planning session held for the sesquicentennial observance at the University of Illinois in 1966, representatives from towns throughout the state expressed their ideas of how they thought the affair should be organized. They did not think on the large scale of reenactments of canoe trips to Canada, the commissioning of traveling exhibits or operas, or the promotion of tourism. Their ideas tended to center around matters derived from personal interest and a local past. A woman from Decatur told the planning conference that they should produce a commemorative quilt and a souvenir mug. Another woman from Vandalia wanted a special stamp featuring her hometown courthouse, a symbol of local importance. Another group from Riatt County described the efforts they had made in erecting a local museum devoted to pioneers.[35]

During the sesquicentennial itself the emphasis on local and personal interests was maintained along with the celebration of national loyalty, progress, and history. In Henry County a strawberry festival, fishing, a rodeo, and a tractor pull were all held in conjunction with the sesquicentennial. In Perry County, in July 1968, demonstrations were held of churning, weaving, spinning, soap making, and "other duties of the householder in olden times." Adams County published a history of the county and developed a "strong historical association." Some counties prepared and sold their own cookbook. Near Peoria two hundred Girl Scouts hiked an old trail used by early settlers in the area in order to gain an "appreciation" of the past. In Galesburg nearly all the attention was devoted to a local hero, Carl Sandburg. Readings of Sandburg's work were presented near "Remembrance Rock" and a new junior college in the town was named in honor of Galesburg's most famous citizen. At a predominantly black high school in Chicago the sesquicentennial meant a celebration of black history. Included in one program were the reading of biographical sketches of famous blacks in Illinois history and musical sketches from old Negro spirituals. In Jo Daviess County an elaborate pageant was created by county residents retelling aspects of local history such as episodes of pioneer life and the "county's great boom days."[36]

But local celebrations were by no means impervious to expressing the sentiments held to be important by cultural leaders as well, and ordinary people could also adopt ready-made suggestions for thinking about the past. Local celebrations, in other words, could consist of layers of public and private, official and vernacular, concerns. In Randolph County members of the National Muzzle Loading Association recreated the march of the by now legendary (in the Midwest) George Rogers Clark. At the Messiah Lutheran School in Chicago, theatrical presentations depicted standardized themes of Illinois history such as a drama of pioneer life and the early life of Lincoln. National history dominated the subjects of four plays presented by Northern Illinois University that included the story of the "great American patriot," Nathan Hale; the personal problems of a "brave man in the South"; during Reconstruction; and the issue of "New England morals" during the westward movement. Lincoln plays, the official state pageant that celebrated material growth in Illinois, and traveling art exhibits and musical productions were incorporated into hundreds of local activities throughout 1968.[37]

CONCLUSION

The nature of commemorative activity in the Midwest revealed both continuity and change when the periods before and after World War II are compared. The stress on patriotism remained vigorous, although much of it was incorporated into officially sponsored celebrations. Many people were involved in centennial planning, but it still remained an activity designed primarily by leaders in positions of authority. These individuals worked persistently to nurture and encourage patriotic sentiment both in the early years of building a Cold War consensus and in the tumultuous days of the 1960s. In fact, an argument could be made that the Cold War consensus that emerged in this country after World War II may have been partially due to the traditional influence that cultural leaders, largely of the professional class, had exerted in the process of reworking reality and creating interpretations of events.

It is also clear that ethnic groups, produced from newer waves of immigration after 1880, received more tolerant treatment in state celebrations after 1945 than they did in the era of a more belligerent patriotism after World War I. No doubt some of this attitude can be attributed to the shared experience and cooperation of the wartime experience between 1941 and 1945 and the increased political power of ethnic groups themselves. Women too probably received an enhanced status in these events from their wartime efforts. Whatever its specific causes, greater diversity and tolerance were evident in the expanded symbolic universe of state centennial activity in the Midwest. Actually the history of the region was still primarily reserved for the pioneer settlers. When newer ethnic groups were discussed it was usually in terms of their "ethnic culture" not their historical experience in the region. And both the culture and experience of women were placed within the dominant framework of contributions to the nation and to progress. Newer immigrants, like pioneers before them, were preoccupied, so the historical interpretation went, with the process of nation building.

Finally, the notion of material progress appeared to be reinvigorated after World War II when messages and ideals were discussed in public discourse. It certainly had fallen from some favor in the 1930s when the prospect for continued material progress appeared more uncertain. But this notion, championed by the middle class since the nineteenth century, now reappeared and was promoted avidly as a major trend of American society in both the past and the present by government officials and members of the business and professional classes who orchestrated so many commemorative events. This pattern was reinforced, moreover, by the international competition that manifested itself in the early Cold War period when society leaders felt compelled to defend and celebrate American progress in contrast to the underdeveloped economies of the Communist states. Attacks upon the American nation-state from domestic sources in the 1960s, as the celebration in Illinois revealed, created a similar desire to defend and assert the historic pattern of American material progress, and as always, the need for unquestioned loyalty.

Part Four

NATIONAL FORUMS

History is no longer a record of past events.
It is an illuminating account of the expanding life of man
in all of its manifestations, revealing how each stage of
civilization grew out of preceding stages, revealing
how the past still lives in us. . . . So considered
history is inspirational.

—A Kansas judge, 1927

Corporate America has conceived a Bicentennial plan
to manipulate the mass psychology of an entire nation
back into conformity with its vision of what
the American life should be. The strategy will be
to speak of the greatness of America to those who feel
insignificant; . . . to speak of patriotic commitment
to those who feel isolated and confused. The long-range
goal is to convince people that the problems facing
America can be solved by existing institutions.

—Peoples' Bicentennial Commission, 1974

CHAPTER SEVEN

The National Park Service and History

PUBLIC MEMORY was not only discussed in ethnic enclaves, urban communities, and regional and state commemorations, but in national forums as well. Beginning in the 1930s, a period in which government attempted to increase its influence over many aspects of American society and culture, the National Park Service (NPS) began a significant attempt to rationalize and centralize the process of selecting historical landmarks and sites. These activities were paralleled by a series of federal commissions that were established to coordinate commemorations of George Washington's birth, and as previously noted, George Rogers Clark and the settlement of the Northwest Territory. In a period when the reality of economic decline accentuated citizen concern over future social and economic change, government leaders moved to consolidate their own authority and reinforce loyalty and calm anxiety about the future by memorializing the history of nation building, a story which implied that change in the past had been purposeful and positive. After World War II federal commissions were created to direct the national celebrations of the centennial of the Civil War in the 1960s and the bicentennial of the American Revolution in the 1970s and further the interests of the nation-state and its supporters in the cultural debates over memory.

It would be convenient to claim that ethnic, local, and state forums and interests were simply replaced by national ones after the thirties. History and the discourse over public memory, however, seldom progressed in such a simplistic way. Indeed, while official culture could dominate vernacular culture, it could not have existed without it. It not only came to contain local interests and expressions but drew its very existence from the challenge vernacular interests posed to national order and unity. In most cases cultural leaders, especially those in the park service and on national celebration commissions, attempted to minimize the importance of vernacular expressions or reformulate them into nationalistic frameworks. Even where they did this, however, they were forced to accommodate such expressions of local interests. Thus, many of the places ultimately selected by the NPS as historic sites certainly reflected themes of national significance but were also promoted by local groups out of pride or out of a desire for stimulating local economic growth. The political and cultural power of the nation-state could administer, harmonize, contain, and reformulate diverse vernacular expressions but it could never remove them completely.

In the 1930s the federal government intervened in the discussion over public memory in a very substantial way and created a national forum for the expression of interests on the subject. As it came to regulate areas like the workplace and the family, the government also attempted to influence and, therefore, distort the discussion over how the past related to the present. Large bureaucratic organizations such as the NPS and the professionals who were tied to the power that such organizations could exercise, attempted to set standards for the creation of national historical landmarks and symbols and impose a nationalist framework upon the public's perception of the past in a more systematic way. This effort did not obliterate the regional, state, ethnic, and local forums from the discussion of memory or erase the messages and symbols that these structures held dear. But the power and the visibility of the park service history programs did tend to alter the nature of the expressions of memory on a local, regional, or ethnic level. Not surprisingly, since park service programs were administered by middle-class professionals, the link between the traditional middle-class promotion of progress and patriotism was actually reinforced. The state in other words not only began to consolidate its already considerable power and use it in the discourse over memory, but it advanced some of the class interests of those who were intimately tied to that power for over a century.

Organized in 1916 to satisfy the desires of conservationists and others who cherished the wilderness and "scenic nationalism," the NPS spent much of its first decade concentrating on the maintenance and preservation of landscape treasures and natural wonders such as Yellowstone Park, acquired by the government in 1872, and Yosemite Park, acquired in 1890. Some historical artifacts were inevitably included in its storehouse, such as the ruins of cliff dwellers at Mesa Verde, Colorado. But the natural landscape dominated the organization's thinking and planning. During the 1920s the park service acquired twice as many natural areas as historic ones, including the Grand Canyon and Grand Teton parks.[1]

The NPS became a powerful shaper of historical images and messages for the American public in 1933. In that year the government, under the influence of the newly elected administration of Franklin D. Roosevelt, reorganized the management of historical resources and transferred all federally owned national parks, monuments, military battlefields, sites under the control of the War Department, eleven national cemeteries, and national capital parks into one national park system. This move, which emanated in part from aggressive leaders and professionals within the NPS, sought to strengthen its political base and professional competence in historic interpretation. It also proved to be pivotal in narrowing the range of symbols and messages from the American past that would receive official sanction. Before that story can unfold, however, the tenor of public commemorative activities in the late 1920s and early 1930s must be understood. Without an appreciation of the climate in which public historical exercises were conducted at the time, the role and ideological direction of the park service can never be fully understood.

THE PATRIOTIC TWENTIES

In the decade after World War I the atmosphere of civic ceremonies and anniversaries was charged with the celebration of patriots and ancestors. Stimulated by the unprecedented efforts of the Wilson administration during the war to excite sentiments of loyalty and devotion to the state and the nation, the twenties and early thirties witnessed a number of extremely large historical celebrations that made a definite impact on the entire nation. Commemorative events in New England, for instance, influenced the organization of similar activities in the Midwest. And officials in the NPS took note of the appeal and impact historic observances launched by local governments and commissions made on the public mind.

The mass distribution of historical information to the public often took place before World War I through international fairs and elaborately staged pageants. Fairs such as the one at St. Louis in 1904 chiefly acclaimed material progress and almost always contained exhibits of the evolution of technology and the marked contrast between Native American culture and industrial culture. The pageants, which persisted in popularity into the thirties, were more pointedly historic in content. Held mostly in cities in the Midwest and Northeast, they invariably involved hundreds of local citizens in the dramatization of local history which usually progressed in stages from a point where Indians occupied the land, through a period of pioneer settlement, to an era of modern states, schools, victorious military campaigns, and technological progress. Historian David Glassberg has ably demonstrated how these pageants celebrated progress and democracy by allowing for the mass participation of countless numbers of local residents. Pageant masters throughout the country found employment plentiful as they organized productions at state centennials, town anniversaries, and civic celebrations. Ethel Rockwell, who was active in the pageant movement in the Midwest, asserted that a pageant was designed "primarily to educate, to revise or maintain a memory of the past, and to awaken a civic pride and a spirit of community cooperation." But the leading pageant writers, such as Thomas Wood Stevens, also wanted to entertain the population as much as educate them and freely mixed factual detail with imaginative fiction in creating historical dramas for public presentation.[2]

Although public commemorative activities before World War I always contained expressions of memory that served local and national interests, the latter clearly predominated in the aftermath of wartime propaganda and mobilization. As the examples of the state centennials of Indiana and Illinois and ethnic celebrations in the 1920s have already suggested, local and communal memories could be commemorated after 1918, but they invariably had to be cast in an ideological framework that expressed loyalty and devotion to the nation in the present and in the past. World War I did not mark the beginning of the nationalization of public culture but it certainly advanced that trend to a very significant extent.

Several large celebrations took place in the twenties and captured much public attention. In December 1920, Plymouth, Massachusetts, hosted the 300th anniversary ceremonies of the landing of the Pilgrims. The festivities emphasized many of the themes found in pageants and fairs, although patriotic fervor and ancestor worship appeared more explicitly as sentiments than the adulation of material growth. A large quantity of Pilgrim bones was actually entombed under reinforced concrete "secure from everything that can destroy them." A huge pageant called "The Pilgrim Spirit" was witnessed by over one hundred thousand people who were reportedly moved not only by spectacular lighting effects but the historical scenes that passed in front of them. A new granite portico was even dedicated at Pilgrim Hall by the New England Society of New York City which sought to honor "the memory of the virtues, the enterprise, and the unparalleled suffering of their ancestors."[3]

Philadelphia organized an extensive if controversial celebration of the sesquicentennial of the adoption of the Declaration of Independence in 1926. The event lasted for months and attracted a considerable amount of positive and negative comment. Protestant leaders in the city led a bitter fight to keep the festivities, which contained exhibits of progress, patriotic gatherings, and carnival features, closed on Sundays, something that was done during the 1876 centennial exposition in the city. Fair officials, mindful of the need to make money, argued that Sunday was the only day that the working classes could attend both the exhibits and the amusements. Although one of the directors of the event claimed that the "Sesqui" should remain open on Sundays so that the "horizons of patriotism" could be broadened for the public, religious leaders eventually got a state order closing the exposition site on the Lord's Day.[4]

By the early years of the 1930s elaborate commemorative ceremonies were plentiful as the United States appeared to feverishly turn to its past for entertainment, consolation, patriotic renewal, education, and inspiration from the deeds of ancestors. The incredibly expensive and privately financed restoration at Williamsburg, Virginia, by John D. Rockefeller had made a definite impact on the public mind by 1930 and reinforced the notion that the past was indeed glorious and a source of inspiration. In 1930 the tercentenary of the Massachusetts Bay Colony opened an even greater awareness of the potential of ceremonies for public instruction. Drawing on state and town governmental structures, the celebration involved nearly every citizen in the commonwealth as it inspired over two thousand separate events attended by over eleven million people. Planners of the event acknowledged that they had to overcome initial apathy on the part of many citizens but persisted because the "morale" of the state's people was threatened by worsening economic conditions. They felt they could reinvigorate civic pride and public optimism by cultivating an appreciation for the region's history and their ancestor's values. The state department of education closed schools on days of great parades and pageants and urged schoolchildren to recite a patriotic creed that bluntly advocated uncritical loyalty and deference:

> I must always in trouble's hour be
> guided by the men in power.
> For God and country I must live, my best
> for God and country give.

Pageants were devised for replication throughout the state and focused attention on the colonial era and the Revolutionary War. When it was all over the tercentenary commission felt that they had successfully achieved their goals of honoring pioneers and of demonstrating the progress that had taken place in America in "spiritual, educational, cultural, and human affairs."[5]

Just prior to the reorganization of the park service in 1933, the federal government itself sponsored several prominent commemorative events. An influential reenactment and pageant celebrating the sesquicentennial of the Battle of Yorktown in 1931 was funded in part by several million dollars from Congress.[6] The year before, the United States Army at its annual military exposition and carnival in Washington, D.C., contributed to the national celebration of the "Covered Wagon Centennial." The event marked the departure of the first wagon train leaving St. Louis for Oregon, and the Army thought it suitable to feature a demonstration of the perils encountered by pioneers in covered wagons "who won and held the West" and the cavalry who often rescued them from Indian attacks. President Hoover was moved to exclaim that the westward trek of the pioneers was a source of pride to all patriotic Americans.[7]

The federal government's furthest intrusion into the business of shaping patriotic and historic sentiment during this era was represented in the work of the George Washington Bicentennial Commission. Staggering in size, scope, and ambition, the commission was appointed by Congress and represented a high point for the orchestrated promotion of patriotism that pervaded the era after World War I. In retrospect it also revealed how reluctant twentieth-century leaders and states were to leave the nurturing of patriotic sentiments and proper modes of historical consciousness entirely to chance. Congressman Sol Bloom, who directed the entire affair, told an audience in 1931, in explaining why the celebration had to be held, that he felt called to "defend that flag, to honor that flag, and to preserve that flag as long as time shall be."[8]

Although the commission to celebrate Washington's birth had its roots in the patriotic twenties, it made its greatest impact in the early years of the depression decade. Composed of prominent individuals such as Bernard Baruch, Simeon Fess, Henry Ford, and U. S. Grant III, the impact of the commission was diverse and widespread. It clearly made an impression on the NPS. By generating popular interest in the first president, the celebration gave impetus to a large restoration project at Washington's birthplace monument in Wakefield, Virginia. NPS officials were given some responsibility for the task and considered it an "honor." They eagerly used it to push further into the field of historic interpretation.[9]

The zeal and promotional thrust of the Washington commission, as it sought to embed images of the first president and what he stood for into the minds of citizens, knew no boundaries. Drawing upon his experience as a "showman," theater owner, and promoter, Bloom asserted that "we must teach the biggest lesson in history ever given." His commission was responsible for encouraging over 4.7 million commemorative activities, an average of over 16,000 per day. Events included department store window display contests; exhibitions of art devoted to Washington and his times; programs that allowed ethnic groups to proclaim their contributions to the American past; student essay contests; the planting of memorial trees; a long list of publications on the first president's life—especially his willingness to serve his country in lieu of pursuing private interests; the dedication of the Washington Masonic National Memorial in Virginia; pageants such as one depicting the surrender of Cornwallis; and a commemorative funeral service. Over seventy-five thousand churches participated in a "Thanksgiving Day service closing the celebration, and students attended over 3.5 million separate school programs that included the introduction of new courses on Washington into the curriculum.[10]

Bloom and his fellow planners were keen on taking their message of civic responsibility and patriotism as embodied in Washington's life to as wide a public as possible. They began by sending a questionnaire to every postmaster in the United States asking for the names of prominent citizens, schools, and civic organizations in localities. They consciously rejected the older idea of an exposition or fair that had been popular after 1876. Such events could mainly influence only the people who attended them. Considerably more effective as an educational, inspirational, and propagandistic technique was a celebration that would be taken to the public and would make "serious appeal to the hearts and minds of men, women, and children." Their objective was a "spiritual celebration" not, as the great fairs had attempted, a veneration of material progress.[11] As the government moved more fully into shaping public commemorative ceremonies, the celebration of material progress—so dear to the hearts of the nineteenth-century middle class—gave way somewhat to the immediate needs of the state itself for emotional loyalty.

THE PARK SERVICE ENTERS HISTORY

No one was more influenced by the historic celebrations taking place around him than the director of the park service, Horace Albright. He was particularly intent on expanding the base of political support for the NPS by moving it further into the realm of historic preservation and interpretation. The nativistic and patriotic attitudes of the 1920s provided him with just the right atmosphere to do so. Albright was acquainted with, among other influential people, Madison Grant, a leading nativist and defender of Anglo-Saxon America, and appreciated his strong support of the park service itself. By 1930 Albright was looking at military and prehistoric sites that were under the jurisdiction of the departments of war and agriculture. He also toiled fervently to bring two colonial sites into the NPS—George Washington's birthplace and the Colonial National Monument which embraced Jamestown and Yorktown.[12]

Albright and the NPS in general also recognized that they could not hope to gain credibility within the government and attract more tourists if they did not raise the professional level of park service staff in historical matters and alter their image as simply keepers of natural wonders. In 1931 the NPS hired its first professional historian, Verne Chatelain. Shortly thereafter, Albright strengthened ties to local historical organizations by directing Civilian Conservation Corps workers in the rehabilitation of state historic sites. In 1933 Albright, with the cooperation of his friend, Secretary of the Interior Harold Ickes, successfully resisted a plan to create a separate national preservation commission to coordinate historical activities. Ickes argued that such a plan would put history back into the hands of amateurs.[13] Instead, Ickes got Roosevelt to sign an executive order that same year reorganizing the NPS and consolidating all federally owned national parks, monuments, military parks, eleven national cemeteries, and various memorials and national capital parks into one National Park System. In a relatively short period Albright saw an unprecedented increase in the authority of the NPS over historical matters as its inventory of historic sites increased from twenty to seventy-seven.[14]

The aggressive posture of the park service toward the acquisition of historical sites, especially in the populous East, can be detected in a quarrel that erupted in 1932. During the Washington bicentennial celebration, Congress became embroiled in a dispute with the proprietors of Washington's home in Virginia, the Mount Vernon Ladies' Association. The issue involved the refusal of the association to grant free admission to a group of children from a Jewish orphanage. The controversy ignited some editorial discussion in the nation's press over the issue of admission fees to and private ownership of patriotic "shrines." At least one congressman argued, in language that reflected the sentiment of the NPS, that the American people were anxious to bring Mount Vernon "under perpetual control of the central government" and called upon the Ladies' Association to donate the property to the government as a patriotic gesture. Local political leaders in Virginia and the Daughters of the American Revolution rejected such an idea. A Virginia newspaper argued that Mount Vernon was already "in safe hands" and that it was a "shrine" not a "picnic ground for all tourists." But Horace Albright favored a federal takeover of the property, and his chief historian wrote that there are so many reasons why the park service ought to administer Mount Vernon that he hesitated to list them all. "No one single historic spot in the east," Chatelain asserted, "has so much interest for the American people."[15]

Increased responsibility for the management of historic sites inevitably caused the NPS to give greater attention to the issue of interpretation. What exactly would they tell the American public about history and what function should that information serve in the first place? These were new questions that had not been so specifically addressed before. They now came to be matters of considerable discussion. When the NPS had only to think about scenic wonders, they could rely on guided tours carried out by a "ranger naturalist" who generally lacked any form of historical training for interpretation.[16]

The small but growing staff of professional historians in the NPS wasted little time in attempting to conceptualize an approach to presenting history to the public in the 1930s. The sudden expansion in historic sites within the NPS demanded nothing less. Their initial assumption was that the public could comprehend neither all the historical detail at a given site nor the entire mass of American history. Necessarily, public presentations would have to be selective and, therefore, symbolic. That is to say that images and messages conveyed to the public would have to "make lasting impressions" because it was not possible to tell everything. Each site and each bit of detail offered for public consumption inevitably became a representation of a larger and more complex reality and concept.

Chatelain, a former history professor from Nebraska, went further and concluded that people needed to be both educated and inspired when visiting sites. He felt deeply that these objectives could best be accomplished by the creation of patriotic sentiments. Historic sites would stimulate patriotism in the same way that scenic ones had for years. He saw the role of the NPS interpreters as one that would "breathe the breath of life into American history" and offer ordinary citizens "something of the color, the pageantry, and the dignity of the country's past."[17]

For policymakers at the NPS education and inspiration could best be achieved through a selective or symbolic presentation of the past. Thus, each site within the system would have to carry an important thematic burden if visitors were to be properly impressed. This was more than simple preservation or a promotion of progress. The object of NPS attention was not people in the past but the minds of citizens in the present. Only sites that were "matchless," entitled to a position of the first rank, and based on "broad aspects of prehistoric and historic American life," would be acceptable within the system. Clearly aware of the increased time Americans enjoyed for touring and travel to historic sites, NPS professionals eagerly sought to penetrate leisure time with educational messages. Chatelain felt strongly, moreover, that a standardized policy of site selection and basic themes would act as a defense against the creation of a park and monument system that would be a disjointed assortment of various concepts, a triumph of vernacular over official interests. If every suggestion from a local, ethnic, or racial group ever became a historic site the symbolic system would become confused and the messages unclear. Chatelain claimed he wanted a puzzle but one where every single piece neatly fit into an overall design.[18]

By 1933 NPS staff was planning a survey of "historical-educational development and possibilities" at each site under its jurisdiction. Concerned about creating a "well-formulated policy" for "public education and recreation, particularly in the teaching of American history," each site was to be examined to learn what events or persons of "historical significance" were connected with it and the extent any facilities for "public education" existed. Staff argued that the park service had to acquire and present historical material in a professional way in order to win the confidence of the "educational world," and that antiquarianism had been "divorced" from the historical activities of the NPS. Specific plans were made to hire more professionally trained historians and not rely simply on "naturalists" to run educational programs; the idea was to publish informational pamphlets of various sites and create a national committee of historical consultants in cooperation with "national learned societies." Staff professionals also suggested that the presentation of history within the NPS be organized in terms of various categories such as economic, military, political, or religious, and that it all be placed under an overarching framework of "stages of American history from prehistoric times to colonial to the present."[19]

The belief in public education and inspiration through history that existed among professionals in the park service received a monumental boost with the coming of the New Deal. Powerful political leaders anxious to enlarge the role of government in nearly all areas of economic, political, social, and cultural life, and to exert mastery over an errant economy now stood ready to provide resources and encouragement for bureaucratic expansion and federal programs. Harold Ickes as head of the Department of the Interior and, therefore, ultimately responsible for the NPS, actually felt that he was partially responsible for the "material and psychological well-being" of ordinary people as well as of natural and historic resources. Under Ickes the historical programs of the park service would reflect both of these concerns.[20]

Ickes and NPS officials firmly established the historical and educational role of the park service by gaining passage of the Historic Sites Act of 1935. A logical extension of steps that had already been taken to some extent to consolidate the administration of historical sites, the act declared that it was a national policy to preserve for public use historic sites, buildings, and objects of national significance "for the inspiration and benefit" of the American people. Ickes, influenced by his staff at the NPS, told Congress during hearings on the measure that the bill would facilitate the building of a system of parks and monuments that would collectively present to the American people a "graphic illustration" of their past. Others offering testimony, including W.A.R. Goodwin of the Williamsburg restoration project, cited the need to avoid commercialism in the process of preserving and interpreting the past. President Roosevelt wrote a special message on behalf of the legislation insisting that the preservation of historic sites for the public benefit, "together with their proper interpretation, tends to enhance the respect and love of the citizen for the institutions of his country."[21]

Specifically, the act formalized procedures by which the government could sanction the creation of historic sites and monuments. It authorized the continuation of a Historic American Building Survey that would compile an inventory of significant structures, empowered the park service to enter into agreements with state and local bodies for the care of historic properties that were not nationally significant, and, most important, established a criteria by which professionals in the NPS could exert greater control over the selection of future historic sites for the system.[22]

SELECTING OUR SYMBOLS

Although the Historic Sites Act would eventually restrict and regulate the ability of the public to propose and create large historic sites and, therefore, symbols of its own choosing, the immediate popular response to the measure was to encourage local boosters and preservationists to submit suggestions to Washington in the hope of receiving governmental sanction and support. To cope with an abundance of proposals from the public, especially during a period when popular interest in the past was so high, the NPS organized an advisory board on parks, sites, monuments, and buildings, something that had been provided for in the Historic Sites Act itself.[23] It was this body that would give added legitimacy to the decisions on future parks and monuments and reinforce the park service's attempts to replace personal, local, regional, and commercial interests with national and professional standards. This step was inevitable in a process that hoped to educate the popular mind as to what historical representations were all about.

The first meeting of the advisory board brought together a group of individuals experienced in fields relevant to the practice of preservation and interpretation. They included Herman Bumpus, who had been the first director of the American Museum of Natural History; Clark Wissler, an anthropologist familiar with the study of American Indians; and Fiske Kimball, a museum director. The board was predisposed to sustain the professional thrust already launched by the NPS staff. Ickes told them at their first meeting, however, that they should remember that there was no better way to "inculcate true patriotism than to preserve and cherish objects which were identified with the evolution of the nation."[24] Any professional goals they might have, in other words, would have to be framed within patriotic terms.

Policies concerning education and preservation at historic sites dominated the initial gatherings of the board and the staff. Chatelain addressed the board and called for thematic guidelines that would shape the process of acquiring and presenting sites and monuments. Chatelain's basic thrust, which would come to represent the central tenet of NPS policy on such matters, involved a conception of the American past as a series of progressive stages illustrative of "man's life on this continent." He criticized the haphazard manner in which historic sites were selected in the past; a process that resulted in a disproportionate number of sites dealing with military and colonial themes. Since the NPS could only acquire a relatively small number of sites, he argued that such sites must be representative, as he had done before, of major themes or "stages of history." In language that was astonishingly similar to that used in most forms of public historical commemoration during the preceding two decades, Chatelain asserted that American history was a "pageant" that should be illustrated through "key sites," arranged chronologically in order to tell a "story." Three months later the board adopted a resolution revealing the influence of NPS staff thinking and the general agreement for order and rationalization among professionals. They declared that federal historic sites should be carefully chosen on the basis of "important phases" of American history and that the areas selected will collectively present "an adequate story of American progress" from the beginnings of human existence on the continent.[25]

The advisory board did more than automatically accept the policy suggestions, however, of NPS staff. Academically trained individuals on the board, especially Bumpus and Wissler, had come to appreciate the value of material culture and objects as educational tools and the power they had in making lasting impressions. Bumpus complained on numerous occasions that historical landmarks were generally disregarded in the teaching of the American past and that he welcomed the influence of the NPS in demonstrating that "objective instruction" was superior to "subjective instruction." Bumpus supported his point by telling of the lasting impression he had carried from his youth of actually seeing President Ulysses Grant speaking from a train.[26]

Wissler, moreover, held a particular view of culture. Before modern anthropologists began to restrict views of culture to "precepts and concepts" or "ideational forms," Wissler argued in *Man and Culture* in 1923 that culture consisted of "material traits" and "social activities" as well as "ideas." Indeed, this inclusion of material objects allowed anthropology to become more influential than, for instance, sociology in American museums in the 1920s. Wissler asserted in his book that culture could best be described by explaining "dominant characteristics" rather than every detail of a people's past or present. At this point he came close to presenting a view that would ultimately minimize the local, the personal, and the vernacular dimensions of American history and would emphasize broad themes in material sites arranged in a time sequence that suggested that the progress and emergence of the state itself were inevitable. It is, therefore, not surprising to learn that Wissler sat on an Educational Advisory Committee to the park service as early as 1929 that recommended that archaeological and historical materials in the NPS be presented by major historical periods and arranged in a sequence that would duplicate the progression of human life in America. This view was based upon scholarly precepts but actually reinforced a progressive and, thus, celebratory notion of the past.[27]

The attempt to be rather inclusive in the treatment of the American past and yet formulate major themes resulted in several years of discussion and reformulation. Eventually a working list of such themes evolved into nine major conceptual areas. Basically, these themes dealt with the process of nation building: European Exploration and Settlement; Development of the English Colonies; Major American Wars; Westward Expansion; and Political and Military Affairs. Attention to the Original Inhabitants was included to stress just how far the nation had moved civilization beyond the level of the Native Americans. Categories such as America at Work, The Contemplative Society, and Society and Social Conscience gave the appearance that other themes would be entertained, but they never accounted for a substantial part of the NPS inventory or budget. Often they could be used to contribute to the dominant celebration of nation building, which was already inherent in the initial properties that the park service acquired at the beginning of its venture into historic interpretation, such as Washington's birthplace and military battlefields.[28]

The American public wasted little time in challenging the attempt to enforce professional standards and dominant themes upon its public memory. Indeed, the files of proposed monuments and sites in the decade or so after the passage of the Historic Sites Act revealed that the ascendency of the NPS in such matters did not end the societal discourse over historical symbols. It was precisely the public demand for historical commemoration that caused Roosevelt to ask Ickes by 1939 to limit the establishment of historic sites in order to keep costs to an "absolute minimum." But no matter how hard the service attempted to keep the process orderly, political influence, local pride, and personal feeling constantly intruded into the deliberations of the NPS professionals.[29]

It is difficult to read proposals from the public for historic monuments without glimpsing the dichotomy between professional/nationalist visions centering on state building, on the one hand, and the widely diffuse set of personal emotions and local boosterism that motivated the public. In many ways the government's insistence on national significance and major themes forced individuals and localities into exaggerated attempts to distort their past, to make their own memories part of the national record and, by implication, to discard or reconfigure whatever appeared inappropriate.

Some ideas, of course, could not bridge the gap between the vernacular and the official. A man in Minnesota suggested a lake that "was the most beautiful in the state" be designated a national monument, and a woman in Michigan made the same request for a stand of timber she owned. From Waukesha County, Wisconsin, came a nomination for a park that had been created by the local historical society in honor of three members of one family that served the nation in the Civil War and the Indian Wars in the southwest. The Wisconsin citizens wrote Roosevelt directly. But the NPS could find no grounds for "national significance" and argued that the park was in "shabby condition" and national shrines were seldom set aside for individuals. Similarly, the Church of Latter-day Saints wanted to mark the spot where Mormon pioneers caught their first glimpse of the Salt Lake Valley in 1847. But the NPS failed to see sufficient merit in the proposal, in part because the site, Emigrant Canyon, was not on a route that was as "important as other westward emigrant routes of United States history." A proposal from Knoxville, Tennessee, to create a national monument at the birthplace of Admiral David Farragut, the Navy's first full admiral, met only defeat as well. The advisory board declared that it was preferable to preserve places associated with historic events rather than individuals. Similar reservations were expressed about a plan to memorialize a woman who allegedly undertook a dangerous mission in South Carolina during the Revolution and for a monument to all who died in World War II from Brainerd, Minnesota.[30] A rare proposal from a minority group met a similar fate. Park service officials decided that they could not help a local organization in the District of Columbia preserve the home of Frederick Douglass because his accomplishments were not of such national significance that they would warrant commemoration through a national historical site. Whether they were patriots or protestors, ordinary people could not move easily into the realm of heroes and symbols.[31]

A positive reaction on the part of the park service was crucial to the attainment of national recognition, but other obstacles had to be overcome. The land upon which a site rested had to be available for donation to the government. Government finances, moreover, were never sufficient to allow for the acceptance and development of many proposed national monuments and sites. And finally, it was difficult to generate widespread congressional support for most proposals because they were based so thoroughly in local pride and enthusiasm.

Two monument ideas that won considerable support if not ultimate approval involved the firmly established themes of westward expansion and military victory. From Kansas came two proposals for sites commemorating the overland movement of pioneers westward. One site was located at Alcove Springs and the other at Shawnee Mission. Neither location eventually gained national status but the reasons the NPS used to select one as being more significant than the other are illustrative of its thinking.

Both sites were on wagon train routes westward that helped to build the nation. Shawnee Mission was preferred, however, because it not only represented a point on the Oregon Trail and, thus, the expansion of the nation, but because in the late 1940s, when it was being considered, its Indian mission represented "an outpost of western civilization" in the world ideological struggle against Soviet communism, a struggle that was a priority for the nation-state itself.[32]

The Shawnee Mission site could only have been acquired and donated to the federal government because of a decision rendered by the Kansas Supreme Court in 1927 that allowed the state to condemn any property for the purposes of acquisition that was invested with universal historic interest. The judges' final verdict in the case not only furthered the cause of preserving the mission but also left a vivid reminder of how widespread the view was that history should serve patriotism in the decade after World War I. The decision proclaimed in language that could have come from the Historic Sites Act of 1935 (but in fact predated it by eight years) that

> the end to be subserved by the State promotion of intellectual and moral improvement is better citizenship; and good citizenship is inculcated by giving attention to history as history is now conceived. History is no longer a record of past events. It is an illuminating account of the expanding life of man in all of its manifestations, revealing how each stage of civilization grew out of preceding stages, revealing how the past still lives in us. . . . So considered history is inspirational. The Santa Fe and Oregon Trails are [not] merely old-time routes of trade and emigration . . . they are highways of indomitable spirit of man in earnest and arduous quest and fired with passion of purposeful endeavor. Considered this way the careers of men stir the emotions, arouse enthusiasm, and awaken zeal which fuses into patriotism, and patriotism is regarded as a worthy quality of citizenship.[33]

Significant interest was also shown in a proposal (which ultimately failed) involving a military achievement that was to be commemorated with a national monument. In this case there was almost no interlude between the idea to create the monument and the actual historical event itself. In 1947, local boosters near Los Alamos, New Mexico, saw both the tourist and historic potential of the place where the first atomic bomb was detonated. The bomb obviously contributed to both the survival and the building of the nation, and the site had strong backing from state and local officials. In this case, however, the idea received some of its strongest support from federal authorities. The manager of the Atomic Energy Commission at Los Alamos requested NPS support for the project, and the Department of the Interior pursued the idea aggressively. J. A. Krug, the department secretary in 1947, revealed that the Defense Department, however, had delayed his requests to take the idea to the president. Military officials apparently felt that contamination at the site was still a problem as well as possible breeches of security. Former Secretary of the Interior Ickes, who lobbied for the proposal, told the Defense Department that such a site would "afford the people of the United States and foreign visitors an unparalleled opportunity" to witness the power of atomic energy and the extent of the American war effort. Chief park service historian Ronald Lee inspected the site in 1947 and became especially interested in using the ranch house where the bomb was assembled as a major exhibit area. When several citizens complained to the NPS that the dropping of the atomic bomb on Japan was considered a "national disgrace" by some, government authorities replied that the "first non-laboratory use of atomic energy" was nevertheless "an historic event."[34]

Shawnee Mission and the atomic bomb site never became national monuments. But the discussion that surrounded these proposals revealed that the alleged objectivity and rationality of professionals could be swayed considerably by sentiments of passionate patriotism. NPS staff could become quite enthusiastic when proposals both related to their major emphasis on nation building and simultaneously allowed them to rush to the service of their nation whether in the fight against communism or in the euphoria of victory in World War II.

Neither professional zeal nor patriotic fervor, however, could prevent the NPS from eliminating some popular and political interests from the process of crafting historical representations for the public. The most effective proposals were sometimes those that simultaneously expressed the interests of local pride and economic development and allowed the NPS to retain its ideological focus on nation building. The successful efforts to memorialize Fort Stanwix in Rome, New York, underscores this point. The fort had been the site of a gallant stand against the British during the Revolutionary War that "raised the morale" of all American troops. Tradition had it that the American flag as adopted in the Revolutionary era was first flown at the fort. The Rome chamber of commerce even claimed that the fort was comparable in significance to the Lincoln Memorial because the "Stars and Stripes were first displayed" there.[35]

Local boosterism, patriotism, and nation building also mustered enough political support to establish a national historic site at the Cumberland Gap that covered parts of Kentucky, Virginia, and Tennessee. Although added to the park service in 1940, the movement to establish a historical park in this area began in the 1920s with entrepreneurs, newspaper owners, and others interested in the history and the economic development of the region. The potential for tourism and recreation in the site was seen by the Louisville Automobile Club and the Bluegrass Automobile Club when they first called a meeting to organize support for a park at Cumberland Gap in 1923. The gap, of course, was celebrated because it was a "key pass" to the West through the Appalachian Mountains "in pioneer days" and a gateway to the settlement of Kentucky. By the 1930s regional meetings were held in Tennessee and Virginia to which NPS officials were invited to discuss the prospects of a park. In 1931, these efforts made an impact as NPS staff informed the secretary of the interior that the gap "could link old historic sites of the Middle Atlantic with historic areas west of the Appalachian Mountains" and that the site was of "prime importance" due to the numerous pioneers who passed through it to "claim the Northwest Territory for the United States."[36]

Eventually a Cumberland Gap National Historical Park Association was formed by 1938 which pressured congressional representatives from the region to promote the idea that the park would stimulate tourism in several states at once. Tom Wallace, editor of the *Louisville Times* and a long-time proponent of historic preservation in Kentucky, told the group that they must forget state jealousies and foster economic development for their entire area. With regional cooperation and widespread congressional support from several states, the proposal inevitably succeeded.[37]

THE ST. LOUIS ARCH

Local and national political interests combined in a most effective way in the creation of one of the most expensive historical monuments to come under the management of the NPS. In planning and constructing the Jefferson National Expansion Memorial (JNEM) or the "arch" in St. Louis, the park service was able to fashion a symbol that certainly honored the rise of the state by calling attention to Thomas Jefferson's acquisition of the Louisiana Purchase and the movement of pioneers out of St. Louis to the West. But very specific local and national political interests were served in the origins of the project, despite the fact that today it is the symbolic representation of the westward movement that has persisted most forcefully.

When an architectural competition was held in 1947 to select an appropriate monument at St. Louis, little public attention was directed to the complex issues that had ignited interest in a monument on the city's riverfront in the first place. The winning plan by Eero Saarinen, in fact, was criticized because his design of a huge arch along the Mississippi River reminded some observers of a similar arch that had been planned but never built for the twentieth anniversary of "Mussolini's Fascism" in Italy. The project, however, was rooted in the issues and consciousness of the American thirties and involved much more than historical commemoration.[38]

In the depression decade a group of civic, business, and political leaders in St. Louis decided to stimulate economic development of the city's riverfront, real estate values, employment, and loyalty to the nation by launching a campaign to tear down a large portion of the riverfront area and build a memorial. Although the size and scope of their plans were almost unprecedented for a memorial outside the nation's capital, the celebration of Jefferson and his vision of expan-

14. History in the making: The Jefferson National Expansion Memorial, St. Louis, Mo., 1965. Courtesy of Jefferson National Expansion Memorial-National Park Service.

sion was a long established one in Missouri. The state acknowledged its origins in the Louisiana Purchase by naming its own capital city after Jefferson in 1820. A granite obelisk at the state university and a statue in a St. Louis park already stood in honor of the third president. In 1931 the state declared his birthday a legal holiday.[39]

It took more than tradition, however, for the NPS to acquire responsibility for building and maintaining a monument and museum at St. Louis. The primary local booster for the project was a prominent businessman named Luther Ely Smith who had served on a federal commission that erected a memorial to George Rogers Clark in Vincennes, Indiana. Smith was deeply impressed by the patriotic sentiment and enthusiasm generated by the Clark memorial but was also interested in arresting the decay that had come to characterize the St. Louis riverfront. He was able to interest the city's mayor, Bernard Dickman, and a local group of businessmen called the Industrial Club that was loosely tied to the chamber of commerce. In fact, it was due to his familiarity with the Clark commission that Smith suggested to local officials that they seek the creation of a federal commission to investigate the feasibility of the project rather than seek federal funds directly.[40]

In 1934 St. Louis leaders, with the help of midwestern congressmen from Iowa, Missouri, Indiana, and Kentucky, persuaded Congress to create the United States Territorial Expansion Memorial Commission. Exploiting sentiments of midwestern pride, patriotism, and the promise of more jobs in a period of hard times, proponents of the measure convinced the federal government that it was a worthwhile endeavor to stimulate the economy in the name of the "vision and genius of Thomas Jefferson and the other patriotic citizens" who pushed the nation's boundaries westward. Within months the new commission began the process of building a rationale for federal appropriations by taking testimony in St. Louis on behalf of the endeavor.[41]

The variety of arguments used to support the proposed monument testified to the complex nature of its origins and the need for historic symbols to incorporate multiple meanings. Some speakers told the commission that the monument's construction would create over five thousand jobs and a representative of the American Federation of Labor claimed labor backed the proposal and wanted "work not relief." But most speakers invoked the traditional language of historical commemoration in the United States. Alben Barkley, a senator from Kentucky, wanted the monument to stand for the "unknown pioneer no less than the unknown soldier." Charles Merriam of the University of Chicago simply wanted to honor Jefferson and claimed that he could not understand why someone so closely connected with the "development of democracy" did not already have a more distinguished remembrance.[42]

Local advocates of the memorial predominated at the hearings. McCune Gill, an expert on St. Louis history, argued that it was important to explain why this country was not divided among five or six different nations but stretched completely across the continent. He felt that the Louisiana Purchase symbolized "completeness, greatness, [and] the unity of the state over sections." To Gill, St. Louis did a great deal to "preserve the ideals set up by the future-looking patriots of the Eastern Colonies" and foster national expansion by serving as an embarkation point for pioneers moving westward. A city official told the commission that "you hear more about pioneers [now] than we have heard in the previous seventy-five years," and they must be "emphasized." Luther Ely Smith made much about the need to incorporate the Midwest into the national ideological system and to honor those who helped make the region part of the nation. He reasoned:

> You will recall . . . there has grown up a new school of history in this country which has turned its eyes away from the exclusive attention that was formerly given to the Atlantic seaboard and has realized that the character of America was made not on the coastal plain of this great country but was forged in the frontier as the pioneers went out to grapple with the conditions which confronted them. . . . We owe this debt to the pioneers, to Jefferson . . . to Daniel Boone and every one of these great men who trod this sacred soil. . . . Let us pay back the debt we owe to the American pioneers who gave us the American nation and gave us the American character.[43]

Not everyone shared Smith's vision or enthusiasm for the project. A national news magazine thought it would lead to unnecessary expenditures of public funds and claimed that Roosevelt supported the plan only because Mayor Dickman threatened to withhold political support from St. Louis in the 1936 election. The *Nation* could not understand how the projected cost could be three times the cost of the Lincoln Memorial and argued that monies could be better spent to help the four hundred unemployed families living in neighborhoods that would have to be leveled if the project were completed. It declared that this was less a memorial to the dead than an enrichment of real estate speculators. The *St. Louis Post-Dispatch* went so far as to charge the Democratic political machine and Mayor Dickman with stuffing ballot boxes in an election held to gain approval of the expenditure of some local public funds to help with the project. Luther Ely Smith replied that he considered the election "freer from fraud than most elections." Local opponents continued their battle in lawsuits that attempted to halt the city from acquiring the thirty-seven blocks it needed for the site of the memorial and the surrounding park. A local Taxpayer Defense Association sent pamphlets to Washington claiming that the monument was a waste of public funds and asked that money designated for the project be donated to the American Red Cross instead.[44]

By 1936 the government had approved the money for the JNEM despite some local opposition, and the NPS had taken charge of the planning. Herman Bumpus of the advisory board visited the city and recommended the NPS acquire the area to memorialize western expansion. The NPS staff review of the idea did criticize some erroneous statements of historical fact that Roosevelt had made in proposing the plan to Congress. In trying to embellish the historical significance of St. Louis, the president had stated that the famous Dred Scott decision had been handed down in the city instead of Washington, D.C. But the staff report ultimately concluded that the project was "nationally significant" enough to warrant federal aid.[45]

It is not entirely clear if the Roosevelt administration coerced the NPS into ratifying the significance of the St. Louis project in order to meet political demands from Missouri or not. There is no doubt that the project served political and economic interests in St. Louis by leading to the renewal of a large portion of the urban riverfront and creating jobs through construction and, in the long run, tourism. Evidence certainly suggests that both Roosevelt and the NPS were not immune to such political pressures. But the president and the park service were also strongly tied to an effort to nurture a nationalist ideology over attachments to sentiments and beliefs that were local, personal, or even foreign. And Roosevelt had a long established emotional link to Jefferson as a symbol of a "great commoner." Every year on Jefferson's birthday F.D.R. placed a wreath at his tomb, and he had served on the board of the Thomas Jefferson Memorial Foundation. Given Roosevelt's proclivities and the ideological pattern of historical commemoration developed in the park service, a rejection of the St. Louis idea by either the president or the NPS would have at the very least been inconsistent.[46]

INHERITED TRADITIONS

It would be a mistake to suggest that the NPS acquired all of its sites because of either political pressures or attempts to enforce national standards of history in this century. Its inventory of historical sites and symbols was also enlarged by a sizable inheritance from a previous era. These representations of the past were shaped just as surely by political tension and social discourse, but it was a contest and a discussion that had largely ended. What remained behind were the material reality of the sites and the images they evoked. Battlefields, heroes, and cemeteries from the era of the Civil War were acquired by the park service with little or no debate. But the lack of discussion should not obscure the fact that most of them served well the cause of nationalist ideology and patriotic sentiment. Many of these surviving symbols from another era, especially the cemeteries, may have represented the expressions of numerous interests including local pride or personal grief in their original form, but what remained—especially after they had come under the jurisdiction of the nation-state—was the symbolic expression of the triumph of the nation-state and the glory of the sacrifice of those who contributed to that goal. With respect to these nineteenth-century memorials the NPS was not creating a symbolic system but perpetuating an aspect of one that most served its needs.

Consider the case of two of the dominant figures of both the Civil War and the cause of national unity, Lincoln and Grant. Certainly both were central to the ideological focus of the NPS on nation building and patriotism. And in this century the park service acquired sites pertaining to both men that were developed and formed by others outside the government long before the NPS took them over and sanctioned their place in its symbolic repertoire.

The NPS acquired the Abraham Lincoln Birthplace National Historical Site from the War Department in the 1930s. For over sixty years, however, efforts had been made to commemorate the location. The cabin in which Lincoln was born had disappeared from the site by 1865, but a congressman from Kentucky did make an unsuccessful attempt to get the federal government to spend $10,000 to raise a granite obelisk on the site in that year. By 1894 an enterprising businessman named Alfred Dennett bought most of what was formerly the Lincoln farm with notions of turning the site into a large park with a hotel for tourists. Dennett re-created the cabin based on educated guesses as to its location and shape and then made an attempt to sell it all to the federal government. Eventually Robert Collier of *Collier's Magazine* acquired the property because of the "highest patriotic motives" and expressed a desire to save the birthplace from "speculators for vulgar show and unwholesome popularity." Collier felt the site could symbolize national unity rather than "lamentable differences" that he saw enshrined at battlefields such as Gettysburg.[47]

Collier cooperated with an organization called the Lincoln Farm Association that was incorporated in 1906, and purchased logs from the cabin that had been used in traveling expositions and which they brought to Kentucky. The group went so far as to organize "Lincoln Leagues" for the purposes of raising funds and sought government support to build a museum on the farm that resembled the White House. The association differed with those who felt the chief monument to Lincoln should be in Washington, D.C., and sought to secure that status for the birthplace site.[48]

Eventually the site came under governmental control. The state of Kentucky acquired it in 1911 and was able to tranfer it to the federal government five years later. Representative Simeon D. Fess of Ohio, a supporter of federal acquisition, asserted that "the site would connect Lincoln's greatness as he left us with the simple beginnings of his life and will refresh the future generations with the inspiration of American opportunity."[49]

After the NPS acquired the site, it continued to present the humble cabin to the public as the authentic place of Lincoln's birth, despite the fact that neither the cabin's reconstruction nor the site's development was ever based on precise research. Internal staff reviews of the site indicated that the reconstruction had been "fictionalized"; the cabin itself had a concrete floor, something that Lincoln surely did not see at the place. Literature distributed to visitors, who numbered more than 280,000 yearly by 1956, stated that the "cabin was traditionally believed to be the one in which Lincoln was born." It was not until 1968 that the NPS literature admitted that the cabin's authenticity was doubtful, although it did not make fully clear the haphazard history of the reconstruction that visitors saw at the Lincoln farm. Apparently professionalization had its limitations. One scholar studying the overall presentation made to the public at the site concluded that most visitors left believing that they had truly seen the original setting as it was at the time of the president's birth.[50]

Little motivation appeared to exist in the park service for the application of rigorous critical standards to a site such as the Lincoln farm partially because the image of Lincoln and the cabin in which he was born already represented powerful historical images when the NPS acquired them. Because they served the basic interest of celebrating nation building and national unity so well, they were essentially presented to the public as received. A similar response can be detected in the acquisition and presentation of the General Grant National Memorial in New York City. The NPS took possession of Grant's tomb in Riverside Park in 1959 at a time when it was consciously trying to bring historic sites closer to urban populations. Again the park service had not been involved in the development or the interpretative strategy at the site which had been administered by the Grant Memorial Association.[51]

The Grant Memorial was conceived as a fitting tribute to the former general and president immediately after his death in 1885. Grant himself had selected New York as his final resting place, and the committee responsible for the gathering of funds and the construction of the monument was composed of "the most influential men in the city and the state," including former president Chester A. Arthur. The monument association issued an appeal for financial support in terms of Grant's "patriotism and rare service to the Nation." They were not interested in simply a tomb but wanted "a national memorial." Most of the money for the project came from New York, however, as citizens from other regions of the country proved reluctant to support a memorial project in New York City regardless of the grounds on which the appeal was made.[52]

After beating back an attempt by veterans' organizations to have Grant's remains moved to the nation's capital, New York officials were finally able to raise sufficient funds. At the dedication of the memorial in 1897 over fifty thousand people from military, patriotic, and civic organizations paraded through the streets, and President William McKinley gave the dedicatory address.

A half-century later it was very difficult to find people to serve the Grant Memorial Association, and city appropriations for the site were extremely modest. New generations of Americans generally did not share the deep attachments to Grant that many of his contemporaries did.[53] By 1955 the memorial association approached the federal government about accepting the site as a "national shrine." The obligatory staff investigation by the NPS recommended the memorial be designated a "national memorial." They based their decision on the fact that the "American people" had long regarded the site as a national memorial anyway, that Robert E. Lee had been memorialized with the acquisition of the Lee mansion in Arlington, Virginia, and that it would be appropriate to designate a federal memorial to Grant in view of the approaching Civil War Centennial.[54]

The park service gave some thought to interpretation at the site but did not and could not alter substantially historical images and exhibits already in place. General Grant's grandson, U. S. Grant III, insisted that the site remain a "memorialization to General and Mrs. Grant" rather than become a memorial to the Civil War. In the end the tomb became both. Visitors received maps from the park service depicting military strategy from the Civil War. They could also view heroic bronze busts of five of Grant's generals and mementos from his military career, presidency, and funeral inside the monument itself. What is pertinent is that the structure and substance of this presentation was fashioned essentially by an earlier generation and largely transmitted rather than reinterpreted by the park service.[55]

The symbolic world of the nineteenth century not only included great leaders but ordinary foot soldiers as well. Their memorialization took no higher form than the care that was invested into Civil War battlefields. The War Department had proposed the transfer of historic parks and monuments under its jurisdiction to the Department of the Interior as early as 1924. But opposition existed in Congress to the move because of a fear that the NPS could not properly maintain such sites. Several critics claimed the NPS would turn sacred battlefields into "playgrounds" and put "hot dog stands" where men had died. Before the actual transfers were achieved in 1933, Horace Albright had to assure Congress that the park service would in no way impair the "natural qualities" of the battlefields and would "preserve them absolutely intact for future generations." Albright also claimed that the NPS could do a better job than the War Department in developing the "inspirational and educational features" for the public. He promised to send literature and photographs concerning the sites to schools around the country.[56]

Suddenly the owner of numerous battlefield sites and national cemeteries in 1933, the park service again was faced with the prospect of promoting historical symbols that were formulated by an earlier generation. Immediately after the Civil War battles themselves, citizens and officials alike called for the proper burial and commemoration of the dead. The establishment of national cemeteries at Antietam, Maryland, and Vicksburg, Mississippi, were clearly hastened by reports of bodies "bleaching in upturned furrows" and being washed away by floods. Although the original intent in creating these memorials seemed to be more of an attempt to pay respects to the dead than to specifically honor the concept of sacrifice for the nation, it was the latter message that would dominate the presentation of these sites to the public in this century.[57]

EDUCATING THE PUBLIC

By the 1950s the park service's association with historical sites as well as national parks was firmly established. Unfortunately the years during and immediately after World War II had resulted in extremely low budgets due to the demands of a wartime economy. When the growth in personal income, leisure time, and travel began after the war the NPS was completely unprepared to meet the demands of caring for its facilities or interpreting its vast historical storehouse to such a large number of visitors. In fiscal year 1935 the NPS hosted 7.6 million visitors and received an appropriation of $11.8 million. Twenty years later the number of visitors had climbed to 56.5 million but federal appropriations totaled only $32.9 million. In other words, total budgetary support amounted to about $1.50 per visitor in the former year but only about 58 cents per visitor in the latter.[58]

The park service's response to declining revenues and increasing numbers of visitors in regard to its historic areas was a plan that sought to improve and upgrade the manner in which historical interpretation was made at its various sites. In a program called "Mission 66" the NPS sought to attract federal support by presenting government officials with a comprehensive and sophisticated plan for reconstruction and improved interpretative facilities such as museums and exhibits at historic sites. With the support of the Eisenhower administration, "Mission 66" initiated a ten-year effort (1956–66) to improve interpretation with the rehabilitation of Independence Hall in Philadelphia and the construction of visitor centers at such sites as Gettysburg, Jamestown, and Yorktown.[59]

Before 1956 historic interpretation in the NPS had been handled in a generally loose and casual manner. NPS officials and the advisory board had worked hard to formulate and enforce thematic standards but at actual sites the training of personnel engaged in interpretation and exhibit preparation was generally inadequate. In the early 1950s, for instance, the site historian at Fort Sumter National Monument in South Carolina arrived by boat each morning with the tourists, unlocked doors, turned on lights, raised the flag, and handed out literature. With "Mission 66" a new emphasis was put on staff training in both historic and natural areas and new training centers were constructed in the East and West. The program also intensified the discussion once again over the nature of historic interpretation in the agency as planners worried more about how to deal with such an increasing number of people.[60]

In an internal memo circulated in 1956, NPS directors told staff that, in part, "Mission 66" was launched because increased use of facilities by the public had made it difficult to provide adequate enjoyment, satisfaction, and education for its patrons. A definite need was indicated for more museums and exhibits at historic sites. Such facilities, it was argued, could expand the "public information and educational services" of the NPS and provide "inspirational content" that would hold America "to her best ideals."[61]

Park Service leaders argued that significant returns could be reaped from greater investments in the system. They claimed that their sites—natural and historic—were "a spiritual necessity" in the modern world. They allowed the visitor to regain "spiritual balance" and served as an "antidote to the high pressures of modern life." Moving beyond its traditional claims of patriotic education, the NPS now saw therapeutic functions in the power of its sites and symbols as well as political ones, something public memory symbols had always served but which the park service had been slow to acknowledge. But the traditional emphasis on creating proper civic attitudes was far from forgotten. The NPS explained: "Where else but on historic ground can Americans better renew the idealism that prompted the patriots to their deeds of diplomacy and valor? Where else do they have such opportunities to recapture the spirit and something of the qualities of the pioneers?"[62]

NPS conceptualization of its role regarding historic interpretation is revealed quite succinctly in presentations made to its staff in training sessions during the early years of "Mission 66." Park and site interpreters and others were told in a 1957 meeting that a need existed for more "personalized historical interpretation." "We are advertisers selling history. We are dramatists!" exclaimed the instructor, Frank Barnes, "above all we are teachers." Barnes went on to argue that many visitors have heard about symbols and sites such as the Liberty Bell for years and have traveled great distances to see them. Because their visit may only be a one-time affair, "we must not let them down." He urged interpreters to be dedicated to the task of "cherishing our historical heritage and making it come alive to the people."[63]

The following year at a training program in Yosemite National Park, John Hussey, a regional historian in the NPS, gave a detailed presentation of "The Role of History in the National Park System." His remarks neatly summarize many of the ideas and currents that pervaded the organization in the postwar decades. Hussey contended that the people of the United States were proud of their heritage of history—"stories of pioneer courage, of heroism and sacrifice in battle, of steadfastness under political and economic pressures." Treasured above all, he asserted, were the "symbols of the past" such as Valley Forge, Gettysburg, and the Liberty Bell. He also stressed that there were over one hundred thousand sites in the country that were recognized by some organization as sufficiently "historic" to be preserved and that historic places were as important as scenic ones to the "fabric of America." Because people visited such sites more and more, the NPS, according to Hussey, must recognize their importance. In 1957 alone, he noted that more people visited Colonial National Historical Park than either Yellowstone or Yosemite.[64]

Hussey also considered the point that nearly every government in the world valued and preserved historic sites, and attempted to explain it. He asserted that such sites and exhibits provided a record of the "past sacrifices" and, consequently, "kindles in us a quiet pride in the accomplishments of our ancestors and makes us determined to put the future in debt to us." This resolve he felt was that "true patriotism" without which no nation or people can hope to survive. He declared in language that strikingly reflected the achievement of the NPS in establishing the supremacy of national history over a personal and a local one that an appreciation of the nation's past was effective in the "conquest of provincialism, the provincialism of self, the provincialism of place, the provincialism of time."

Hussey also revived earlier NPS perceptions about the apparent power of material culture over the human mind that had been used in the early 1930s. He noted that historic sites have the capacity to make more vivid impressions on the minds of people than traditional sources of history such as the written word. "The person who walks on the very field where Cornwallis surrendered," he reasoned, "receives a vivid impression, a thrill of kinship with the past." Finally Hussey recognized the ability of sites and symbols to stir emotions beneficial to the nation. To him historic sites along with documents such as the Declaration of Independence and the Constitution were the "most tangible symbols of our unity as a Nation." He concluded in language that was by now entirely consistent with NPS ideology: "They inspire patriotism and love of country by recalling the events and ideals which made our nation great; they remind us of our common social, cultural, and spiritual background, of that national history which forms perhaps our strongest single social bond."[65]

In many respects the aspects of "Mission 66" that related to historic interpretation represented an aggressive outward thrust on the part of the NPS to promote its ideals and values. Less interested in acquiring existing sites and ratifying new ones, the stress now was on consolidating its thinking regarding historical messages and formulating a clear conception of how these messages would be transmitted most effectively to the widest possible audience. In doing so, the NPS discovered that its basic devotion to patriotism and national unity that had served it well in the past could be readily adopted to new needs generated by a society becoming conscious of dealing with political problems in its growing urban areas. In the decade of the 1960s, when urban unrest became a paramount concern of the government, the NPS moved quickly to serve the state again by bringing its interpretative and inspirational program to city people. In the thirties the NPS found that symbols of patriotism and unity were viewed as crucial by national leaders who determined its budget and who wished to lessen the appeal of any ideology that appeared to threaten national unity. In the 1960s urban populations, especially disaffected minorities, posed a threat to national unity and civic order, and the NPS recognized again that it must direct its symbolic messages in strategic directions.

The park service was already moving its attention away from the wilderness areas of the West somewhat by 1960 and planning more historic sites near the urban East. The acquisition of the Grant Memorial in 1959 and the rehabilitation of Independence Hall under "Mission 66" were two examples of the growing importance of such sites. During the 1950s the chief historian of the NPS, Ronald Lee, had continuously preached on the subject of "Bringing History to the People." Lee, like many of his colleagues, held a firm belief in the power of historic sites and symbols to create "rich and vivid impressions" among the public. In 1956 Lee presented the advisory board with results from a poll that indicated that visitors to NPS sites tended to come from "the professional, business, and managerial segments of the population," and much less so from "wage earners" who, he felt, failed to understand how much they could derive from historical and natural wonders. By 1960, NPS director Conrad Wirth told the advisory board how impressed he was over the gathering of forty thousand people at Fort McHenry National Monument in Baltimore for ceremonies to raise the first fifty-star flag. "The mobilization of [patriotic] sentiment and feeling which is an important element in the overall basis of the National Park System was gratifying," Wirth exclaimed. At the same meeting the board also discussed plans with New York developer David Rockefeller for the integration of urban renewal and historic site development for lower Manhattan Island that included the building of the World Trade Center and improvements to be made at the Statue of Liberty.[66]

The shifting attention directed to urban populations manifested itself in a 1957 decision by the NPS to build a museum at the Statue of Liberty site devoted to the history of ethnic minorities called the American Museum of Immigration (AMI). Again the park service responded to political rather than professional demands. Powerful local leaders were able to influence the NPS, such as U. S. Grant III (grandson of the Civil War general and a prominent figure in American civil and commemorative activity in this century) and Pierre Dupont III, both members of the AMI's board of directors. Grant, who had already served on a committee that made recommendations to the NPS advisory board on historic matters, and Dupont contacted the park service about funding the museum project. The AMI's board had previously failed in an attempt to raise sufficient funds from a public appeal campaign through a program called "Operation Unity." The NPS staff review recommended the project in 1956 in part because it saw the theme of unity implied in the idea of celebrating immigrant contributions to the nation. It also suggested that it would be important to stimulate unity out of ethnic diversity during the Cold War—"a time in our history when the competition of conflicting ideologies was intense."[67] Although born in the political climate of international tensions, however, the NPS quickly saw the symbolic appeal of the project for urban populations in the following decade.

The "urbanization" of NPS educational activities went even further under the administration of Richard Nixon. "Parks to the People" became a central program in continuing to keep the NPS involved in the contest for people's hearts and minds in cities often torn with strife, decay, and impoverishment. Secretary of the Interior Walter J. Hickel declared in 1969 that the NPS represented "those precious and irreplaceable remnants of our national world and landmarks of our cultural inheritance." He declared that the recognition of these "roots" of our society will generate a sense of "stability" in millions of citizens "isolated by asphalt and concrete in our metropolitan centers."[68] The previous administration of Lyndon Johnson had already pushed a program of "Outdoor Recreation for America" which was designed to provide more recreation and wilderness areas. After 1968 "Parks to the People" consciously sought to maintain the effort to influence the leisure time and civic attitudes through a public educational program that would sustain patriotism and unity in a society perceived by government officials to be factious.[69]

NPS staff wasted little time in devising methods by which their urban sites could educate and inspire local populations. As the staff surveyed properties near cities such as the Statue of Liberty, the Jefferson National Expansion Memorial, Fort Stanwix, Fort McHenry, and Independence Hall, it concluded that all such parks represented powerful values but had often failed to involve local residents in their activities and celebrations. Ways were now conceived to make these sites "better relate to their local and regional audience" and make them part of community recreation and "inner-city programs." Planners in the NPS developed programs to hold summer day-camps, ethnic performances, sound and light shows, and historical pageants at these locations. In Atlanta and Richmond plans were devised to use nearby Civil War battlefields for programs that would require large amounts of space.[70]

The process of using the past to serve the present can be seen at the Grant Memorial in New York in the 1960s. The 1966 master plan of the NPS stressed that the "memorial character" of the tomb was desirable and that an atmosphere "conducive to meditation" and "an aura of martial splendor" should be maintained. But by the mid-sixties the site had become largely ignored by the local populace. A sad state of affairs existed that included acts of malicious mischief such as the stoning of the curator, the burning of a sentry box, the cutting of flag poles, and the use of the tomb as a "granite bulletin board." Under "Parks to the People," consultants recommended that the agency "sensitize itself to the delicate relationships already established in the neighborhood" and indicated that the majority of local residents felt that there was not enough to see inside the tomb and that there was no one to explain the material on display. Proposals in the study directed that more of an emphasis be placed on Civil War artifacts in the tomb, greater attention be paid to Grant's life and the history of the immediate neighborhood (something the men who built the tomb would have never considered), and information be provided on Afro-American participation in the Civil War.[71]

The park service not only attempted to make history more relevant—and, perhaps, more "provincial"—by the late 1960s and 1970s, but reconsidered its entire policy concerning historic preservation. In a 1972 planning document it created an even more elaborate scheme of topics under which possible sites and monuments could be considered. One student of the NPS felt that this effort represented more of a triumph for "balanced preservation" over the "glorification of the sacred and the special." But the nine major themes stated by the NPS in 1972 appeared to ultimately reaffirm the basic plot of progressive nation building. Thus the sequence again ran from the "original inhabitants," through "major American wars," and "westward expansion." And yet this reaffirmation of professional and nationalistic objectives could not stave off continued efforts by localities to gain national recognition for their own historical interests as evidenced by plans to create historical parks along the Cuyahoga River in Ohio and in Lowell, Massachusetts.[72]

The approaching celebration of the bicentennial of the American Revolution caused the NPS to reconsider one more time how and what it would present to the American public on a vast scale. Program objectives devised by the staff in 1972 indicated that the agency had no intention of changing its commitment to influencing the psychological needs and collective memory of citizens. The bicentennial program would continue to "inspire" the public and initiate "a discussion in consonance with the times." Planners in the organization asserted that the pace of modern social change was simply bewildering and that modern man was faced with an "overloading of his psyche and his institutions."[73] To help citizens cope, the NPS sought to forge philosophical objectives that would effectively exploit its environmental and historical treasures. National parks would not only be promoted as refuges, but historical sites would be used as places of renewal from the tedium of modern life and centers where messages could be communicated about the need to manage and preserve cultural resources. Both a conservation ethic and a concern with urban problems, major issues of the 1970s, weighed heavily on the minds of the NPS staff.[74]

Essentially, the NPS attempted to direct its bicentennial activities through existing parks and sites. Although willing to cooperate with public organizations[75] and other governmental bodies such as the American Revolutionary Bicentennial Commission, the NPS selected twenty-two major sites pertaining to the Revolution from its holdings for attention in 1976. The goal here was to provide solace, inspiration, and education of a very general level and to "identify, communicate, and interpret the relevancy of the Revolutionary years to the peoples of 1976." The agency moved with ease to three of its nine major themes in formulating a foundation for its program. They were the development of the English colonies, major American wars, and political and military affairs. Major sites involved in the effort included Independence Hall, Colonial National Historical Park, Morristown (New Jersey) National Historical Park, and the Saratoga battlefield site in New York state. Of "secondary importance" were sites at Fort Stanwix, Guilford Courthouse in North Carolina, and the George Rogers Clark Memorial in Indiana.[76]

Much of the attention at Revolutionary War sites revolved around restoration, renovation, research, and interpretation of those locations as they related to the progress of the Revolution. This was certainly logical and consistent with the tradition of venerating the rise of the nation-state that had dominated historical interpretation in the agency. But the NPS was not about to rely solely on its existing inventory of sites and symbols to instruct the public in the history of the Revolution. It aggressively moved beyond the limitations imposed by its material collections and commissioned the preparation of short plays or dramatizations that could be performed at NPS sites with no direct link to the events of 1776. If all visitors could not come to Revolutionary War sites, relevant bicentennial messages would be taken to visitors at other locations. The results of this zealous educational bent was the production of two traveling shows: *We've Come Back for a Little Look Around* and the *People of '76*. Both productions toured NPS sites in

1976 and taken together allow a further glimpse into the ideology and psychology of public historical commemoration that characterized the agency in modern times.[77]

We've Come Back for a Little Look Around consisted essentially of dialogue between a guide and a maintenance man at an NPS site and prominent historical figures such as Ben Franklin and Abraham Lincoln. The objective of the presentation was to raise questions about the present more than the past and to impart certain messages to the audience. Historical figures return to measure the progress America has made in fields close to their own interest. Thus, Franklin explores issues related to science, and Lincoln asks questions about national unity.

The segment on science begins when the maintenance man attempts to get a photograph of Franklin with a Polaroid camera. Franklin expresses amazement that the camera was developed at all and that it was made in America. He recalls for the audience how the French thought American science was "primitive" in his era and contended that he knew there would be an industrial and technological revolution after the Revolution of 1776. The maintenance man assured Franklin that the United States won that second revolution "hands down."

But the performance was structured around the notion of a debate rather than the straightforward exposition of ideas. Every view the maintenance man presented to a historical figure was countered by the character of the NPS guide. In the case of industrial and scientific progress, the guide told Franklin that we endangered the entire world with environmental pollution and built crowded and dangerous highways. Franklin was ultimately able to conclude that he could not say for sure whether the United States had experienced success or failure in its experiment with progress, a significant admission that would not have been possible in the political culture of the decades just prior to 1960.

Lincoln faced a similar debate when he appeared to evaluate the degree to which national unity had been achieved. The maintenance man told Lincoln that his Civil War was the "first and the last" and "us Americans are one big happy family." But the guide countered strongly: "Who's kidding who? . . . What about our little civil wars? The ones that go on all the time . . . like between the blacks and whites . . . between the rich and poor. . . . I'm serious. This country is dangerously divided in dozens of ways." Lincoln also could not decide if American unity had been achieved.

Although this dramatization introduced an unprecedented amount of balance in its portrayal of the past, it did not leave completely open the question of whether the process of nation building was successful or not. The last word was left to an ordinary person, the maintenance man, and it carried a strong sense of patriotism and citizen responsibility—themes that were by now firmly established in all NPS messages. He mused aloud, "maybe I paint too rosy a picture of America because, well, I just happen to love this place." He admitted that others may paint a gloomy picture, but he claimed that that was not the real point. The most important issue was that the "Great Experiment" will continue, and that it was the responsibility of everyone in the audience, not historical figures such as Franklin and Lincoln, to see that America achieves goals such as progress and unity.

The other performance sponsored by the NPS, *People of '76*, consisted of a play depicting internal tensions in the fictitious colonial town of New Bristol during 1776. The major issue in the dramatization is the division that existed among the colonists over whether to support the "rebels." The issue divides the town into fervent loyalists, who were usually of the upper class; people in the middle who could not decide which way to move; and ardent backers of the revolution. One of the local men, Tom Fowler, eventually ends up at Valley Forge with Washington and writes to a friend in New Bristol that the rebel troops "are an army now" and that "the seed that the *Mayflower* bore has blossomed here," a hint that the birth of the nation was an inevitability. After the success of the revolution the discord among the people is ultimately forgotten and unity, a favorite NPS theme, triumphs. An old man in the play observes that those small colonial towns were all pretty much alike, "torn apart and then united again. Time heals all."

People of '76 was a much more explicit form of instruction than *We've Come Back for a Little Look Around*. It allowed for less variation and complexity in its thematic thrust and presented social change as a temporary aberration, and national unity as established once and for all. The devotion to unity and, therefore, the national state, was just as desirable as a goal in *We've Come Back* but it was pointed out that it was not so easily achieved and could not be maintained without citizen action in the future.

Both shows were extremely popular with audiences. After *We've Come Back* the historical figures moved into the crowds and asked people whether they thought the American experiment would succeed. In *People of '76* crowds had an opportunity to see authentic artifacts used in the play such as weapons and spinning wheels; these objects proved to be favorite attractions for those who attended.

CONCLUSION

Three distinct ideologies converged in the early 1930s to substantially shape the nature of historical activities within the NPS. As the NPS entered the public historical business in a meaningful way, it was heavily influenced by the current of zealous and belligerent patriotism that had moved through American society after World War I. This sentiment was actually reinforced in a way by the highly nationalistic programs of the early New Deal which sought to revive public loyalty to and enthusiasm for American culture and traditional American historic symbols. Finally, in acquiring a collection of nineteenth-century battlefields and national monuments at the time, the park service inherited the ideals and symbolism of much of the previous century that focused on national unity and service to the nation rather than on vernacular interests, and became their custodian. This preservation of the symbols of national unity and greatness was so powerful that it proved difficult for vernacular symbols and messages to be widely discussed in public discourse over the past. As Edward Shils has argued, such inherited beliefs can be accepted in a powerful way because their presence "reduces the imagination of alternatives."[78]

But the past that was presented to the public by the park service was more than simply a collection of inherited traditions. Professionals concerned with order and centralization of authority attempted to rationalize the process of selecting historic sites and monuments. Their discussions over this process led to a large and valuable collection but in no way superseded the larger effort to describe and celebrate the process of nation building which formed the basic narrative structure of park service ideology. Products of a complex economic and political process themselves that nurtured people who valued expertise and ordered procedures, these professionals exhibited an inclination to serve national power. To this extent they differed from nineteenth-century merchant elites, often leaders in commemorative activities, whose fortunes were tied more directly to economic rather than national political structures. They continued to serve national political power in the 1960s and 1970s in the form of Congress and the office of the presidency. The rationale for "Mission 66" was cast partially within the rhetoric of the Cold War, and the service moved quickly to conform to the goals of Nixon's "Parks to the People" agenda. This acquiescence may have been understandable and inevitable, but it was also a long-established tradition in the historical programming of the NPS. The central role of rising merchants and industrialists in the previous century had now been supplanted by government officials, planners, and their professional advisors.

Local pride and boosterism, moreover, continued to fight for space and recognition within the constellation of ideas and messages of public memory. In part it succeeded in some instances and still survived in monuments such as the St. Louis arch and the site at Cumberland Gap. But the major symbolic thrust of these and other sites was ultimately a victory for a nationalistic ideology—one that saw the actions of historical actors directed to a narrow and specific goal of nation building. Local initiatives were powerful interests with which the park service had to deal. When a local plan and interest could reinforce nationalist themes, it stood a chance of gaining national recognition, although a number of factors could intrude to shape the final decision. But hundreds of expressions of local and personal feeling were rejected for inclusion within the system of sites and monuments by the NPS. And ultimately the agency fostered the triumph of a public memory that served the cause of a powerful nation-state.

CHAPTER EIGHT

Celebrating the Nation, 1961–1976

In the 1960s and early 1970s political discourse in the United States was dominated by conflict and divisiveness. Citizens argued passionately over issues of war, race, and authority, while the ability of the nation-state to reconcile these differences was in doubt. Frequently lost in the historical preoccupation with disorder and conflict was the fact that the period began and ended with two large celebrations that attempted to foster order and national unity. The language and activities of these celebrations seldom referred directly to arguments over civil rights or Vietnam, for instance. Rather, the celebration of the Civil War Centennial between 1961 and 1965 and the American Revolution Bicentennial in 1976 were heavily influenced by government officials who urged widespread citizen participation, respect for patriots who died for the cause of national unity, and loyalty to the nation. But the commemorations of the Civil War and the Revolution were never far removed from the disunity that was manifested in the era. They stood as massive cultural bookends that attempted to contain volumes of dissent and indifference to the civic messages of leaders. On a cultural level they boldly attempted to fashion memories of past conflict and actually transform them into symbolic struggles for unity. As with commemorative activities before them, however, they were only partially what authorities wanted them to be. Ordinary people continued to use them for entertainment, for the celebration of a past that was mostly local, ethnic, or personal, and for other unintended purposes.

THE NATIONAL CELEBRATION OF THE CIVIL WAR CENTENNIAL

In 1957, prompted by popular interest throughout the country and by the lobbying of Civil War Round Tables, the federal government created the Civil War Centennial Commission. Round Tables, particularly one based in Washington, D.C., consisted of citizens who held a passionate interest in the Civil War era and its military dimensions. The Washington group, which lobbied directly for the commission, included Karl S. Betts, the first executive director of the national commission, and U. S. Grant III. Both of these men, in fact, had military backgrounds. Betts was a veteran of World War I, and Grant, who graduated from West Point, had spent his entire career in the military.[1]

Like most other commemorative commissions in this century, this one was composed entirely of prominent members of society and middle-class professionals. Congressional representation included Fred Schwengel of Iowa and Ralph Yarborough of Texas. Members of the historical profession included author Bruce Catton and professors Avery O. Craven of the University of Chicago and Bell Irvin Wiley of Emory University in Atlanta. Also members of the group were William S. Paley, chairman of the Columbia Broadcasting System; Conrad Wirth, director of the National Park Service; and Vice Admiral Stuart Ingersoll of the Naval War College.[2]

Much like the George Washington Bicentennial Commission of the early 1930s, this commission used a historic event to promote patriotic instruction. These planners and officials were fully aware of the ability of such an event to advance a number of goals such as tourist travel or popular merrymaking. They chose to emphasize, however, language and activities that were ceremonious and ritualistic. U. S. Grant III told the commission in 1960 that Congress had created federal leadership for the centennial in order to prevent "popular interest" from being unduly commercialized and forgetful of historical and educational values. Grant elaborated:

> The flood of popular interest is running high and cannot now be stemmed. Our children and their parents will be inspired by a better knowledge of what Americans have done for the principles they held dear, and, perhaps recapture some of the enthusiasm and patriotism of that time for American institutions. We are confident that the results will lead to a better popular understanding of America's days of greatness, a more unified country.[3]

Betts and other national planners of the event clearly recognized that a federal commission with several hundred thousand dollars a year could not completely reshape popular and vernacular interests. That, in fact, was never their intent. Their approach was not to control events but disseminate ideals and values such as national unity and patriotism that would restrain commercial, entertainment, and popular activities. To that end, Betts, Grant, and others worked tirelessly to encourage the formation of state centennial commissions and circulated lists of local activities from various regions throughout the country to offer ideas on how the centennial could be celebrated. Eventually, commissions were established in forty-four states and the District of Columbia. Betts declared in his first annual report that he had worked diligently to "decentralize" the actual execution of the program (but not the formation of ideology) to the various state commissions and local groups. He reasoned, "It would be impossible to supervise hundreds of observances, pageants, and reenactments. We must confine ourselves to encouraging the preparation of educational programs, marking historical sites to arouse the pride of all Americans in the heritage handed down to us by our Civil War ancestors."[4]

In the end the commission adopted a fifteen-point program that accommodated many interests. It encouraged local and state celebrations and actually provided awards for some. It supported a number of scholarly projects involving the Civil War which included the microfilming of Civil War records, and attempted to assist the National Park Service in improving interpretive facilities at Civil War battlefields and sites.[5]

Betts and the commission promoted civic education with vigor and imagination. "Our market is still 170 million Americans whom we hope will join in the commemoration," he remarked. To reach them he developed plans with major travel agencies for stimulating visitations to Civil War battlefields. Maps combining tourist and historical information were developed in conjunction with the American Automobile Association and the National Association of Travel Organizations. In cooperation with a company that prepared syndicated news stories, the commission developed a program to produce an illustrated "Newspaper Story of the Civil War" that would reach some 32 million readers of Sunday newspapers. The project would include "professionally prepared" articles and illustrations in a format that resembled newspapers of the Civil War era. Costs could be covered through advertising. This particular program received the enthusiastic endorsement of Dwight Eisenhower in 1959. The President thought that the newspaper format would make a deeper impression on the public mind than history books. He argued that it was fitting that the war, "its causes, lessons, and heroism," be described for people "in the direct language of today."[6]

Eisenhower's use of the term heroism was important. It struck a theme that centennial planners could use effectively to interpret the Civil War in a manner that would suit their purposes. These officials desperately wanted to avoid rekindling any feelings of regionalism or any other forms of disunity. Their goal was to reinforce loyalty to the nation in an era when it was ostensibly threatened internally and externally by foreign ideologies. They, therefore, needed symbolic language that would allow both the North and South to find common ground in the centennial, and they found it in the idiom of the heroic ideal. Heroism became an explanation for the fighting that took place on both sides. The complexity of all combatants and of the past itself was reduced to one symbol that would best serve the interests of those who promoted the power of the state in the present. If everyone who carried a gun was a hero fighting for what he or she believed, ordinary people could find another source of pride in the past and both the North and the South could participate in a commemoration that ultimately affirmed the power of the nation over any of its constituent parts.

Grant was specific on this point. He told a meeting of the commission in 1960 that he had heard a few complaints that the centennial might arouse sectional antagonisms. But he claimed that the Civil War could not be forgotten and expressed his belief that the "heroism and self-sacrifice" of even the Confederates was worthy of mention. "They too were Americans," he asserted, "who were heroically fighting for what they thought was right."[7]

Unable to influence all forms of popular celebrations, the federal commission did design several formal ceremonies that symbolically emphasized its major theme of national unity. All commemorative activities included varied and competing themes and, consequently, they could commemorate complex historical struggles such as the movement for racial equality. But the opportunity to teach lessons of "patriotism and heroic devotion to principles" and stimulate national unity was always foremost. This was apparent, for instance, in solemn ceremonies at Grant's tomb in New York City and Lee's crypt in Lexington, Virginia, that officially launched the centennial in January of 1961.

The simultaneous tribute to Grant and Lee, by now a patriot for calling for peace and reunion after the fighting, afforded the commission the opportunity to establish the central metaphors by which they hoped the war would be interpreted by citizens in the 1960s: national unity and heroism. The former promised to stimulate a sense of loyalty and patriotism that would relegate other loyalties—regional, racial, ethnic, political—to a secondary status. This served the needs of the nation-state completely. Secondly, on a personal rather than political level, heroism offered a place in the historical record for common people in much the same way that the symbol of the pioneer had done. Ordinary foot soldiers were transformed into model human beings who followed their leaders and fought for the larger political structures in which they lived. Eisenhower certainly saw it that way. In a message to mark the occasion he claimed that the observance afforded all citizens an opportunity to pay tribute to the "heroism and sacrifice" exhibited in the war. He suggested that these qualities were necessary to maintain the "national spiritual unity which has been nurtured and developed over the years."[8]

In New York the opening ceremony centered around themes that reinforced loyalty to authority—religion and the military. In fact, the national commission had asked that special religious services be held on Sunday, June 8, and had distributed a booklet entitled *The Role of Religion in the Civil War Centennial*. At Grant's tomb troops in full dress uniform stood at attention as taps sounded "in memory of the thousands of Union and Confederate dead" and wreaths were laid in honor of the "victorious Union commander." Bells also rang out from the gothic tower of Riverside Church as a procession moved up the steps of the Grant Memorial. The ceremony, sponsored by the Military Order of the Loyal Legion of the United States—a group composed of descendants of Union officers in the Civil War—included remarks from Major General Ulysses S. Grant III, who stressed that the Civil War was important because it demonstrated that the country was able to preserve its unity.[9]

At Lexington, Virginia, ceremonies at the grave of Lee essentially repeated the messages of unity and loyalty. A former governor of Virginia actually praised Grant as "a magnanimous leader." A telegram from U. S. Grant III, calling Lee "a great and knightly American soldier and citizen," was read. And religious and military symbols were combined when the ceremony was held in the chapel at Washington and Lee University, an institution that Lee headed after the Civil War, while students from Virginia Military Institute appeared in full dress. Congressman William Tuck of Virginia, in his address, reminded his audience of the familiar point that Lee had called for an end to the bitterness after the war and urged Southerners to apply themselves to the task of strengthening the union. "A large part of the concord and harmony which we as a nation enjoy today," he asserted, "is due to the righteousness of spirit and the nobility of character of the great Southern chieftain."[10]

Despite the primacy placed on national unity and loyalty by the national commission, the issue of racial divisiveness in both the past and the present could not be ignored. On September 22, 1962, the commission sponsored a formal rite at the Lincoln Memorial to mark the centennial of the Emancipation Proclamation.[11] The ceremony focused on Lincoln as a symbol of national unity and not only on the symbolic end of slavery in the United States, partially because the administration of John F. Kennedy was reluctant to take a strong stance in public at the time on civil rights. Poet Archibald MacLeish honored Lincoln, and gospel singer Mahalia Jackson, the granddaughter of a slave, sang "The Battle Hymn of the Republic." The president did not appear, having resisted attempts by black leaders to issue a second Emancipation Proclamation during the centennial, and simply sent a recorded message praising blacks for the effort they had made on their own behalf for better schools and housing. And, as a national leader, Kennedy emphasized the theme of patriotism. He thought it remarkable that despite humiliation and deprivation, blacks had retained their loyalty to the nation and "democratic institutions." He praised blacks for demonstrating loyalty in wartime, rejecting "extreme or violent policies," and working for civil rights "within the framework of the American Constitution."[12]

In an interesting contrast to the program at the Lincoln Memorial, a ceremony at Lincoln's tomb in Springfield, Illinois, sounded a slightly different note. Although Kennedy did acknowledge in his speech that much remained to be done to eradicate vestiges of discrimination, the ceremony sponsored by the national commission basically placed black history in the framework of national history and emphasized black contributions to national progress on civil rights and material progress. In Springfield, in an event organized by the American Negro Emancipation Centennial Authority of Chicago, less optimism prevailed and speakers lamented the continued existence of racism and the need for a much fuller integration of blacks into American society. A black judge from Chicago, James Parsons, argued that America must still learn to accept blacks in every facet of life not merely offer them a "pretense toward equality." Parsons expressed dismay that the "democratic process" is still a "farce" in American cities that remain "patchworks of ethnically separated peoples who have retained their ideas of group superiority and hatred."[13]

Any attempt to emphasize progress in the field of race relations since the Civil War by the national commission, however, had already been destroyed by the reality of continued racial animosity. In April of 1961 the commission planned to hold its annual National Assembly in Charleston, South Carolina. These meetings were held in different locations and featured various commemorative events designed to stimulate enthusiasm for the centennial and discussions about the Civil War. On this particular occasion, however, a member of the New Jersey Centennial Commission attracted national attention when she charged that she was unable to make reservations at a Charleston hotel because of her race. State Civil War commissions from New Jersey, California, Illinois, New York, and Wisconsin threatened to "secede" from the assembly, and the Kennedy administration, worried about offending white Southern Democrats, ordered Major General Grant to "solve the problem."[14]

A solution of sorts was reached when the federal government arranged for the assembly to be held at the Charleston Naval Base. At this federal facility an integrated luncheon was held to open the meeting. But attendance was smaller than expected because a number of Southern delegates to the assembly held a separate luncheon meeting, "informally styled the Confederate States Convention." At this gathering a speaker openly attacked New Jersey for being "schizophrenic and discriminatory in its race relations" and felt northern states such as New Jersey were in no position to "rebuke" other states for any reason whatsoever.[15]

The assembly at Charleston was a fiasco and brought the leadership of the national centennial commission under sharp attack. Commemorative activities were not meant to portray divisiveness so starkly in either the past or the present. At an executive meeting of the commission the following August, Karl Betts was forced to leave his position as executive director. Grant attempted to defend Betts and told the commission that he had talked to the Charleston Chamber of Commerce before the assembly and was told that while blacks did not normally stay at the headquarters hotel of the event, they could certainly find lodgings at other hotels in the city. Grant also praised Betts for his devoted service to the commission and claimed those who wanted him removed should offer more facts to support their case. Grant was supported by Conrad Wirth who recalled how diligently Betts had worked with the park service in formulating legislation for the centennial in the first place.[16] And John Krout of Columbia University, who had served on the George Washington Bicentennial Commission along with Grant, claimed that he was impressed with the way Betts had used his national office to encourage the formation of so many state centennial commissions.[17]

At this point most members of the commission were not prepared to accept a continuation of the current leadership, however, and voted to remove Betts, an action that prompted Grant's resignation. Historian Bell Wiley felt that the executive director had not used wisdom and statesmanship. Other members charged that "a great feeling of malaise" now existed on the commission. By December, 1961, Betts and Grant were gone and Allan Nevins, a professional historian and, in the words of one commission member, "a distinquished interpreter of our heritage," was appointed as director of the commission. James I. Robertson, a former editor of *Civil War History*, was named to replace Betts. With new leadership in place many commissioners now hoped that the proper focus of the centennial from their point of view, the promotion of loyalty and unity, could be restored. Congressman

Schwengel told the members of the meeting at which Nevins assumed his duties that the commission, with its past difficulties, was missing a great opportunity to develop an interest in and an understanding of the history of the war. He declared that such an interest was necessary for young people "so that we will be better prepared for an intelligent and adequate patriotism to meet the challenges to freedom in this, the most dangerous time in the history of the human family." Nevins himself joined the effort at education and civic loyalty by declaring that the commission would not encourage any "cheap and tawdry" ceremonies that might diminish the "magnanimity of spirit shown by Lincoln and Lee" or "that fall short of honoring the heroism of the 600,000 men who gave their lives." Nevins exclaimed, "Above all our central theme will be unity, not division. When we finally reach the commemoration of Appomattox, we shall treat it not as a victory or defeat, but as a beginning of a century of increasing concord, mutual understanding, and fraternal affection among all the sections and social groups."[18]

No matter how diligently the national commission may have worked to keep the focus of the centennial on unity, loyalty, and heroism, ordinary people still used the commemoration for purposes of their own. Commercial ventures involving the celebration were endless in number, and thousands of citizens engaged in battle reenactments which tended to trivialize warfare and certainly distracted attention from the tone of solemn commemoration struck by the national commission. Numerous companies looked to the centennial with the anticipation of increased profits, an indication that commercial interests were coming to rival official ones. The fireworks industry reportedly planned for a one-third increase in annual sales during the event, and publishers anticipated expanded sales of books about the war.

Increased profits were planned for the tourist industry as well. The director of the centennial in Mississippi estimated that pageants and guided tours of the state's seven hundred battlefields would more than double the annual profit from tourism in the state. When Montgomery, Alabama, spent over $100,000 for five nights of parades and pageants for its commemoration of Jefferson Davis's inauguration in 1961, its retail stores experienced an increase in sales of 30 percent. At Manassas, Virginia, the First Manassas Corporation spent over $200,000 to plan the first and possibly biggest reenactment of the celebration in July 1961. The corporation "drafted infantry" units from all twenty-three states who fought in the original battle of Bull Run and even bought 165 horses and conditioned them to the sound of gunfire.

So much of this effort went on in the South that Karl Betts was reported to have exclaimed that the South may have lost the war, but it was sure going to win the centennial.[19]

This commercial use of the memory of the war and, especially, the popularity of battle reenactments continually disturbed national centennial planners and others who hoped to confine commemorative activities to the realm of somber ceremony and civic education. Ralph McGill, publisher of the *Atlanta Constitution*, called for an end to "tourist-bait attractions" that attempted to celebrate the centennial. He deplored the fact that people now wandered the South "wearing sleazy-imitations of Confederate uniforms, growing beards, making ancient wounds bleed again, reviving Ku Klux Klans, recreating old battles, and otherwise doing a great disservice to the memory of those who fought and died." Nevins basically concurred. He despised the "carnival atmosphere" of the reenactment at Manassas. After Manassas Nevins claimed that if the national commission ever attempted to reenact a battle, it would be over his dead body. And he called for an end to events that were "trashily theatrical."[20]

The reenactment at Manassas had a profound effect on government planners. In its initial conception it caught the imagination of many, including centennial administrators, officials in the National Park Service, and individuals in Virginia who saw the popular and commercial possibilities of the event. Major General Grant himself was listed on the letterhead of the First Manassas Corporation, the group that organized the reenactment. Early funding came from the state of Virginia, and the park service provided the battlefield site which it now owned. Park service files show that some critics existed in the agency who felt the reenactment would be too much of a celebration rather than an event "commemorating a tragic event in our history." Others in the agency, however, felt that they could not deny the American public the "excitement" of such an event.[21]

Shortly after the Manassas affair, little division was evident in the park service or in the offices of the national centennial commission. Federal officials were not upset that history was distorted. In the actual first battle of Bull Run, Union troops had broken and fled in disorder toward Washington, D.C. In the reenactment, Northern and Southern units came together on the field of battle at the end to sing "God Bless America." Officials condemned the event only when they were stung by criticism that reenactments dishonored the men who had fought and turned serious commemorations into carnivals. A newspaper in Virginia charged that the "sham battles" threatened to turn the memory of "the greatest tragedy" into a farce. Another reporter wrote that live ammunition should be used in the next reenactment, so that America would "be free of one of the sicker elements" in its society.

Voices defended such performances, of course. Thousands of ordinary people paid their own way to perform in these events and took personal pleasure in what they were doing. One "soldier" at the Manassas reenactment thought that the experience was worthwhile because it served as a "solemn reminder of a time when Americans fought in defense of principle without the inducements of the G.I. Bill." But government officials had heard and seen enough. Conrad Wirth wrote to Betts shortly after the Manassas affair telling him that any further reenactments would be "unwise" to authorize. Wirth thought that the interpretative value derived from such events was not sufficient to expend the energy, cost, and risk of injury. For the rest of the centennial he advised park service staff to substitute other forms of "pageantry" that people had come to expect. He suggested, for instance, flag presentations, infantry drills, the sounding of Civil War bugle calls, and special parades of soldiers in Civil War uniforms. Such activities would restrain popular participation in commemorative events, leave the explanation of the past more in the hands of trained interpreters (an approach that would tend to turn citizen participants into spectators), and, Wirth felt, form "a dignified and impressive commemoration completely beyond reproach." Both the park service and the centennial commission frowned on reenactments after 1961. "We feel that reenactments possess too much celebrative spirit and too little commemorative reverence," James I. Robertson exclaimed. "This soldier playing mocks the dead."[22]

Despite the fears of the popularization and commercialization of commemorative activity expressed by government officials, the Civil War Centennial Commission did a great deal to promote local celebrations of the war and its era. It certainly knew that it could not control the content and direction of all of this activity, which was absolutely staggering in extent, but it did make an attempt to influence the nature of local events by rewarding certain activities and maintaining an awareness of symbolic goals it held dear. Thus, in 1964, for instance, the commission gave "Awards of Distinction" to the Butternut Ridge Memorial Association in Eaton, Ohio, for public ceremonies at a local cemetery that were held each year since 1959 and which honored local war veterans in "dignity and solemnity." A woman in Arlington, Virginia, was honored for leading a movement to preserve Fort Ward, a fortification that was erected to protect the nation's capital during the war. The Blue and Gray Memorial Association of Fitzgerald, Georgia, was honored for presenting a historical drama, *Our Friends, The Enemy*, because the production stressed the bonds of fraternal affection "among all Americans."[23]

Ethnic groups were particularly rewarded for demonstrating their *contributions* to the Civil War era. An award was presented to the American Polish Civil War Centennial Commission for organizing a four-year program that commemorated Polish-American participation in the war through the publication of articles on Polish soldiers, lectures, and broadcasts. Similarly the Civil War Centennial Jewish Historical Commission was honored for an exhibit that traveled throughout the country. Supported by a consortium of Jewish-American organizations such as the Jewish War Veterans, the American Jewish Historical Society, and B'nai B'rith, the exhibit described Jewish attitudes toward slavery and the war, their military participation in the North and the South, and the relationship between Lincoln and the Jews.[24]

LOCAL CELEBRATIONS OF THE CIVIL WAR

At the urging of the national commission, individual states formed their own commissions and bodies to administer celebrations and commemorations of the war era. Public support and enthusiasm for such activity was never a given, however, and the process of organizing state commissions could be slow or uneven. Several state legislatures were reluctant to appropriate substantial funds and many citizens remained indifferent to commemorative plans. On the other hand, several states did not hesitate to participate in the centennial to the fullest extent.

Obstacles to forming state programs could come in a variety of forms. In Pennsylvania, a state that had played a central role in the Civil War itself, a fiscal crisis in state government in 1959–1960 and a competing organization formed by the state in 1956 to celebrate the centennial of the Battle of Gettysburg and Lincoln's Gettysburg Address hindered the creation of a state commission to commemorate the Civil War. Correspondence between national commission officials and supporters of a new commission in the state, including Roy Nichols, a historian, and Herman Blum, a businessman and collector of Lincoln memorabilia, suggested that the governor, David Lawrence, and the legislature were not interested at all in any celebration that would cost money. An ultimate compromise gave responsibility for "public enlightenment" in matters dealing with the Civil War centennial to the existing Pennsylvania Historical and Museum Commission and the task of arranging commemorative events at the Gettysburg battlefield to the commission that had already been created for that purpose.[25]

In Illinois negative criticism of the intended celebration was expressed frankly in several newspapers. An editor in Benton argued that the war resulted from a rebellion against the United States, was started over a "shameful cause," and thus, should not be celebrated. In 1961 a newspaper in Carlinville felt that the war should be forgotten and that a celebration would only lead to "less unity." The *Herald-Whig* in Quincy reacted to the national controversy that erupted over the segregationist policies of hotels in Charleston, South Carolina, by stating that the events in the South were a "disservice to the memory of Lee and Grant." The journal insisted that it was already sick and tired of the "whole ill-advised business" and the nation could not afford any form of sectional friction.[26]

Limited financial support and a relatively small amount of criticism, however, were never sufficient to prevent the formation of active state commissions in most states. In the North these commissions tended to express rhetoric and goals that sounded very similar to ones articulated by the national centennial commission. They also called for dignified celebrations of unity, loyalty, and heroism. These bodies were generally run by government officials, various professionals, and institutional leaders who valued order and deference to established authority. The chairs of the state commissions in Illinois and Massachusetts were state senators. Moving forces behind the celebration in Illinois and Pennsylvania were businessmen Ralph Newman and Herman Blum, who worshiped Lincoln and held an extraordinary interest in the history of the war itself. They gave quick agreement to speakers from the national commission who visited their states and urged that their programs be "dignified" and promote a serious interest in the history of the era.[27]

State planners and officials were adamant in their support for themes that expressed the ideals of unity and heroism. The Massachusetts Commission declared that the commemoration in the state should impress upon the "coming generation" the "high standards and moral values of the men who preserved the Union." Planners felt that the vast public had only a "cursory knowledge" of the period and thus all events should be covered widely by the news media and be "elevating rather than enervating." The Indiana commission resolved that the centennial in the state would "honor the thousands of men and women who displayed extraordinary patriotism and heroism during the Civil War," stimulate an interest in the period, "inspire all people to follow the guidance of that day," and illustrate "our common heritage" and "the role of unity" in the development of the nation. In Illinois the state commission wrote to U. S. Grant III in 1961, expressing some concern over the extent that commissions in the South were promoting tourism rather than praising "our forefathers for preserving the union." No state ever lost sight of the possibilities for tourist travel the centennial would create, but Clyde Walton, the secretary of the Illinois commission, declared, "This [celebration] is a serious purpose but one tempered with joy—the joy, not of battles won or enemies killed, but of national unity and lasting peace."[28]

State-sponsored events in the North generally assumed a commemorative tone that national and state officials wanted, but still managed to reveal a preoccupation with a local past and people who participated in the war itself. Illinois made arrangements to refurbish monuments it had erected on the Gettysburg and Vicksburg battlefields to its own citizens who had gone off to war. Commemorative ceremonies marked the 150th anniversary of the birth of Stephen Douglas at his tomb in Chicago in 1963, and a book on Illinois' military contribution to the Civil War was commissioned. In perhaps the largest celebration in the state, local and national themes were addressed when an observance of the centennial of Lincoln's funeral was held in Springfield in 1965. Common people participated by wearing period costumes and laying wreaths at Lincoln's tomb. But links to the present were established as well as links to the past. State Representative Adlai Stevenson III, read a speech from his father who served as ambassador to the United Nations, which drew upon an admonition of Lincoln's to do everything possible to achieve a "just and lasting peace." Stevenson felt that such an effort could be applied in 1965 to bring "hope" to "suffering masses from the Mississippi to the Mekong."[29]

In Massachusetts events were organized around the work of committees in four major areas: education, historical displays, industrial activities, and publicity. Educational activity was aimed at school children and sought to teach them about the Civil War era through essay contests and art and music projects. Displays of historical items from the era such as diaries and photographs were mounted in many public buildings. Industrial displays were encouraged for businesses that planned to celebrate their own centennials between 1961 and 1965. The goal here was to link the plans of the business firms to the larger centennial celebration. Finally, the area of publicity and public relations was a major concern. The widest possible audience was desired for centennial programs and the advice and cooperation of various publicity outlets was sought.[30]

Indiana struck upon a commemorative event that was especially supportive of the theme of national unity, although it clearly celebrated state citizens who had fought in the war. Early in 1962 Confederate flags from Tennessee, Arkansas, and Mississippi were found in the basement of the War Memorial in Indianapolis. The state centennial commission suggested that unity could be celebrated and the "brave men" who fought for their respective colors could be honored if the state governor, Matthew Welsh, returned the flags to officials in those southern states. The commission drew upon the memory of southern states returning Indiana flags to state representatives at an annual reunion of the 57th Indiana Volunteer Regiment in 1875.[31]

The scope and breadth of commemorative activities in Ohio was representative of northern states. Local historical societies called upon citizens to look for diaries, letters, and other items for local displays. In Columbus the state board of education directed that during the 1961–1962 school year attention be focused on the part Ohio played in saving the Union by means of assembly programs and reading assignments. In Gallipolis, in May 1961, the state centennial commission sponsored "Muster Day," an event that re-created the mustering of the Ohio militia a century ago for an invasion of western Virginia. Also, Boy Scouts marked a U. S. Grant trail between Point Pleasant, the town where Grant was born, and Georgetown, where he attended school. A collector of Civil War weapons in Bucyrus built a cannon of the era that actually worked, and local newspapers ran thousands of articles on the Civil War.[32]

Pennsylvania's major celebration was centered at Gettysburg but was carefully designed to tone down the brutality and bitterness of the conflict and emphasized national unity and patriotism. On the 100th anniversary of the battle in early July 1963, a three-day celebration was held in the small Pennsylvania community. The Postmaster General dedicated a stamp commemorating the battle, and federal officials accepted deeds to tracts of land purchased by patriotic and preservationist groups who wished to protect the battlefield from "commercial encroachment." A large parade was also held in the town consisting mostly of modern elements of the United States military, reactivated Civil War regiments from the North and South, and sixteen high school bands arranged in an order that expressed the theme "Strength Through Unity."[33]

On the third day of the celebration a dramatization or reenactment of the final phase of the struggle at Gettysburg, Pickett's charge into the Union line, was held. Some observers thought this event was not only the "high water mark" of the Confederacy but of the commemorative event as well. The "charge" was carefully staged before a crowd in excess of forty thousand people. A narrative historical background was relayed to the crowd via a loudspeaker system and sound and smoke effects were carefully orchestrated to give "the audience a real sense of immediacy." As at Manassas, however, the battle reenactment did not end in victory or defeat but in the joining of both sides on the field for a flag salute and the singing of patriotic songs. One Pennsylvania official remarked that he thought the event actually recreated the atmosphere of a century ago "without overemphasizing the shooting and killing but rather the more vital outcome of a reunited nation."[34]

Interest in the centennial in the South was immense. Most of the actual battles had been fought in the region, and this allowed for more celebrations and reenactments. But many Southerners displayed a clear determination as well to treat the Southern cause in an uncritical manner. They talked of national unity but could not merge such a theme as easily with the memories of their role in the larger conflict. Numerous southern newspapers rejected the idea that the Civil War should be forgotten. In Montgomery, Alabama, a local paper editorialized that the centennial was a time to "praise famous men" and recall unknown soldiers of the Confederacy "who gave their all for the right as they saw it." At a time when citizens of Montgomery could read about attempts by whites to limit the political power of blacks in the state, they could also attend a reenactment of the arrival of Jefferson Davis in the city. In fact, at this very same time a libel trial was in progress in Montgomery against four preachers of the Southern Christian Leadership Conference at which defense lawyers objected to the Confederate symbolism apparent in the beards five members of the jury had grown for the local centennial celebration. The judge overruled the objection, and the defendants were found guilty.[35]

When southern state centennial commissions announced their stated aims, they walked a fine line between expressing loyalty to the symbol of national unity and pride in the Southern cause and soldier. In reality the tension was never actually resolved and, when viewed in retrospect, the South celebrated a regional more than a national past. The Georgia Civil War Centennial Commission, created in 1959, listed as one of its objectives the desire "to perpetuate a knowledge of the deeds and traditions of a valiant people who . . . forged one nation under God." The Georgia commission also wanted to "educate the public" about the Civil War campaigns in the state and "honor the valor and sacrifice of Georgians who fought and died for principles which they believed eternal."[36] At best these statements implied a certain ambiguity in the expression of national loyalty.

Virginia used language similar to Georgia and also was a bit more explicit in revealing its interest in stimulating tourism. The state's centennial commission claimed that it was "just and right" to remember the valor and sacrifice of Virginia's sons who fought for what they believed. It also sought to honor the "deeds and traditions of a valiant people who helped forge one nation." The state certainly knew that it possessed a wealth of Civil War sites and built a visitor center in downtown Richmond that attracted over six hundred thousand people between 1961 and 1965. The purpose of this project was not only to educate the public about Civil War activities in the state but to encourage tourists to remain in the state longer by creating a desire to visit other sites. As the commission declared, it wanted to "promote Virginia as the place to come during the centennial."[37]

In Mississippi the goals and plans developed by the state commission did not appear to be particularly concerned about national themes. In this case the agenda was more explicitly a celebration of local historical events and tourist promotion. A central program of the state commission was to encourage the formation of units of "Mississippi Greys" or "Centennial Military Forces in Memorium" in each locality that would participate in reenactment ceremonies of Mississippi's Act of Secession in January 1961. Clearly such activity looked more to the celebration of an old order than to the celebration of new structures of power that tended to diminish state autonomy and, perhaps, even racial segregation. The commission also saw its role as one that would encourage towns to sponsor pageants commemorating "the special events of 1861–65." And like Virginia, it had a keen eye on tourist revenues. S. T. Roebuck, executive director of the state centennial commission, wrote to mayors in Mississippi reminding them that tourism resulted in over $300 million in revenue per year and that millions of Americans would visit the South during the centennial. Roebuck used this point to stress the need for each locality to organize committees to assemble various types of centennial activities.[38]

Southern states did many of the things that northern states did during the centennial. They produced films about their participation in the war, supported educational and publication projects aimed at informing the public about the war, and preserved letters, diaries, and documents. But they also had more battlefields and, therefore, used them extensively as centers of commemorative activities and reenactments, regardless of the reservations federal officials had expressed toward such events. Georgia was a good example of a place where battles and military exploits formed a central feature of Southern celebrations. In contrast to the years just after the Civil War when Southerners focused memories on the dead and built cemeteries, in the

1960s they created a past they could enjoy and revived old war regiments, displayed thousands of weapons from the era, and held parades and pageants on the fields of battle themselves. In the fall of 1963 the Georgia state commission coordinated a series of seven different ceremonies at the Chickamauga Battlefield Park. It was the first of the Civil War national parks, and, consequently, was well marked with tablets and monuments from various states throughout the nation. During the summer of 1963 various days were devoted to particular states that had sent troops to the battle. On Louisiana Day, for instance, a high school chorus presented a musical program especially written for the occasion. During 1964 the Georgia commission sponsored reenactments at five different sites alone. At Resaca local citizens arranged and again "fought" a battle that was part of the campaign to capture Atlanta. On June 27, 1964, the people of Marietta and Cobb Counties carried out a reenactment of the battle of Kennesaw Mountain. Local groups had worked for months to arrange the affair and had attracted over twenty-two hundred people from twenty-six states to assume the roles of soldiers. A large number of cavalry and artillery were engaged and the commission felt that it had achieved "a very high degree of realism." The commission also felt that three important battles around Atlanta were not adequately recognized. With the donation of local funds, the commission was able to erect text markers and battle maps at the sites of the battles of Peachtree Creek, the Battle of Atlanta, and the Battle of Ezra Church. It was even able to raise funds to publish a special issue of *Civil War Times Illustrated* devoted entirely to the Atlanta campaign. When it was all over, the commission could claim that it was justified in focusing on the exploits of fighting men. It argued that acts of bravery and courage were typical of all Americans and suggested that a willingness to die for one's beliefs was indigenous to the "American Character" and a quality that was necessary to perpetuate the nation in the future.[39]

One of the central events of the centennial celebration in Arkansas revolved around a battlefield as well. In 1956 the state appointed a committee to promote the nomination of the Civil War battlefield at Pea Ridge, "where three confederate generals died," as a national park. This was an old idea that had first originated among citizens of the state in the 1920s. In fact, the fiftieth anniversary of the battle was observed in 1912, markers were erected on the field by local citizens in 1932, and a seventy-fifth anniversary pageant was held near the site in Elkhorn in 1937. Local interest and pride pushed for national recognition in the years just before the Civil War Centennial and the state of Arkansas was able to muster some $500,000 for the acquisition of land that included the battlefield and the land around it so that it would be "protected." In 1960 at Pea Ridge ceremonies were held transferring the site from the state to the National Park Service. Karl Betts spoke at the occasion and praised the state for this donation to the federal government, and stressed the importance of the battle for the course of the Civil War in the West. In the 1860s it ended a Confederate threat to launch an invasion into Missouri. In 1960, however, Betts asserted that the preservation of the site was an act that would "keep alive the American heritage" and place Arkansas alongside Virginia as an important place for visitors interested in the war's battlefields to visit.[40]

North Carolina paid the traditional homage to national unity that other states did but, clearly, spent a good deal of time on the Southern military effort. A celebration at Fort Fisher in 1962 attracted over six thousand people who watched a reenactment of a conflict at the site as "cannon roared, muskets barked, and flags waved." Seven reactivated Civil War units put on military demonstrations and Fort Fisher was designated a National Historical Landmark. The state centennial commission also produced a half-hour television drama about a military raid by Confederate troops into Pennsylvania and helped in the process of recruiting volunteers for reactivating Confederate military units. More than one hundred "reactivated Confederates" from the state were sent to the reenactment of the Battle of Antietam in September 1962. The commission also took pride in the fact that the reactivated Sixth North Carolina Regiment was featured in a film entitled *Stonewall Jackson's Way,* that was produced by the state of Virginia. Local groups in the state also took part in activities that attempted to raise a Confederate boat that had been sunk by hostile forces, develop local Confederate forts into "shrines," and display Confederate rifles and swords.[41]

One of the largest state-sponsored ceremonies took place near the end of the centennial at Durham in 1965. Vice President Hubert Humphrey was invited to participate in a "Centennial of National Unity" at the Bennett Place. At the same location a century before, the Confederate General Joseph E. Johnston surrendered nearly ninety thousand troops to General William T. Sherman, the last and largest Confederate army still in the field. "At the same time," according to publicity put out by the North Carolina Centennial Commission, "all civil resistance of the Confederate government ceased, thus paving the way for the reunification of the United States." Pageantry at the site included the presentation of flags from all fifty states to North Carolina as a symbol of national unity. Humphrey himself used the event to make a plea for social order and unity in a year of growing domestic and international tension. He attempted to soothe regional feelings by claiming that the "radicalism" that dominated the Reconstruction era was an example of the "senseless, revengeful extremism that even today, if left unchecked, could bring our great democracy to its knees." He declared that only an undivided America will be able to carry the burden of freedom in the world.[42]

No state exceeded Virginia in its effort to honor its own role and its leader, Robert E. Lee, and attract tourists. The commemoration opened on April 23, 1961, in Richmond with a parade marking the one hundredth anniversary of the acceptance by Lee of the command of the military and naval forces of Virginia. Cadets of the Virginia Military Institute passed in review and seven Virginia National Guard units whose origins date back to the Civil War were honored. The actual ceremonies in which Lee accepted his charge were reenacted in the state capitol, and the governor, William Tuck, declared that Virginia was not refighting the Civil War but restudying it. The state centennial commission also made an initial investment of funds and a loan to the First Manassas Corporation to help stage the reenactment of the first Battle of Manassas in 1961. Also, in the initial year of the centennial, the commission financed two special exhibits. Support was given to the Mariners Museum at Newport News to build an animated diorama of the historic battle between the ironclads CSS *Virginia* (formerly the USS *Merrimack*) and the USS *Monitor*. The Richmond Academy of Medicine also received support for reconstructing a large-scale model of a Confederate hospital.[43]

In addition to these centralized programs and activities, the Virginia commission also developed a "grass roots" program to coordinate and encourage local activities and ceremonies. Toward this end local centennial committees had been appointed in twenty-nine Virginia cities and ninety counties. In these areas, headstones were placed on the graves of "forgotten soldiers," old war fortifications were excavated and cleared of debris, and lectures, plays, and exhibits were presented. Near the Richmond airport a battle map and cannon were installed near "old trenches" and an electric map was erected in Harrisonburg that depicted Stonewall Jackson's "valley campaign."[44]

Military activities also attracted much public interest and participation in Virginia. In 1962 the clash between the *Monitor* and the *Virginia* was reenacted twenty-two times near Norfolk. In the same year the first Battle of Winchester was performed with a "reactivated" unit of the Stonewall Brigade. In this as in other reenactments ordinary people volunteered for "duty" and assumed most of their own expenses. On seven successive weekends in the spring of 1962, "reactivated" units of the Confederate army marched along paths taken by Stone-

15. Reenactment of a North-South skirmish, Civil War Centennial, Richmond, Virginia, 1961. Courtesy of Virginia State Library and Archives.

wall Jackson and foot soldiers a century earlier. Pictures of these celebrations show men in uniform carrying Confederate flags and being followed by wagons and horses. Finally, in June of that year, cavalry members of the North-South Skirmish Association reenacted a four-day "ride around McClellan" which had been carried out a century earlier to determine the size of McClellan's army that was advancing toward Richmond.[45]

The centennial ended in Virginia with the observance of Lee's surrender to Grant at Appomattox on April 9, 1965. The ceremony was relatively simple, in part because the park service prohibited reenactments on its property "because of the undignified experience at Manassas." Historian Bruce Catton spoke at the event and called upon those present to remember the "spirit of reconciliation." The great grandson of Robert E. Lee and the grandson of Ulysses S. Grant III were on hand to symbolize national unity. But a *Washington Post* reporter astutely noticed that most of those in attendance were from Virginia. Despite the fact that there were no Confederate flags on the speaker's stand, the reporter observed that the crowd got only "two big moments to cheer." They were when Lee's great-grandson was introduced and when the United States Marine Band from Quantico, Virginia, played "Dixie." Apparently deep interest in purely regional symbols remained despite the official rhetoric of national unity. Even the governor of Virginia, Albertis Harrison, revealed a vague sense of attachment to regional sentiments. He told the crowd that Virginians could recall the surrender of 1865 without bitterness not only because of the passage of time but because "beliefs and principles for which the Confederate forces fought are still with us." The state centennial commission itself declared in its final report that it felt it had not only stimulated tourism but actually gained a more "sympathetic appreciation everywhere of the Southern position."[46]

THE NATIONAL CELEBRATION OF THE BICENTENNIAL

The modern commemorations of the Civil War and the American Revolution were separated by a decade of disunity and dissension but still connected by an acute concern for citizen loyalty to the state and national cohesion. The conflict and opposition to established authority that were inherent in both events never emerged as prominent features of either the Civil War Centennial or the American Revolution Bicentennial. Rather acts of rebellion and dissent were reinterpreted by government officials and some celebration planners in ways that actually solemnized loyalty to higher authority, a message that explicitly favored the continuity of present structures over any form of substantial change.

For many Americans the weekend celebration surrounding July 4, 1976, marked an end to a period of social unrest and dissent and a renewal of American consensus and patriotism. This is not to say that commemorative events can necessarily effect widespread social and political change. But they can be used by people and institutions to symbolize trends and interpret changes whose actual roots stretch much deeper into the social and political structure. Taking stock of several days of intense commemorative activity and years of planning and celebrating, *Time* magazine proclaimed that "after a long night of paralyzing self-doubt" people felt good about the United States again. The *Washington Post*, recalling the desecration of the American flag during protests over the Vietnam War, felt that the flag was "common property again, to be stapled onto parade floats, stuck in hats, and hung from front porches." The paper felt the weekend had produced a moment of deep and moving reconciliation. And a newspaper in Akron, Ohio, concluded from the weekend events that the American people still have faith in the patriot's dream and in each other.[47]

Despite the diversity of the July 4th celebrations, a feeling of shared participation among millions of people was achieved through widespread television coverage. The weekend like the bicentennial period was characterized by much of what John Warner, head of the American Revolution Bicentennial Administration (ARBA), hoped it would be. By allowing for a diversity of vernacular expression within the framework of one official celebration, Warner wanted to create an image of massive citizen participation in a common cause of exhibiting loyalty to the nation and unity. He proclaimed that "the achievement of all the diverse factions of a community having come together to work in harmony will remain as a lasting memory of the event." And, of course, that was the point. The objectives were to encourage citizen involvement as a display of social unity and national loyalty, symbols that stood higher than those of personal, local, or regional significance. Warner expressed the hope that citizens would reach into their hearts "and find the deepest sense of patriotism."[48] His hope, in other words, was for patriotism as a symbol to mediate official and vernacular concerns in such a way that the former would dominate the latter.

Millions of citizens were exposed to rituals and symbols in common. Although they were presented in an unstructured and often cluttered manner, as event after event was flashed on television screens, the dominant theme was never lost. All that was happening was being done on behalf of the nation; it was the nation, with its past, present, and future themes and symbols, that merited loyalty and respect. Religious services were televised on the morning of July 4th, as loyalty to authority was again reinforced by an association between religion and patriotism. Traditional national symbols were also honored. Marian Anderson read the Declaration of Independence from Independence Hall and pioneer wagons arrived for an encampment at Valley Forge in a curious mixture of periods of history. The wagon trains carried the signatures of twenty-two million citizens who had signed scrolls along the routes that wagons followed from all over the country to Pennsylvania. By signing their names, citizens were told that they were rededicating themselves to the principles of the Declaration. Pickett's charge was also reenacted again at Gettysburg as a sign that serious threats to divide the nation in the past had failed, and patriotic feeling was stimulated with a televised performance of the Mormon Tabernacle Choir singing "The Battle Hymn of the Republic." At a naturalization ceremony at Monticello on July 5, President Gerald Ford could not be explicit about what all of the past and all of the celebrating was about but he did attempt an exegesis. He told a crowd of new citizens, "After two centuries, there is still something wonderful about being an American. If we cannot quite express it, we know what it is. You know what it is or you would not be here today. Why not just call it patriotism."[49]

There was no doubt that government officials and planners were extremely anxious to use the occasion of a bicentennial celebration in the 1970s to reaffirm the existence of national unity and citizen loyalty after a decade of dissent and divisiveness during which governmental authorities had actually inflicted violence upon some of its youngest and poorest citizens. The 1960s were very much on the mind of ARBA when it prepared its report to the people on its bicentennial achievements. "We entered the Bicentennial year having survived some of the bitterest times in our brief history," the celebration planners wrote. "We cried out for something to draw us together again." They reasoned that after a decade of racial tensions, assassinations, scandals [explicit references were made to Watergate in the report], embattled campuses, and eroding public trust, many may have felt that there was little to observe. In the aftermath of the bicentennial, these same planners were moved to exclaim that there was actually plenty to celebrate. "America had kept faith with its people, and its people had kept faith with America."[50]

The bicentennial celebration of 1976 was more than a simple commemoration of the birth of the nation. Just as the celebrations of the 1920s and early 1930s were influenced by the immense wave of patriotism that emerged from the experience of World War I, the bicentennial was in many ways very much a product of the turbulent times that immediately preceded it. On the one hand, like most commemorative events in this century, it was intent on reaffirming the status quo, the authority of existing institutions, and the need for loyalty to the nation-state itself. But it was also a tremendous expression in both design and achievement of local pride and perceptions of a local past. As in the Civil War celebration, the official orchestration of commemorative activity could not take place without a simultaneous celebration of vernacular interests.

President Lyndon B. Johnson signed a bill on July 4, 1966, creating the American Revolution Bicentennial Commission (ARBC). Johnson told Congress that the commission would recall to the nation and the world the "majestic significance" of the Revolution. Sensitive to criticisms his administration was receiving over its war policies in Southeast Asia, Johnson argued that the bicentennial would not only celebrate the birth of American ideals but the birth of ideals for which people around the world still fight. He quoted Casmir Pulaski that "wherever on the globe men are fighting for liberty, it is as if it were our affair." Johnson declared that these words were of special significance for his own generation. "Today, the Vietnamese people are fighting for their freedom in South Vietnam. We are carrying forward our great heritage by helping to sustain their efforts."[51]

The ARBC lasted from 1966 to 1974 and struggled with essentially two plans for celebrating the two hundredth anniversary of the birth of the nation. Led by a succession of prominent individuals, including a university president and a business executive, the commission was plagued by the fact that Congress, preoccupied with fighting a war, gave its needs a very low priority. In fact, seventeen months passed from the creation of the commission until it received any congressional funds at all. During its tenure it established several themes that would eventually guide much of the planning activity, and it took steps to make the national planning group more responsive and sensitive to diverse interests throughout the country. To guide the celebration the commission adopted the themes of "Heritage '76," "Festival USA," and "Horizons '76." The point of this structure was to encourage activities that looked to the past, celebration in the present, and projects for the future. In this respect planners simply codified what had taken place in commemorative activities for years. The past or heritage would be honored and used as an explanation of the origins of current institutions and why they deserved respect. The theme of festival allowed for celebrations that ordinary people would engage in anyway. The appeal to think about the future was meant to stimulate activities such as the construction of a hospital, for instance, that would make "a lasting contribution" to future generations. This program, symbolically allowed for a continuation of the "American way of life" and a reaffirmation that substantial changes would not be necessary in the present or the future because the future was meant to emerge from the past in an orderly way.[52]

During the early 1970s, under the direction of David Mahoney, the commission began to solicit opinions on exactly how a bicentennial celebration should take place. In a move that was somewhat unprecedented for centennial planners and probably reflective of the elevated state of public criticism of government and powerful institutions that had characterized the preceding decade, Mahoney held public meetings in San Francisco, Dallas, Chicago, and Boston that heard from state organizers, community leaders, special interest groups, youth, ethnic and racial spokesmen, and others about what they wanted in the 1976 anniversary. As a result of these meetings, in fact, the commission was enlarged to include more youth and minorities and a conclusion was reached by some government officials that the eventual celebration would probably have to embrace the desires and visions of a multiplicity of groups and localities.[53]

Until the commission had encountered growing public demands for participation in the bicentennial, it had focused a good deal of its attention on two plans that were viewed as possible focal points for a national celebration. The most widely discussed was the effort to hold an international exposition in Philadelphia that could have cost as much as 1.5 billion dollars. This idea was pursued vigorously by an organization of Philadelphia business and civic leaders who wanted to combine commemorative activities with entertainment events. In fact, at one of their planning meetings the Philadelphia group heard from the director of entertainment of Expo '67 in Canada. Philadelphia civic groups were simultaneously pressuring the National Park Service and the federal government for $18 million to complete the restoration and interpretive work at Independence National Historic Park. Toward both of these ends, Philadelphia leaders, such as William Wilcox of the Greater Philadelphia Movement and Robert McLean of the city's bicentennial corporation, attempted to arrange for visitation and receptions of federal officials and their spouses in the city.[54]

An alternative to the Philadelphia exposition developed by the ARBC was more sensitive to the need to decentralize the celebration but nearly as expensive. In 1972 Mahoney unveiled a model of a Bicentennial Park that would provide cultural and recreational opportunities in each of the fifty states and would serve as the focus of a state's participation in the Bicentennial and as a "lasting remembrance of the celebration afterward." Since the costs of the project were so high, however, budget planners in the Nixon administration advised the president not to go forward with the idea.[55]

The failure of the "two grand plans," however, was not due entirely to their high costs. The ARBC was severely criticized by 1972 and discredited by charges that it was overly "politicized." In memos obtained from the commission's files and released to the press by the People's Bicentennial Commission (PBC), a private organization that attempted to turn the commemoration into a critique rather than a celebration of institutional power in the United States, the ARBC was portrayed as a body interested primarily in serving the interests of reigning political leaders. In a front page article in the *Washington Post*, the commission was characterized as being more interested in the political goals of the Nixon administration than in commemorative events. The PBC charged that individuals such as Max Bond, a "black Republican," were appointed to bicentennial committees because they could be an "asset" to the Republican party. In fact, Nixon's appointments to the ARBC included a former director of White House communications and the chairman of the Mississippi Republican party. David Mahoney himself had taken a three-month leave from his job in 1960 to work for the Nixon campaign and had contributed to the party again in 1968.[56]

The disclosures of the PBC prompted increased congressional attention toward the ARBC. A study conducted by the Government Accounting Office and the House Judiciary Committee dismissed for the most part charges of undue political interference and commercialism but the House committee did conclude that their investigation revealed a "startling lack of concrete ongoing programs" initiated or coordinated by the ARBC. Added to the sting of these charges was widespread criticism from the states that the federal commission was not giving them enough direction and support.[57]

Rendered ineffective by 1973, the ARBC was replaced by an entirely new organization with a more focused charge. The Nixon administration announced the creation of the American Revolution Bicentennial Administration (ARBA) in 1974 and established goals for the organization that clearly institutionalized the idea of cooperation between divergent sources of power and various interest groups. The concept of a centralized celebration with one major geographical or even thematic focus was simply not possible given the diverse structure of American society. ARBA was responsible for seeing that the federal government and the states cooperate in a common effort and that each individual should have a right to participate. It was also given the responsibility of seeing that federal funds for citizen programs be divided as evenly as possible among bicentennial organizations chartered in each state. As the final report of the ARBA made explicit, "The experience of the years since the establishment of the ARBC in 1966 had clearly solidified agreement that no single government entity—federal or state—and no single geographical locality should dominate the Bicentennial."[58]

The attempt to decentralize the celebration and encourage wider citizen participation was reflected in the structure of ARBA. A board that determined policy and budgets was composed entirely of governmental officials, something that was characteristic of such bodies in this century. The board was to be bipartisan and included members of the House and Senate, the Secretary of the Interior, and three state Bicentennial Commission officers. Additionally, public representation was strengthened in the planning process by the appointment of a twenty-five member Advisory Council. The council was supposed to provide for a broader public role in the planning process and the participation of a wider section of the social structure in the discussion over the celebration of the past and present. The group included a homemaker; two students; four writers, including Alex Haley and James Michener; five women, including Betty Shabazz, the widow of black activist Malcolm X; Mrs. Lyndon B. Johnson; and seven executives. The Secretary of the Navy, John W. Warner, was selected to become the administrator of the new organization. Shabazz was particularly outspoken in calling upon blacks to participate in the commemoration after leaders such as the Rev. Jesse Jackson called for blacks to boycott the official celebration.[59]

Under Warner ARBA launched a vigorous program designed to stimulate the broadest possible level of citizen participation in the celebration regardless of what form that participation took. While federal officials were not particularly interested in sponsoring a carnival or an undignified celebration, they had little to say about the need for solemn ceremony. Solemn ceremony certainly took place but officials in charge of the national celebration did not talk about it as much as they did during the Civil War Centennial, and expressed more concern about maximizing the participation of ordinary individuals. In fact, when critics charged that ARBA lacked a "centerpiece" project, the organization answered that the Bicentennial "would involve all our communities, institutions, and citizens" as its major focus.[60]

Widespread citizen participation under the direction of an organized national authority could convey a traditional message of the efficacy of national power and still allow for the realization of local and personal interests. Consequently, ARBA promoted citizen participation in numerous ways. A "Bicentennial Communities Program" was created in which towns and localities throughout the country could apply for recognition as an official "Bicentennial Community." This program, which had actually originated with the ARBC, required communities to plan as many programs as they wished under the three major themes of "Heritage '76," "Festival USA," and "Horizons '76," and also to initiate at least one project that would provide a "lasting reminder" of its bicentennial activity. Eventually the federal agency would designate over twelve thousand "Bicentennial Communities." It was clearly a successful way to generate community participation and citizen involvement in a common purpose. And such an approach symbolically reinforced the notion of national unity after a decade in which public space was punctuated with expressions of divisiveness and acknowledged the stubborn persistence of local and personal ties to the past and the present.[61]

ARBA not only stimulated citizen involvement but formally sanctioned links between commemorative activity and commercial endeavors. Over the course of the bicentennial over 241 American business organizations committed $38.9 million to official programs. The "American Freedom Train," for example, was sponsored in part by the Prudential Insurance Company, Pepsico, General Motors, and Kraftco, and carried an exhibit of five hundred historical documents, objects, and models spanning two centuries of American history. "The Bicentennial Wagon Train Pilgrimage to Pennsylvania," was first funded by the Commonwealth of Pennsylvania which saw potential in the project for stimulating tourism to the state, and the Gulf Oil Corporation. The event was the brainchild of a Pennsylvania advertising executive who sought to re-create the trek of pioneer wagon trains in reverse and generate income by negotiating contracts for the use of "approved Wagon Train" merchandise. The project eventually attracted over sixty thousand volunteer riders who moved wagons and horses over several routes from throughout the nation that all culminated in Valley Forge for an immense encampment on July 4, 1976. ARBA proclaimed that the wagons "kindled our imagination by evoking memories of the hopes and bravery of pioneers making the long trek through the wilderness that was America." The Smithsonian Institution's "Festival of American Folklife" was a joint venture of the federal government and corporations such as American Airlines and the General Foods Corporation. It involved a summer-long exhibition of regional songs, ethnic crafts, and dance. Exxon Corporation gave

$1.5 million to the American Issues Forum, a program that attempted to provoke local discussions about "our national aspirations" and "our form of government." And Eastman Kodak spent $1 million to build a national visitor reception center near the Washington Monument. ARBA also worked closely with an informal advisory group called Travel Associations in the Bicentennial to encourage and facilitate travel to and within the United States.[62]

Despite the obvious achievement of ARBA in generating widespread popular participation, not everyone was happy with the nature of the celebration. Reservations over the commercial aspects of the celebration were frequently expressed, and someone even exploded a bomb at Plymouth Rock in June 1976. Other forms of potential disagreement were defused by allowing for almost any sort of activity to pass as a bicentennial event. Although most criticism was relatively modest and certainly weak in relation to the energy invested in commemorative activities, the actions of the People's Bicentennial Commission did raise interesting challenges to events and served to illustrate how this celebration, like others before it, relied on particular interpretations of the past.

Basically and implicitly ARBA treated the American Revolution as the end of history. That is to say that it was not celebrated because it had demonstrated that people could engage in radical social and political change whenever they so desired, but it was commemorated because it had produced a nation and a political system that deserved citizen support in the past, present, and future. John Warner said as much in a letter to the *New York Times* in 1976 when he asserted that America would "honor the great men who forged and then steered a nation so strong and so flexible that one revolution has proved enough."[63]

The PBC was started in 1971 by Jeremey Rifkin and other social activists who had challenged the policies of powerful institutions in the 1960s. In an interview in 1976 Rifkin claimed that the PBC began as an effort to find the roots of "leftist ideology" in American history. Rifkin felt that it was not possible to get most Americans to identify with historical figures such as Mao Tse-tung, Ho Chi Minh, Castro, or Che Guevara. Rather, he and his associates sought to find examples of radical behavior in the American past itself. This, of course, was antithetical to the views of the past that were usually discussed in commemorative activities and were designed to inculcate notions of patriotic loyalty and the immutable character of existing institutions. Rifkin claimed that the bicentennial should not be a time for a "grandiose display of chauvinism but rather a time for the reaffirmation of the principles of democracy and equity for all." He claimed that the "government group, whose members would have been labeled Tories during the American Revolution, planned to have a jamboree for its corporate mogul friends and others that control the institutions that try to manipulate our lives." Thus, the PBC attempted to organize counter-celebrations to the official programs and generate support in Congress for measures that would curtail the influence of corporations such as government takeover of major industries including oil, electricity, and chemicals, and community control of capital in a public banking system.[64]

In 1974 the PBC published a guide for citizen participation during the bicentennial which further elaborated its views. It argued that in the 1770s there was a revolution in this country but that "in the 1970s the White House and Corporate America are planning to sell us a program of 'Plastic Liberty Bells,' red, white, and blue cars, and a 'Love It or Leave It Political Program.'" The PBC believed that the programs did not have to be commercial but could be channeled into a new movement to "reclaim the democratic ideals upon which this nation was founded." The PBC observed, "We will be celebrating radical heroes like Jefferson, Paine, and Adams, and radical events like the Boston Tea Party. . . . All the while, modern-day tories will attempt to present themselves and the institutions they control—the corporations, the White House—as the true heirs and defenders of the struggle waged by the first American revolutionaries."[65]

The commission warned citizens that "corporate America has conceived a bicentennial plan to manipulate the mass psychology of an entire nation back into conformity with its vision of what American life should be." PBC leaders charged that the celebration will attempt to foster patriotic commitment and convince people that the problems facing America can be solved by existing institutions. In a special appeal to teachers and students, the PBC's guide asked schools to reconsider how they were participating in a process that simply fitted people into niches in the economy rather than created well-rounded individuals in the mold of Jefferson. They also urged that classrooms consider how closely our society today approximates the principles articulated in the Revolutionary era.[66]

Rifkin and his group did not hesitate to put their ideas into practice, although they often sparked controversy. In their efforts in 1972 to discredit the ARBC, they actually generated some public and institutional support; many looked with favor upon their attempt to expose political agendas within the agency. Their attack upon corporate power, however, produced a decidedly different stance. The PBC took out a large advertisement in the *New York Times* in 1976 claiming that a band of "troublemakers we now call the Patriots" started a revolution two centuries ago over many of the same problems we face today: high prices, shortages of vital goods, unfair taxes, discrepancies in wealth, and corruption in government. In the past, revolutionaries pointed the accusing finger at the British government and its rich merchant friends, the PBC declared. "Today, we at the People's Bicentennial Commission are pointing the finger at big business and its friends in the American government."[67]

Among the most controversial moves by the PBC was the mailing of cassette tapes to the wives of Fortune 500 executives asking the women to interrogate their husbands at the dinner table about possible corporate misdeeds and benefits they derived from tax loopholes. The tape was followed by a letter to eight thousand corporate wives discussing tax loopholes for the rich, the disparity of wealth in America, and industrial pollution. Several wives angrily responded to the messages arguing that their husbands paid plenty of taxes and that the tapes were a waste of time. The *New York Times* attacked the measure and claimed that the PBC's "transparent anti-capitalist bias has led it to resort to dangerously dirty tricks." The latter charge brought a sharp reply from Rifkind who accused the *Times* of protecting its own "big business management."[68]

During the July 4th celebration of 1976 some authorities feared that opposition groups such as the PBC would instigate violence, but events sponsored by such organizations were relatively peaceful. A large counterrally held in Fairmont Park in Philadelphia attracted a crowd of approximately thirty thousand. The gathering, according to a reporter, included Puerto Rican nationalists, blacks, Indians, women's rights activists, and "various leftist organizations and homosexual groups." In another part of the city a smaller group called Rich Off Our Backs marched several thousand people to Norris Park, which a reporter called a "scruffy square." This march moved through run-down areas of North Philadelphia where large minority populations lived and where windows of abandoned buildings were boarded up and covered with graffiti. Only one American flag was seen on a drive through dozens of blocks in the area. In the larger demonstration at Fairmont Park, Puerto Rican nationalists called for independence from the United States and a bicentennial without colonies. At the same rally, which the *New York Times* described as an "echo of the protest days of the 1960s," Elaine Brown of the Black Panthers charged that the country's history had been one of murder and plunder. Karen De Crow, the president of the National Organization for

Women, reread the speech with which Susan B. Anthony disrupted the celebration of the 1876 Centennial to claim that women had made relatively little progress. The group Rich Off Our Backs, which included a contingent of Vietnam veterans in their old fatigues, marched and proclaimed that social problems in the country could be attributed to "the elites of society."[69]

In Washington the PBC rallied near the Capitol and denounced big business and called for a "new economic revolution." Using symbolic acts to make points, Rifkind read a "Declaration of Economic Independence" to an interreligious "jubilee" service marked by the ringing of liberty bells and the blowing of shofars or biblical ram's horns. The *Post* reported that the crowd was small, about five thousand, and "leisurely" when compared to the better attended demonstrations of the antiwar and civil rights era. The rally had begun that morning with a religious service at the Jefferson Memorial and a march by demonstrators who carried banners such as "Mobil, Exxon, ITT—down with corporate tyranny" and "Independence from Big Business."[70]

Groups critical of ARBA not only attacked the organization from the outside but sought to work within its confines to achieve goals of their own. This was especially true of many minority and ethnic bodies. ARBA had initially tried to establish connections with these groups by convening many of their representatives in an informal fashion to solicit advice about how to shape the celebration. Unexpectedly, however, a 1974 meeting of ethnic and racial representatives decided to seek official status and power within the structure of ARBA and perpetuate itself rather than simply offer suggestions or take part in a "pleasant conversation." Interested especially in contemporary problems that affected urban ethnic communities, this group called itself the Bicentennial Ethnic Racial Coalition. One of its leaders, Geno Baroni, told Warner that the bicentennial should not be just another Fourth of July parade but should do something about the problems that existed in urban communities and should recognize America's cultural diversity. Coalition members pursued these objectives by promoting bicentennial programs that attempted to stimulate economic development in ethnic neighborhoods and rewrite American history texts that would include more minority history as a way of combating ignorance and prejudice. In Boston the group helped organize an "Ethnic/Racial Forum" in 1976 that passed a resolution calling for the rewording of the "Pledge of Allegiance." The new version attempted to balance pluralistic and statist interests by calling for loyalty to "one nation of many people, cultures, languages, and colors under God, indivisible, with respect, liberty, and justice for all."[71]

THE LOCAL CELEBRATION OF THE BICENTENNIAL

In numerous towns and communities the celebrations did not directly attack national institutions and planners. The challenge of vernacular culture was always more subtle. Local activities revealed more of an attachment to vernacular and personal interests than to official expressions of patriotism. There were certainly expressions of national loyalty at the local level. Such expressions, however, generally took place within the context of local participation in programs that had been organized by national planners and officials. Thus, communities hosted stops of the Freedom Train, an Armed Forces Caravan, or the Wagon Train. Most of the sixty-six thousand activities, however, listed in the *Final Report* of ARBA were not planned by national officials and could not have taken place without an intense expression of local interests and personal experience. The building of a community hospital, the honoring of an ethnic group, or the commemoration of a local past were the types of endeavors that usually explained how citizens commemorated the nation's anniversary when left to their own resources. This was especially true in the decisions that local people made of what to place in the hundreds of time capsules that were buried across the country: family photos, footballs, mugs, money, toys, fishing licenses, street signs, cookbooks, city council minutes, and local newspapers.[72]

Vernacular themes were a staple of the bicentennial celebration in the South. Activities in Alabama included an archival project on Methodism in the state and an oral history project in Birmingham on the lives of "plain Alabamians." Tours of antebellum homes were held in Centerville, a log cabin was reconstructed in Jasper, a pioneer burial ground was restored in Lanett, and letters written during the Civil War were cataloged in Mobile. In Georgia a program was begun to acquire "endangered sites" important to the state's natural and cultural heritage and a booklet was prepared for schools providing biographical sketches of "Famous Georgians." A major exhibition was staged featuring early Georgia furniture in Atlanta. In Colbert local residents researched the history of the town and made it available to citizens "to facilitate their understanding of the past," and in Chickamagua a local train depot was restored to its former glory.[73]

Local history was important in the North as well. In Illinois a display of local Civil War artifacts was presented and a Civil War battle was reenacted at Broadview. At Cahokia an exhibit was presented on prehistoric Indian culture relevant to the area, and a reenactment took

16. Reenactment of Washington crossing the Delaware, Veterans of Foreign Wars group, Elyria, Ohio, 1976. Courtesy of Ohio Historical Society.

place of George Rogers Clark's trek. Carbondale compiled an inventory of its historical architecture and a center on regional history was established in DeKalb. In Decatur a replica of "Lincoln's log cabin" was constructed, and the home of a prominent local citizen, James Millikin, was restored. In Galena Grant was not forgotten, as an authentic Civil War camp was reconstructed and a cannon was fired in tribute. In Galesburg the route the earliest settlers took to the town from New York state was retraced. In Moline markers were placed on "certified pioneer homes" in the area. At the Chicago Historical Society demonstrations of pioneer spinning, weaving, and cooking were held.[74]

In Indiana similar themes were recalled. A museum was established for Warrick County in Boonville and three hundred local citizens in "authentic costumes" put on skits concerning Jackson County history in Brownstown. A year-long exhibit on women prominent in local history was mounted in Evansville. And in Warren Township

17. Bicentennial Commemoration at a pioneer school, Schoenbrunn, Ohio, 1976. Courtesy of Ohio Historical Society.

the community's history was researched and written by honor students for local schools. In May 1976, men from Lafayette dressed as eighteenth-century French explorers and traveled by canoe from Fort Wayne to Vincennes, much as earlier men had done two centuries before. At Vincennes people viewed the restoration of an eighteenth-century French home and watched a reenactment of the capture of Fort Sackville by George Rogers Clark.[75]

The interest in minority and ethnic themes on a local level was reinforced by the influence these groups held within the structure of ARBA itself. By 1975 a formal advisory committee of ethnic and minority representatives informed ARBA's deliberations and pushed for special consideration of projects related to them.[76] A few were national in scope such as *Many Voices*, a film produced by ARBA. The production said of America's diversity:

> Together we make up America,
> strong and rich in cultural variety,

a vivid mosaic of our entire society,
yet with each piece retaining
its own bright and essential integrity.[77]

Despite criticisms by blacks of bicentennial activities, moreover, federal officials worked to create programs that brought special attention to Afro-Americans. The National Park Service awarded a contract to the Afro-American Bicentennial Corporation in 1970 to identify historic sites associated with blacks. The project resulted in an increase from three to sixty in the number of such sites on the National Register of Historic Places. ARBA sponsored a program in several cities that discussed the achievements of black women and published a booklet on blacks who had served in Congress. Under a matching grant program, over half a million dollars went through state bicentennial commissions to 156 separate programs involving blacks.[78]

Celebrations focusing on local racial and ethnic themes flourished throughout 1976. The point can be suggested by simply looking at two cities: Atlanta and Chicago. In the southern metropolis, bicentennial events included workshops to encourage black artists to paint scenes of the city from a black perspective, recordings made by black composers, and an exhibit entitled "Georgians Creating a Culture," which featured the contributions of blacks, Jews, Scotch, Irish, and other ethnic groups to state history. Other projects included the establishment of a Chinese-American cultural center, an award program to minority businesses, a Turkish festival, and a Hellenic festival.

Chicago's attention to minorities was also strong. The city hosted a lecture series on the black experience in America and exhibits on the contributions of black scientists and black women. At Hull House, a structure that had served as a settlement house for the foreign-born earlier in the century, an exhibit told of ethnic settlement of Chicago's west side. A symposium was held on the Greek experience in America, and Japanese-Americans held a reunion. Students conducted an oral history project of Ukrainians in Illinois, Mexican-American artists organized their own exhibit, Lithuanian Folk Dancers presented a festival, and the St. Patrick's Day parade in 1976 depicted Irish contributions to America.[79]

It cannot be said that activities focusing on patriotism and national themes did not emerge from the minds of local planners. Obviously some ethnic groups attempted to honor both local and national histories when they stressed "contributions." And any survey of local activity cannot ignore a relatively impressive amount of patriotic ceremony. The point is not that themes honoring the nation were forgotten by local planners. After two centuries of commemorative activity, public ceremonies were infused with both local and national, personal and public, themes. The point is, rather, that national themes were distorted to a greater extent in local celebrations by vernacular interests.

National culture was clearly celebrated in places such as St. Louis which held a celebration of American music that included choral music, Afro-American songs, American operas, and Native American song and dance. Florence, Alabama, sponsored a seminar on the "American Heritage" and a dramatic reading entitled "Carl Sandburg's America." Jasper, Alabama, initiated a community-wide flag display during the summer of 1976 and presented a pageant about the Revolutionary War. The town also marked the graves of three Revolutionary War soldiers from the area. In Albany, Georgia, citizens could attend five lectures on the principles of the Revolution; a performance of *1776*, a musical play concerning the signing of the Constitution; and "a Bicentennial salute to the American flag," involving the participation of representatives of the U.S. Marine Corps. In Atlanta the public schools initiated a discussion program "to instill in students . . . a comprehensive knowledge and appreciation of the richness of our national heritage," and performances by drum and bugle corps from throughout the nation offering a "musical marching salute to the Bicentennial." Other communities commemorated Washington and local citizens who served in the Revolutionary War. In Augusta, Georgia, a Washington Day parade commemorated Washington's visit to the city in 1791. In Cochran, Georgia, a publication was produced listing "all patriots" who were ancestors of local citizens who served in the Revolutionary War.[80]

In the North celebrations of the nation and a national past took similar forms. In Chicago performances of music from the period of the Revolution were presented and the Chicago Historical Society mounted an exhibit entitled "Creating a New Nation: 1763." At Galesburg a monument was erected to war veterans, and in Kewanee veterans were honored by the construction of a park. At Peoria an exhibit was presented on American folk art, the American Freedom Train visited in late July, the Armed Forces caravan visited in August, and actors re-created the arrival of the La Salle expedition in 1681. In addition to commemorating Lincoln, Springfield set up a program by which organizations could rent films about the Revolution, restored graves of Revolutionary War soldiers buried in the area, hosted the national Wagon Train pilgrimage, and presented a multimedia show designed to take an "inspiring look at American heritage" and "inspire the viewer for the future of Americanism." In Indiana, Girl Scouts in Evansville sponsored a program called "Wake Up America" that "stressed patriotism." At the state museum in Indianapolis an exhibit depicted the expedition of George Rogers Clark "which was the most revolutionary action west of the Allegheny Mountains." On August 15, 1976, Seymour, Indiana, celebrated America's victory over Japan in World War II and expressed pride that it had sponsored the longest continuously celebrated VJ Day in the nation.[81]

CONCLUSION

Officials who planned national commemorations of the Civil War and the American Revolution desperately wanted to interpret the past in ways that would reinforce citizen loyalty to a nation-state and diminish attachments individuals may have held toward a region, a locale, or a communal group. These contemporary political goals transformed the interpretation of the past to such an extent that acts of outright rebellion against political authority, such as the Civil War and the Revolution, became dramatic stories in which great men made irrevocable decisions that now deserved praise, and ordinary people deferred to higher authority and fought heroically for political dogmas.

But the political goals of national officials did not entirely define the nature of commemorative events in the 1960s and 1970s. When ordinary citizens expressed their historical interests they generally demonstrated a preoccupation with a past that had been formulated and discussed locally and still held meaning for them in the present. Often this expression honored national power and institutions in the present as government officials desired. Thus, ethnic groups listed their "contributions" to the nation. But often these expressions simply reflected their interest in personal and local themes unrelated to the civic goals of national planners or a desire for leisure and entertainment. After the widespread discontent and civil disobedience of the 1960s, moreover, national officials appeared to be more inclusive in their planning for the bicentennial and more tolerant of alternative forms of celebration. Bicentennial officials did not take quite the high moral tone of those who shaped the national celebration of the Civil War and were less predisposed to orchestrate formal rituals. Rather, in 1976, these planners appeared more accepting of popular choices for commemorating the past in the context of local or ethnic memories. This is not to say that no attempt was made to maintain a national framework around the celebration. In fact, the creation of several keynote activities such as the Wagon Train and the widespread use of official emblems and sanctioning procedures turned out to be another, perhaps more subtle, attempt to maintain the symbol of national unity and power amidst activities that actually stood somewhat opposed to that power in its most complete form. After the 1960s the cultural power of the nation-state certainly remained but appeared to be less effective than it had been in the decades after World War I.

Certainly national planners were not the only ones to advocate allegiance to national symbols and interpret the past in ways that would facilitate the achievement of that end. Countless expressions of loyalty to the nation-state emanated from local people in various regions during both celebrations. By this time, however, the existence of national power was both too real and too well established within the consciousness of most people for such expressions to be surprising. What was unexpected was the continued expression of uncertainty over this power in numerous forms, whether it be in the southern celebrations of the Confederacy, the forceful assault of the PBC, or in the continuing preoccupation with a communal, racial, and ethnic past.

CONCLUSION

Subcultures and the Regime

How do the worlds of private life,
the group meanings and interests of smaller
social units, affect and effect the configuration
of public life? How does the character and
quality of relations with public life affect life
and the life of social groups?
—*Thomas Bender*

CITIZENS drew upon the past and the present to invest public commemorations and memorials in America with meaning. This public expression of memory was entirely dependent upon a process of symbolic communication that simultaneously allowed for a diversity of expression and privileged some expressions over others. To the degree that these expressions were official and abstract, their pluralist dimensions were obscured. On the other hand, their multivocal and pluralistic quality tended to constrain both their ideal restatements of reality and the political objectives of officials. Public memory was never clearly or permanently defined but, rather, it was continually constructed in a realm where the small- and large-scale structures of society intersected.

The essential contest that shaped commemoration and the interpretation of the past and the present was waged between the advocates of centralized power and those who were unwilling to completely relinquish the autonomy of their small worlds. Cultural leaders, usually grounded in institutional and professional structures, envisioned a nation of dutiful and united citizens which undertook only orderly change. These officials saw the past as a device that could help them attain these goals and never tired of using commemoration to restate what they thought the social order and citizen behavior should be.

Defenders of vernacular cultures, however, had misgivings about centralized authorities and their interpretations of the past and the present. Their cultural expressions and public memory were not always grounded in the interests of large institutions but in the interests of small structures and associations that they had known, felt, or experienced directly. These attachments could change from time to time and include interests that served the needs of leaders as well. Because their ultimate aim was to serve a subculture rather than the regime, however, they were inherently threatening and oppositional.

Fashioned from political debates and cultural exchanges, public memory was part of American political culture. It changed as the structure of social and political power changed, and its diversity and its symbolic expressions were rooted in the material reality of the dominant political forces and organizations of the times. It was discussed in forums throughout the social structure because it was part of the process by which that structure resolved basic issues of power and constructed interpretations of the very meaning of its existence. When veterans were a powerful political entity in that structure they became a significant force in shaping memory symbols. When ethnic groups were highly influential, so too was the attempt to accommodate their interests in commemoration. And, most significant, when the nation-state itself grew and expanded in the twentieth century, so did its cultural power.

The vast amount of energy and effort that went into the formulation of public memory also suggested that the material reality and operation of the political structure with its leaders, parties, elections, and legislation was never sufficient to fully resolve some very basic issues. The survival of the American political system for over two hundred years did not mean that the triumph of a consensual belief in the "American way of life" was complete. In ways that the traditional study of political history has never fully revealed, the examination of commemorative activity suggested that political issues were not entirely about economic power, military agendas, or class and status issues, but were also about the small-scale realm of personal and communal anxieties and feelings or what George Lipsitz called the "emotions close to home." The need for symbols such as pioneers and patriots emerged partially from the existence of that realm and those emotions.[1]

Regardless of the number of forums that existed or the complexity of communication over the past, however, the dialogic activity examined here almost always stressed the desirability of maintaining the social order and existing structures, the need to avoid disorder or dramatic change, the dominance of citizen duties over citizen rights, and the need to privilege national over local and personal interests. Accounts of fundamental change such as the Revolution, industrialization, or migration were usually reinterpreted in ways that fostered patriotism and made them seem inevitable and desirable. Dramatic episodes of citizens asserting their rights such as minority protest movements were almost never commemorated once the colonialists had asserted their rights in 1776. This was so primarily because cultural leaders, concerned with preserving unity and authority, usually invested more time and energy into the planning and structuring of commemorative events than ordinary people. It was not that ordinary people were disinterested in the past or failed to state their interests. Rather, they tended not to take the lead in organizing public events and, at times, appeared indifferent to supporting such activities.

Cultural leaders were effective, moreover, because they were able to minimize opposition to their own drive for change and growth by making their activities appear consistent with changes and actions of people in the past and by successfully promoting the symbol and concept of the nation itself. Attempts to place vernacular interests in the service of official ones were continual. Thus, the exploits of immigrant pioneers and veterans in the past were usually told as a story of nation building and valor rather than of uncertainty and death. Anxiety that people may have had about events in the present—the depression, the Cold War—was minimized by the continual tale of progressive and orderly transitions in the past. We can suggest that the reduction of such tensions was as eagerly sought by leaders as it was by ordinary people.

Promoters of official culture had another advantage. Much of the power of vernacular memory was derived from the lived or shared experiences of small groups. Unlike official culture which was grounded in the power of larger, long-lasting institutions, vernacular interests lost intensity with the death and demise of individuals who participated in historic events. Immigrant pioneers were celebrated in the Midwest most seriously when they or children that knew them still lived. Civil War veterans were commemorated until the end of the generation that experienced the war firsthand. The emotional force of the vernacular dimension of commemoration was seldom felt in subsequent generations. Thus, the National Park Service preserved Civil War cemeteries but not really feelings of grief and sorrow. In the same way, descendants of immigrants still in Cleveland did not return to the city's cultural gardens. Indeed, the public's attitude toward those gardens and memorials such as Grant's tomb in New York City had degenerated to apathy and indifference by the 1960s. To make matters worse, these sites eventually were victimized by random acts of vandalism and defacement.

But vernacular interests survived even if they changed. In part they had to survive because they were the basis for the existence of official culture and the concerns of cultural leaders in the first place. One helped give life to the other. Secondly, the powerful historical symbols and messages that cultural leaders continuously used actually contained dimensions of vernacular culture. If such symbols reduced or transformed the meaning of vernacular culture from time to time, they also preserved aspects of it. Thus, vernacular culture was sustained both by the power of ordinary people in the social structure and their ability to put commemorative activity to unintended uses and also by the mediating capacity of culture itself. The real question was never whether vernacular interests would go away but which interests would predominate from time to time.

In the period from the American Revolution to the 1830s the nation-state managed to achieve status as a dominant interest and symbol. Concern about preserving the structure and the symbol of the new nation was widespread. Heroes such as George Washington and symbols such as the Declaration of Independence honored both federal authority and the act of separation from England. This arrangement would not change until the expression of class and regional interests grew more pronounced after 1830 with the economic expansion of the nation itself.

The Civil War had a major impact on discourse over a past for the present. It certainly resulted in a renewed emphasis on the mobilization of national sentiment. In the aftermath of that conflict numerous groups expended much energy to instill national loyalty as a means of fostering reunification. But the participation of millions of ordinary citizens in the protracted war left a powerful vernacular need to understand what had happened—the dying and the sacrifice. This need could not simply be met by recalling deeds of patriotism or the tradition of national unity. Ordinary people desired to express memories and feelings of sadness and caring in commemorations and ceremonies. Battlefields and cemeteries, symbols of both patriotism and grief, now entered the memory system on an extensive scale.

In the period following the war, the competition between divergent memory interests became even more aggressive. A rising middle class, bent on the attainment of material progress and political power, promoted symbols and messages that celebrated both that progress and their own role in attaining it in commemorations. For this reason they had much to say during the national centennial celebration of 1876 and the huge international fairs of the late nineteenth century. But ordinary people who settled farms and towns also expressed an interest in celebrating different themes from the past. Anxious about the accelerated pace of change, they seemed less interested in honoring material progress and the growth of the nation and more interested in honoring people who had founded their families and towns or preserved their traditions. As political time in the form of widespread social change intruded upon their private lives, they drew upon a private and local past which they understood more readily than one invented by distant leaders. In the culture of this era the entrepreneur stood opposite the pioneer.

At the end of the nineteenth century, the clash of interests in both the social and cultural realm led to an increased willingness on the part of many social groups to invest more authority in the nation-state itself. Perceived to be a neutral entity that could ultimately protect vernacular interests such as business organizations or even ethnic institutions and promote order and unity, the nation-state acquired sufficient material strength and cultural power by 1900 to actually dominate those interests. It now became the center of a political structure and culture that rested upon a recognition of a pluralistic set of societal interests under the aegis of a powerful state.

In the twentieth century the administration of commemorative activity by government officials at both the state and national levels ended any doubt of which symbols and messages were to be considered dominant in public commemorative activities. Stimulated by an aggressive patriotism and the mobilization of thought during World War I, government officials joined the mercantile and professional classes that had been the leading promoters of official patriotism and loyalty to the nation in the previous century. The celebration of the nation's growth, always an important focus of public commemorations in the nineteenth century, now achieved a privileged status in the discourse over memory and the past.

In the 1920s the promotion of patriotic and nationalistic memory was conducted in a very belligerent manner that favored the idea of statism over pluralism, a tendency that threatened the "liberal consensus" forged earlier in the century. In the Middle West local government officials and members of the professional classes built monuments to patriots and cleverly transformed the interpretation of pioneers from people who founded local places to citizens who built a nation. Pioneers became a cultural equivalent of the founding fathers for ordinary people. Ethnic commemorations in the 1920s also reflected the power of uncompromising patriotism and became an increasing and unpredictable mixture of cultural threads. Both the Cleveland Cultural Gardens and ethnic celebrations in Illinois and Minnesota gave dramatic evidence to the curious ways in which vernacular and official interests could blend.

During the 1930s vernacular interests were able to assert themselves somewhat more vigorously than they had in the previous decade. Public interest in the pioneer symbol was very evident in the celebration of the Northwest Territory and somewhat more tolerance was demonstrated toward vernacular interests on the part of government officials. Pluralism survived but statism actually prospered as the federal government expanded its cultural activities and political power. The National Park Service, for instance, consolidated many federal resources for the preservation and promotion of the past and began to influence the symbolic inventory of American public memory tremendously. The park service was able to combine the older stress of the professional classes on a progressive history with its desire to tell the story of national development. In a period of intense social conflict and anxiety, the cultural power of the nation-state was again reinvigorated by cultural leaders.

The need to sustain loyalty to the nation during World War II and during the earliest days of the Cold War obviously did not diminish the enthusiasm of authorities in the federal government and the states to use commemorations to foster patriotism. This was evident in state centennials held in the Midwest in the late 1940s and 1950s. These activities always honored patriotism and governmental institutions in an unquestioning way. But they also celebrated numerous vernacular interests—ethnic groups, pioneers, material progress, business, women. Their structure, in fact, suggested that the promotion of official culture was done in a less aggressive way after World War II than it was after World War I. Although this study cannot demonstrate all the factors that accounted for this difference, it is possible that the increased political power of ethnic groups, for instance, and the need to maintain a coalition of supporters of the nation during the threatening days of the Cold War muted more extreme expressions of political ideology.

Social divisiveness after 1960 caused "those whose function it was to do so" to reinvigorate their commemoration of official patriotism and loyalty. This was evident in the Illinois sesquicentennial celebration of 1968 and the 1976 bicentennial celebration. It was also a part of the agenda of cultural leaders in the Civil War Centennial. In this effort leaders could draw upon existing memories and traditions that had become thoroughly familiar to much of the population. Thus, they honored soldiers who fought for the beliefs of their leaders and pioneers who built a nation.

Despite the renewed attempt to promote official culture, however, vernacular interests were not so easily managed. Evidence from Cleveland and Indianapolis suggested that public commemorations were now less concerned with the serious matters of life and devoted more to the pursuit of leisure and entertainment, an indication of the growing power of commercial rather than official culture after 1945. Where serious matters were still discussed, ordinary people did what they had always done to a considerable extent: expressed their vernacular interest in local, ethnic, or regional pasts. Official interests were expressed strongly both by leaders and by ordinary people who by now had fused numerous cultural threads in their consciousness. Thus, local celebrations in 1976 contained strong expressions of both vernacular and official patriotism, although the latter was fostered to a great extent by centrally organized programs and commercial interests. The strength of vernacular interests should not be surprising, however, since the political culture of the previous decade had done much to weaken the power of the nation-state.

Thus, the stages of public memory in the United States developed unevenly and reflected the changing nature of structures of power. In the early nineteenth century the power of the new nation as a center of public memory was real but tenuous. Its fragility was revealed during the rest of the century when it was effectively contested by an assortment of class, regional, and personal interests. Cultural nationalism and a state-dominated memory system were most powerful during the first half of the twentieth century and were fostered by a continuing series of crises such as war, class conflict, and economic depression, although vernacular interests endured with vigor and strength. In recent decades the power of the nation-state has been contested to a greater extent, and public expressions of vernacular memory have become more pronounced.

The debate between vernacular and official interests was also more dynamic over time in the United States than in other western societies. In France, for instance, successive stages of national memory were characterized by the constant expansion of the idea of national power and greatness over a long period. In the nineteenth century Pierre Nora explained how national memory became a project that used symbols such as the splendor of Versailles to stir loyalty. In Fascist Italy and Germany in the 1930s the state organized festivals and parades in a successful effort to replace local folk memories and beliefs with ideals of national loyalty. Local cultural patterns in the United States in both the nineteenth century and in the 1930s remained more independent of official interpretations than they did in some European states.[2]

In many European countries, however, the power of national culture over local culture did wane after periods of devastating national wars. Nora felt that this happened in France after World War I when the nation was celebrated less in commemorations. Other scholars locate such a decline in England and Germany after World War II. George Mosse believes the citizens of England and Germany were somewhat insulated from devastation during World War I because most of the conflict was fought on the western front and away from the civilian population. In World War II these populations experienced destruction firsthand and, consequently, were less likely to recall war in terms of heroic nationalism after 1945.[3] The penetration of the American homefront by televised accounts of the Vietnam War in the 1960s may have led to similar flights from the heroic ideal in commemorative patterns by the 1980s and more powerful statements of grief and sadness.

Some scholars such as Todd Gitlin feel that the political culture of our own times is no longer dominated by a central symbol as powerful as the nation-state. In this postmodern era various interests and cultures mix more freely in the public sphere—nationalism, internationalism, consumerism, ethnicity, race, gender, private feelings, and official concerns. Certainty has been replaced by doubt and the present is no longer seen as something that emerged neatly and purposefully from the past, a view that was implicit in the story of nation building. A commercial culture, centered in the electronic media, has challenged the supremacy of state power, something that was evident in commemorations as early as the 1920s. Both commercial and state culture, in fact, seek to weaken and transform a vernacular past: the former to gain loyalty to products, the latter to sustain ties to the nation-state.[4] In this unpredictable exchange of interests and messages, however, vernacular culture can find opportunities to be free of dominant interests and assert itself with vigor, something that might explain the power of the vernacular in the Vietnam Veterans Memorial.[5] During the war with Iraq in 1991, vernacular sentiments of concern for ordinary people were symbolized by the proliferation of yellow ribbons as much as were expressions of official patriotism.

But no one can be sure what such a free mixture of vernacular interests will produce or how the United States will be remade in the future. In the past unregulated pluralism led to a growth in state power. Yet state power may be on the wane. Conservative interests in the United States have attacked the ability of the state to intervene in economic and social affairs and support entitlement programs that are capable of sustaining some level of national loyalty. An apparent end to the Cold War may create less of a desire for official patriotism in the United States. It is certainly forcing eastern European nations to find new forms of public culture to accommodate ethnic identity and personal rights and reduce the heavy reliance on officially enforced patriotism. Public memory will change again as political power and social arrangements change. New symbols will have to be constructed to accommodate these new formations, and old ones will be invested with new meaning. Pluralism will coexist with hegemony. But the central question for public memory will continue to be what it always has been: just how effective will vernacular interests be in containing the cultural offensive of authorities?

Notes

Prologue

1. *Washington Post*, Oct. 13, 1988, sec. B, pp. 1, 3; Jan C. Scruggs and Joel L. Swerdlow, *To Heal A Nation: The Vietnam Veterans Memorial* (New York: Harper and Row, 1985). Also see Christopher Buckley, "The Wall," *Esquire* 104 (Sept. 1985): 61–73.

2. Scruggs and Swerdlow, *To Heal A Nation*, 16; *Hearings Before the Subcommittee on Parks, Recreation and Renewable Resources of the Committee on Energy and National Resources*, 96th Cong., 2d sess., 1980, 96–111.

3. The letters cited here are to be found in the Records of the Vietnam Veterans Memorial Fund (RVVMF), Library of Congress. Grace Tallman to Vietnam Veterans Memorial Fund (VVMF), n.d.; Mrs. J. C. Hayward to VVMF, n.d., RVVMF, cont. 74. See Scruggs and Swerdlow, *To Heal A Nation*, 21–28.

4. Jean Dick to VVMF, n.d., and Ann Lapin to VVMF, n.d., RVVMF, cont. 74; Mrs. Peter Baxter to VVMF, Nov. 4, 1980; Mr. and Mrs. Paul Burton to Bob Hope, Dec. 6, 1980, RVVMF, cont. 81; Wayne Buckner to VVMF, May 25, 1981, cont. 74; Roxane Lambie to VVMF, Nov. 11, 1913, VVMF, cont. 72, RVVMF.

5. Scruggs and Swerdlow, *To Heal a Nation*, 66; Rick Atkinson, *The Long Gray Line* (Boston: Houghton Mifflin, 1989), 463–80. See Tom Carhart, "Statement to the U.S. Fine Arts Commission, Oct. 1981," cont. 76, RVVMF.

6. Muriel Bargar to VVMF, Oct. 22, 1981; Robert Snell to Ronald Reagan, Nov. 11, 1981; J. Goerhing to Ronald Reagan, Sept. 9, 1981, cont. 76, RVVMF.

7. See Patrick Buchanan, "A Memorial on the Mall," *Washington Inquirer*, Jan. 15, 1982, p. 5. Many letter writers took their language directly from Buchanan's article after it was published. Emitt G. Moore to Ronald Reagan, Feb. 3, 1982; Ken C. Mazoch to Ronald Reagan, Jan. 3, 1982; and John Gustafson to Ronald Reagan, Feb. 1, 1982, cont. 81, RVVMF.

8. Regis Brawdy to Ronald Reagan, n.d., cont. 81, and G. S. Robinson to Jan Scruggs, May 14, 1981, cont. 78, RVVMF.

9. Scruggs and Swerdlow, *To Heal A Nation*, 73–83, 101; *Washington Post*, Mar. 25, 1982, sec. B, p. 3; Sept. 25, 1982, sec. A, p. 25; Oct. 12, 1982, sec. C, p. 2.

10. *Washington Post*, Nov. 11, 1982, pp. 1, 10.

11. Ibid., Nov. 13, 1982, p. 3.

12. Ibid., Nov. 14, 1982, p. 1.

13. Ibid., July 8, 1985, pp. 1, 4. *USA Today*, Nov. 11, 1987, sec. A, p. 6, published a list of hundreds of Vietnam memorials that had been erected in localities throughout the nation. A very few proclaim explicit patriotic messages and celebrated the notion of national greatness and strength. Most, however, stood as tributes to ordinary individuals who lost their lives and expressions of sorrow. For instance, a monument of a dead soldier wrapped in a tarpaulin was unveiled in Denver. Many communities listed the names of

local residents who had been killed or had been wounded in action. In Winston-Salem, North Carolina, a brick memorial was built consisting of one brick for each of the fifty-eight local residents who were killed or missing in Vietnam.

14. Christie Norton Bradley, "Another War and Postmodern Memory: Remembering Vietnam" (Ph.D. diss., Duke University, 1988), 17–27, 198. Paul Fussell, *The Great War and Modern Memory* (New York: Oxford University Press, 1975) suggests that ordinary people—in this case writers in Great Britain—tended to remember World War I with the more somber metaphor of the "trenches" rather than with any metaphors of glory and valor.

Chapter One
The Memory Debate: An Introduction

1. For a discussion of the dogmatic quality of some cultural forms and their ability to privilege abstraction over experience, see George Lipsitz, *Time Passages: Collective Memory and American Popular Culture* (Minneapolis: University of Minnesota Press, 1990), 14. The impact of oral histories upon the dogmatic quality of traditional historical studies is addressed in Paul Thompson, *The Voice of the Past: Oral History* (Oxford, Eng.: Oxford University Press, 1988), 72–99. My use of the terms official and vernacular has been influenced by the discussion in Susan G. Davis, *Parades and Power: Street Theater in Nineteenth-Century Philadelphia* (Philadelphia: Temple University Press, 1986), 16–18.

2. On "contradictions" in the social system see Mark Poster, *Foucault, Marxism, and History: Mode of Production Versus Mode of Information* (Cambridge, Eng.: Polity Press, 1984), 48, 60, 84–85. On patriotism see Hans Kohn, *The Idea of Nationalism in the Twentieth Century* (London and New York: Basil Blackwell, 1979), 8, 87–88, 205–6; Raphael Samuel, "Introduction: Exciting to be English," in *Patriotism: The Making and Unmaking of British National Identity*, ed. Raphael Samuel, 3 vols. (London: Routledge, 1989), 1:xix-xl.

3. Anthony D. Smith, *The Ethnic Origins of Nations* (New York: Basil Blackwell, 1986), 156, 201.

4. On the rise of middle-class professionals see Robert Wiebe, *The Search for Order* (New York: Oxford University Press, 1967), 111–32, and Thomas L. Haskell, "Professionalism versus Capitalism: R. H. Tawney, Emile Durkheim, and C. S. Pierce on the Disinterestedness of Professional Communities," in *The Authority of Experts*, ed. Thomas L. Haskell (Bloomington, Ind.: Indiana University Press, 1984), 180–225. Samuel, "Introduction: Exciting to be English," xix-xxx. For a discussion of the role of intellectuals in helping to generate cultural rather than political nationalism see John Hutchinson, *The Dynamics of Cultural Nationalism: The Gaelic Revival and the Creation of the Irish Nation-State* (London: Allen and Unwin, 1987).

5. Benedict Anderson, *Imagined Communities: Reflection on the Origins and Spread of Nationalism* (London: Verso, 1983), argued the symbol of a nation attracted strong feelings of attachment partially because it incorporated many "natural" meanings such as kinship or home and because it appeared to be an

entity outside the exclusive control of any one group or class. The idea of symbols containing discordant meanings is drawn from Clifford Geertz, *The Interpretation of Cultures* (New York: Basic Books, 1973).

6. Maurice Godelier, "The Ideal in the Real," in *Culture, Ideology, and Politics*, eds. Raphael Samuel and Gareth Steadman Jones (London: Routledge and Keegan Paul, 1982), 12–38. This mediation of diverse interests in symbols is part of the reason that most myths and symbols have what Victor Turner has called a "multivocal quality"; see Turner, *The Ritual Process* (Ithaca, N.Y.: Cornell University Press, 1977).

7. Victor Gondos, "Karl S. Betts and the War Centennial Commission," *Military Affairs* 27 (Summer 1963): 51–75.

8. Eric Hobsbawm, "Introduction: Inventing Traditions," in *The Invention of Tradition*, eds. Terence Ranger and Eric Hobsbawm (Cambridge, Eng.: Cambridge University Press, 1983), 1–14, suggests that public commemoration was created mainly to serve the interests of national leaders and national power. His hegemonic notions allow little room for the role of public discourse and exchange in the creation of traditions or for an appreciation of the multivocal quality of such inventions. A hegemonic view of commemoration is contained in W. Lloyd Warner, *The Living and the Dead: A Study of the Symbolic Life of American Communities* (New Haven, Conn.: Yale University Press, 1959), 116–20. For a more complex view on the creation of a usable past see the pioneering work of David Lowenthal, *The Past is a Foreign Country* (Cambridge: Cambridge University Press, 1985), 35–73.

9. The distinction between personal or autobiographical memory and historical memory is made in Maurice Halbwachs, *The Collective Memory* (New York: Harper, 1980); T. J. Jackson Lears, "The Concept of Cultural Hegemony: Problems and Possibilities," *American Historical Review* 90 (June 1985): 567–93; and Samuel, "Introduction: Exciting to be English," lx.

10. Maurice Agulhon, *Marianne into Battle: Republican Imagery and Symbolism in France, 1789–1880* (Cambridge, Eng.: Cambridge University Press, 1981), 144, 181–84. Pierre Nora sees a democratization of national memory symbols in the latter part of the nineteenth century in France in "La Nation Memorie," in *Les Lieux De Memorie*, vol. 2, pt. 3, *La Nation*, ed. Pierre Nora (Paris: Gallimard, 1986), 747–58. See William Cohen, "Symbols of Power: Statues in Nineteenth-Century Provincial France,"in *Comparative Studies in Society and History* 31 (July 1989): 491–513.

11. Mary Douglass, *Implicit Meanings: Essays in Anthropology* (London: Routledge and Paul, 1975), 160–61. My argument that public memory could be simultaneously multivocal and hegemonic was shaped by a reading of the work of Anthony Giddens and Clifford Geertz. Both scholars stress the importance of public exchanges in the restatement of reality. But Giddens allows for a good deal of manipulation and hegemony by locating the origins of ideological expressions in specific regions of the social structure. For Giddens the study of ideological systems is ultimately the examination of how structures of signification are mobilized to legitimate the sectional interests of hegemonic groups. He accepts the need for discourse but feels it cannot be free of distor-

tion. "The repressions which distort communication are equivalent," he claims, " to the social sources of ideology."

Geertz, on the other hand, tends to locate the power of ideology not in the sectional interests of the social structure but in the power of ideological representations and symbols themselves. He stresses the degree that culture is independent of social structure rather than the social origins of cultural systems. For Geertz the power of symbols lies in their cognitive capacities that help people grasp, formulate, and communicate. Metaphors, for instance, can integrate discordant meanings from reality in such a way that multiple meanings or positions are coerced into a "unitary conceptual framework." A multiplicity of "referential connections" to social reality exist and are expressed in the metaphors and semantic structure of ideological systems. See Anthony Giddens, *The Constitution of Society* (Berkeley, Calif.: University of California Press, 1984), 45–49, and *Central Problems in Social Theory* (Berkeley: University of California Press, 1979), 175–88; Clifford Geertz, *The Interpretation of Cultures*, 210–16. The increasing multivocal nature of public discourse can be viewed over time in Jürgen Habermas, *The Structural Transformation of the Public Sphere: An Inquiry into a Category of Bourgeois Society* (Cambridge, Mass.: MIT Press, 1989), 17–54, 216.

12. Leslie T. Good, "Power, Hegemony, and Communication Theory," in *Cultural Power in Contemporary America*, eds. Ian Angus and Sut Jhally (New York: Routledge, 1989), 59–61; Stuart Hall, "The Rediscovery of 'Ideology': Return of the Repressed in Media Studies," in *Culture, Society, and the Media*, ed. Michael Gurevitch et al. (London: Metheun, 1982), 56–90.

Chapter Two
Public Memory in Nineteenth-Century America

1. Robert Wiebe, *The Segmented Society: An Introduction to the Meaning of America* (New York: Oxford University Press, 1975), 7–8.

2. Merrill D. Peterson, *The Jefferson Image in the American Mind* (New York: Oxford University Press, 1960), 13; Michael Kammen, *A Machine That Would Go of Itself: The Constitution in American Culture* (New York: Knopf, 1986), 75–77.

3. Merle Curti, *The Roots of American Loyalty* (New York: Atheneum, 1968), 140–41; Barry Schwartz, *George Washington: The Making of an American Symbol* (New York: The Free Press, 1987), 13–15, 31–45; Karal Ann Marling, *George Washington Slept Here: Colonial Revivals in American Culture, 1876–1986* (Cambridge, Mass.: Harvard University Press, 1988), 53–84.

4. Philip F. Detweiler, "The Changing Reputation of the Declaration of Independence: The First Fifty Years," *William and Mary Quarterly* 19 (Oct. 1962): 559–73; Wesley Frank Craven, *The Legend of the Founding Fathers* (New York: New York University Press, 1956), 6–11; Fred Somkin, *Unquiet Eagle: Memory and Desire in the Idea of America, 1815–1860* (Ithaca, N.Y.: Cornell University Press, 1967), 175–77.

5. Kammen, *A Season of Youth: The American Revolution and the Historical*

Imagination (New York: Knopf, 1978), 38–43; Peterson, *The Jefferson Image in the American Mind,* 4–5. Mary Ryan, *Women in Public: Between Banners and Ballots, 1825–1880* (Baltimore: Johns Hopkins University Press, 1990), 21, says that July 4th was the chief source of new holidays in the period.

6. Somkin, *Unquiet Eagle,* 131–63.

7. George Washington Warren, *The History of the Bunker Hill Monument Association* (Boston: J. R. Osgood, 1877), 9, 31, 94, 153, 231; David G. Hackett, "The Social Origins of Nationalism: Albany, New York, 1754–1835," *Journal of Social History* 21 (Summer 1988): 659–81.

8. William Tufant Foster, *Washington's Farewell Address to the People of the United States and Webster's First Bunker Hill Oration* (Boston: Houghton Mifflin, 1909), 45–47, 100–101.

9. Ibid., 100–101.

10. Warren, *The History of the Bunker Hill Monument Association,* 318–19.

11. "The Completion of the Bunker Hill Monument (June 17, 1843)," in *The Great Speeches and Orations of Daniel Webster* (Boston: Little, Brown and Co., 1897), 145–46; "The Landing at Plymouth," ibid., 496–97. *Proceedings of the Bunker Hill Monument Association at the Annual Meeting, June 23, 1875* (Boston: Bunker Hill Monument Association, 1875), 143–51. At the fiftieth anniversary of the ground breaking in 1875 a much more complex set of interests were expressed that included pride in ethnic and religious heritages on the part of ordinary people as well as celebrations of patriotism and national unity.

12. Curti, *Roots of American Loyalty,* 126–28; Somkin, *Unquiet Eagle,* 63–64, 184–88; Richard Rollins, "Words as Social Control: Noah Webster and the Creation of the American Dictionary," in *Recycling the Past: Popular Uses of American History,* ed. Leila Zenderland (Philadelphia: University of Pennsylvania Press, 1978), 50–52.

13. Craven, *Legend of the Founding Fathers,* 66, 86–89; Daniel J. Boorstin, *The Americans: The National Experience* (New York: Random House, 1967), 363; David Van Tassel, *Recording America's Past: An Interpretation of the Development of Historical Studies in America, 1607–1884* (Chicago: University of Chicago Press, 1960).

14. Boorstin, *The Americans: The National Experience,* 327–39.

15. Anthony F. C. Wallace, *Rockdale* (New York: Knopf, 1978), 312; see Susan G. Davis, *Parades and Power: Street Theater in Nineteenth-Century Philadelphia* (Philadelphia: Temple University Press, 1986), 67–71. Kathleen Neils Conzen, "Ethnicity as Festive Culture: Nineteenth-Century German Americans on Parade," in Warner Sollors, ed., *The Invention of Ethnicity* (New York: Oxford University Press, 1989), 45.

16. Curti, *The Roots of American Loyalty,* 104–6; Eric Foner, *Tom Paine and Revolutionary America* (New York: Oxford University Press, 1976), 264–70; Sean Wilentz, *Chants Democratic: New York City and the Rise of the American Working-Class, 1788–1850* (New York: Oxford University Press, 1984), 14.

17. George Appling, "Managing American Warrior-Heroism: Award of the Congressional Medal of Honor, 1863–1973" (unpublished Ph.D. diss., Cornell Univ., 1979), 11–32; Mary H. Mitchell, *Hollywood Cemetery: The History of a*

Southern Shrine (Richmond, Va.: Virginia State Library, 1985), 68–69, 83–91; Gaines Foster, *Ghosts of the Confederacy: Defeat, the Lost Cause, and the Emergence of the New South* (New York: Oxford University Press, 1987), 36–37; Charles Reagan Wilson, *Baptized in Blood: The Rebellion of the Lost Cause, 1865–1920* (Athens, Ga.: University of Georgia Press, 1980), 105; Ryan, *Women in Public*, 42.

18. Richard West Sellars, "Vigil of Silence: The Civil War Memorials," *History News* 41 (July–Aug. 1986): 20–23; Curti, *The Roots of American Loyalty*, 190–93; John S. Patterson reveals how the war department encouraged the South to place memorials at Gettysburg in an attempt to promote national unity in "From Battle Ground to Pleasure Ground: Gettysburg as a Historic Site," in *History Museums in the United States: A Critical Assessment*, eds. Warren Leon and Roy Rosenzweig (Urbana, Ill: University of Illinois Press, 1989), 128–57. Kirk Savage, "Race, Memory, and Identity: The National Monuments of the Union and Confederacy," paper delivered at the conference on "Public Memory and Collective Identity," Rutgers University, March 1990. Savage argues that a standardized version of the Civil War soldier monument was mass produced for both the North and the South by the late century.

19. Marling, *George Washington Slept Here*, 132. On the Columbian celebration see *Harper's Weekly* 36 (Oct. 22, 1892): 1009–18; *Chicago Tribune*, Oct. 13, 1892, p. 1; Oct. 21, 1892, p. 1.

20. Robert C. Post, ed., *1876: A Centennial Exhibition* (Washington, D.C.: The Smithsonian Institution, 1976), 13–22.

21. The centennial celebration did generate enough public enthusiasm to help bring the Washington monument to completion. See Robert W. Rydell, *All the World's a Fair: Visions of Empire at American International Expositions, 1876–1916* (Chicago: University of Chicago Press, 1984), 35; Craven, *The Legend of the Founding Fathers*, 124; Theodore Johnson, "The Memorialization of Woodrow Wilson" (unpublished Ph.D. diss., George Washington University, 1979), 4–5. Congress made the "Star-Spangled Banner" the national anthem in 1931.

22. Rydell, *All the World's a Fair*, 2, 127–30, 155–60.

23. Ibid., 6, 24–25, 235; Virginia R. Dominquez, "The Marketing of Heritage," *American Ethnologist* 13 (Aug. 1986): 548–49.

24. See Dorothy Ross, "Historical Consciousness in Nineteenth-Century America," *American Historical Review* 89 (Oct. 1984): 909–28. Ross claimed that "historicism," the doctrine that all events in historical time can be explained by prior events, was slow to gain acceptance in the United States because many saw the Revolution as the end of historical time.

25. Foster, *Ghosts of the Confederacy*, 79–81; Morris Janowitz, *The Reconstruction of Patriotism: Education for a Civic Consciousness* (Chicago: University of Chicago Press, 1983), 53; John Shelton Reed, *The Enduring South: Subcultural Persistence in a Mass Society* (Lexington, Mass.: Lexington Books, 1970), 45.

26. Wilson, *Baptized in Blood*, 25–33, 119–43; Thomas L. Connelly, *The Marble Man: Robert E. Lee and His Image in American Society* (New York: Knopf, 1977), 4–5; Foster, *Ghosts of the Confederacy*, 100–101.

27. Leon Fink, *Workingmen's Democracy: The Knights of Labor and American Politics* (Urbana, Ill.: University of Illinois Press, 1983), 12–13, 93; Nick Salva-

tore, *Eugene V. Debs: Citizen and Socialist* (Urbana, Ill.: University of Illinois Press, 1982), 11.

28. Francis G. Couvares, *The Remaking of Pittsburgh: Class and Culture in an Industrializing City, 1877–1920* (Albany, N.Y.: SUNY Press, 1983), 65–73.

29. Ibid., 96–110; William H. Cohn, "A National Celebration: The Fourth of July in American History," *Cultures* 3 (1976): 141–56; Raymond W. Smilor, "Creating a National Festival: The Campaign for a Safe and Sane Fourth, 1903–1916," *Journal of American Culture* 2 (Winter 1980): 611–12; Roy Rosenzweig, *Eight Hours For What We Will: Workers and Leisure in an Industrial City* (Cambridge, Eng.: Cambridge University Press, 1983), 153–57, 171–72.

30. Craven, *The Legend of the Founding Fathers*, 123; David Lowenthal, "Pioneer Museums," in *History Museums in the United States: A Critical Assessment*, 115–27; Homer L. Calkin, "Iowa Celebrates the Centennial of American Independence," *Annals of Iowa* 43 (Winter 1976): 175–78. For a discussion of family reunions as an attempt to preserve familial cultural ties in opposition to societal pressures for mobility and individualism, see Gwen Kennedy Neville, *Kinship and Pilgrimage: Rituals of Reunion in American Protestant Culture* (New York: Oxford University Press, 1987).

31. "Centennial Sketch History of Grant Township, Lyon County, Iowa," handwritten manuscript, Rare Book Collection, Library of Congress. Also see "A Compilation of the Centennial Celebrations and Orations Deposited with the Librarian of Congress in Response to the Joint Resolution of Congress (Mar. 13, 1876)," ibid.

32. *Michigan Pioneer and Historical Society Collections* 21 (1882): 84. "The Centennial Anniversary of the City of Gallipolis, Ohio, Oct. 16–19, 1890," *Ohio State Archaeological and Historical Society Publications* 3 (1891): 37.

33. Henry S. Lucas, *Ebenezer: Memorial Souvenir of the Centennial Commemoration of Dutch Immigration to the United States Held in Holland, Michigan, 13–16 August, 1947* (New York: Netherlands Information Bureau, 1947), 20, 37–40.

34. See David Donald, *Lincoln Reconsidered: Essays of the Civil War Era* (New York: Knopf, 1956), 144–63.

35. Martin Sklar, *The Corporate Reconstruction of American Capitalism, 1890–1916: The Market, the Law, and Politics* (Cambridge, Eng.: Cambridge University Press, 1988), 13–14. Theodore J. Lowi, *The End of Liberalism: The Second Republic of the United States* (New York: Norton and Co., 1979), 3–4, 23–24.

36. Sklar, *The Corporate Reconstruction of American Capitalism*, 34–35.

37. Michael E. McGerr, *The Decline of Popular Politics: The American North, 1865–1928* (New York: Oxford University Press, 1986), 103; Curti, *The Roots of American Loyalty*, 172–220.

38. Ellis Hawley, "Herbert Hoover, the Commerce Secretariat, and the Vision of an 'Associative State,' 1927–28," *Journal of American History* (June 1974), 171–74; Hawley, *The Great War and the Search for Modern Order* (New York: St. Martin's Press, 1979), 141–44; Alan Brinkley, "The New Deal and the Idea of the State," in *The Rise and Fall of the New Deal Order, 1930–1980*, eds. Steve Fraser and Gary Gerstle (Princeton, N.J.: Princeton University Press, 1989), 85–90.

39. John Patrick Diggins, *The Proud Decades: America in War and Peace, 1941–*

1960 (New York: W. W. Norton, 1988), 111–15, 175, 250; Godfrey Hodgson, *America in Our Time* (New York: Vintage, 1970), 67–68.

40. Wiebe, *The Segmented Society*, 7–8.

Chapter Three
The Construction of Ethnic Memory

1. Barbara Ballis Lal, "Perspectives on Ethnicity: Old Wine in New Bottles," in *Ethnic and Racial Studies* 6 (Apr. 1983): 154–73; Kathleen Neils Conzen, "Ethnicity as Festive Culture: Nineteenth-Century German America on Parade," in *The Invention of Ethnicity*, ed. Werner Sollors (New York: Oxford University Press, 1989), 44–76. Conzen studies German festival culture and sees it created largely by immigrant middle class and artisanal leaders as an attempt to re-create a feeling of "communitas" that had been growing in early nineteenth-century German provinces and as a defense against nativists who tended to disparage immigrant culture and assertions of pluralism. Thus, for Conzen the mobilization of immigrants was aimed not so much at the achievement of political power but at the retention of feelings that some newcomers had known and as a defense against outsiders.

2. Werner Sollors, *Beyond Ethnicity: Consent and Descent in American Culture* (New York: Oxford University Press, 1986), 6–10. On the concept of interweaving see Michael Fisher, "Ethnicity and the Post-Modern Arts of Memory," in *Writing Culture*, eds. James Clifford and George E. Marcus (Berkeley, Calif.: University of California Press, 1986), 230.

3. See "The Meaning of the July Fourth for the Negro," in *The Life and Writings of Frederick Douglass*, ed. Philip S. Foner, 2 vols. (New York: International Publishers, 1950), 2: 181–204. I would like to thank Professor Richard Blackett for this reference. William B. Gravely, "The Dialectic of Double- Consciousness in Black American Freedom Celebration, 1808–1963," *Journal of Negro History* 67 (1982): 302–5. Robert L. Harris, "The First Jubilee of Freedom," unpublished paper in the author's possession. I would like to thank Professor Harris for a copy of this paper. William Wiggins, *O Freedom: Afro-American Emancipation Celebrations* (Knoxville, Tenn.: University of Tennessee Press, 1987), 49–134. See also Philip Kasintz and Judith Freidenberg, "The Puerto Rican Parade and West Indian Carnival: Public Celebrations in New York City," in *Caribbean Life in New York City*, eds. C. Sutton and E. Chaney (New York: Center for Migration Studies, 1987), 330–34.

4. Sollors, *Beyond Ethnicity*, 234, discusses the metaphorical use of the term generation. The idea of family reunion as rituals in a mobile society is drawn from Gwen Kennedy Neville, *Kinship and Pilgrimage: Rituals of Reunion in American Protestant Culture* (New York: Oxford University Press, 1987).

5. "Semi-Centennial Celebration of the Settlement of Bishop Hill Colony, Sept. 23–24, 1896," 2–6.

6. Ibid.

7. "Illustrated Souvenir, Seventy-Fifth Anniversary, Historic Bishop Hill, Ill., 1921."

8. "Celebration of the Seventieth Anniversary of the Founding of the Bishop Hill Colony," *Journal of the Illinois State Historical Society*, 9 (1916–17): 344–59.

9. "Program of Old Settlers Reunion, 80th Anniversary of the Founding of Bishop Hill, Sept. 23, 1926;" *Cambridge [Ill.] Chronicle*, Sept. 24, 1936, p. 1. For additional celebrations of Swedish-American pioneers see the account of the dedication of a pioneer monument at Luther College in "Scandinavians in America," *American-Scandinavian Review* 24 (Winter 1936): 364–68.

10. Vilas Johnson, "Reminiscences of the Swedish Pioneer Centennial," *Swedish Pioneer Historical Quarterly* 20 (Oct. 1969): 170–79; Conrad Bergendoff, "The Beginnings of the Swedish Pioneer Centennial," ibid., 161–79; *The American Swedish Monthly* 42 (June 1948): 33.

11. Johnson, "Reminiscences of the Swedish Pioneer Centennial," 171–72; Bergendoff, "The Beginnings of the Swedish Pioneer Centennial," 161–67.

12. Bergendoff, "A Centennial of Swedish Pioneers," *American Scandinavian Review* 34 (Summer 1946): 114–16.

13. Johnson, "Reminiscences of the Swedish Pioneer Centennial," 175; *Chicago Tribune*, June 5, 1948, pp. 1, 8.

14. *Chicago Tribune*, June 6, 1948, p. 22; June 7, 1948, p. 14; Johnson, "Reminiscences of the Swedish Pioneer Centennial," 175–77. See the discussion of attempts by Finnish-Americans to discover "historical milestones" and instruct their youth in A. William Hoglund, *Finnish Immigrants in America, 1880–1920* (Madison, Wis.: University of Wisconsin Press, 1960), 144–48. For a stimulating but slightly different view of "the invention of tradition" in ethnic communities see Dag Blanck, "An Invented Tradition: The Creation of a Swedish-American Ethnic Consciousness at Augustana College, 1860–1900," in *Scandinavia Overseas*, eds. H. Runblom and D. Blanck (Uppsala: Uppsala University Centre for Multiethnic Research, 1986), 98–115.

15. *Rock Island Argus*, June 5, 1948, p. 1; June 7, 1948, p. 2. "Heroes of Faith," pamphlet in Records of the Swedish Pioneer Centennial Association, Swedish Immigration Research Center, Augustana College. I would like to thank Kermit Westerberg for his assistance in locating this material.

16. *Rock Island Argus*, June 7, 1948, pp. 2, 11; June 19, 1948, p. 15. "Centennial Celebrations of the Bishop Hill Colony, Sept. 23, 1948." See "Minutes of the Executive Committee," Records of the Swedish Pioneer Centennial Association.

17. *Rockford [Ill.] Register-Republic*, June 9, 1948, pp. 1–2.

18. Larry Danielson, "The Ethnic Festival and Cultural Revivalism in a Small Midwestern Town" (unpub. Ph.D. diss., Indiana University Press, 1972) provides the material for this account of the Lindsborg festival.

19. Ibid., 182.

20. Ibid., 188.

21. Ibid., 151.

22. Ibid., 152–54.

23. Ibid., 156–57. On the "resocialization" function of family reunions see Neville, *Kinship and Pilgrimage*, 4–5.

24. Danielson, "The Ethnic Festival and Cultural Revivalism in a Small Midwestern Town," 159.

25. Ibid., 162–63.

26. Ibid., 202–6.

27. Odd Lovoll and Kenneth O. Bjork, *The Norwegian-American Historical Association, 1925–1975* (Northfield, Minn.: Norwegian American Historical Association, 1975), 7–17. Tora Bohn, who made a tour of the United States in 1949 and 1950 in search of Norwegian antiques, described what he found kept in midwestern museums and homes in "A Quest for Norwegian Folk Art in America," *Norwegian-American Studies and Records* 19 (1956): 142–59.

28. Carl H. Chrislock, *Ethnicity Challenged: The Upper Midwest Norwegian-American Experience in World War I* (Northfield, Minn.: Norwegian-American Historical Association, 1981), 15–19.

29. Ibid., 7–8; John R. Jenswold, "Becoming American, Becoming Suburban: Norwegians in the 1920s," unpublished paper in the author's possession. I would like to thank Professor Jenswold for furnishing me with a copy of this work.

30. Chrislock, *Ethnicity Challenged*, 7–8.

31. Jenswold, "Becoming American, Becoming Suburban," 2–11.

32. John Appel, *Immigrant Historical Societies in the United States, 1880–1850* (New York: ARNO Press, 1980), 364–65. Odd Lovoll, *A Folk Epic: The Bygdelag in America* (Boston: Twayne, 1975), 163–64.

33. Rasmus Anderson, "Restaurationen—The Norse Mayflower," *American Scandinavian Review* 13 (June 1925): 348–60.

34. *St. Paul Pioneer Press*, June 5, 1925, pp. 1, 21.

35. Ibid., June 9, 1925, pp. 1, 4; *New York Times*, June 8, 1925, p. 2. Pamphlets describing the celebration and minutes of the corporation can be found in box 6, Norse-American Centennial Papers, Norwegian-American Historical Association, Northfield, Minnesota. Lloyd Hustvedt assisted me in locating this material.

36. At one point during Coolidge's visit five hundred school children from St. Paul transformed a formation of the Norwegian flag they had made into an American flag; see *New York Times*, Apr. 12, 1925, sec. 9, p. 17.

37. *St. Paul Pioneer Press*, June 7, 1925, p. 1; June 8, 1925, pp. 1, 2.

38. Ibid., June 10, 1925, pp. 1, 2. Appel, *Immigrant Historical Societies in the United States*, notes that in the summer of 1925 the Society for the Preservation of Historic Relics and Records of the Norse-American Pioneer and Cultural Life was organized by individuals such as Theodore Jorgenson and Ole Rolvaag. A pamphlet describing the pageant is to be found in box 6, Norse-American Centennial Papers.

39. "The Story of Red Wheat," pamphlet in Mennonite Library and Archives (MLA), North Newton, Kansas. I would like to thank Barbara Thisesen for helping me find this material. *Mennonite Weekly Review* (Newton, Kansas), June 20, 1974, p. 1.

40. *Newton Kansan*, Nov. 22, 1974, clipping in MLA.

41. Ibid., July 19, 1974.

42. *Mennonite Weekly Review*, Aug. 8, 1974, clipping in MLA.

43. *Newton Kansan*, Aug. 13, 1974, clipping in MLA.

44. *Mennonite Weekly Review*, undated clipping in MLA.

45. *Newton Kansan*, Sept. 28, 1974, clipping in MLA.

46. Ibid., Sept. 25, 1974.

47. John O. Crimmins, *St. Patrick's Day: Its Celebration in New York and Other American Places, 1737–1945* (New York: The Author, 1902), 15–56.

48. Ibid., 58–63, 70–71.

49. Timothy J. Meagher, "Why Should We Care for a Little Tro or Walk through the Mud? St. Patrick, Columbus Day Parades in Worcester, Massachusetts, 1845–1915," *New England Quarterly* 58 (1985): 5–7.

50. Ibid., 22–23, suggests that in the twentieth century a stronger Irish (and more respectable) Catholic identity was advocated by organizations such as the Knights of Columbus. The Knights sponsored a Columbus Day parade to honor someone associated with the United States more than just Ireland.

51. Jane Gladden Kelton, "New York City St. Patrick's Day Parade: Invention of Contention and Consensus," *The Drama Review* 29 (Fall 1985): 93–99.

52. Ibid., 99–101.

53. See Appel, *Immigrant Historical Societies in the United States*, 179–80. For a commemorative event that attempted to portray Irish-Americans of all ranks as respectable and loyal citizens see *Centennial Celebration of the Declaration of Irish Independence at the Convention Held at Duncannon by Irish Descendents of Ireland* (Chicago: Donnelley, 1882), 15–16.

54. "Field Day, 1912," *Journal of the American Irish Historical Society* 12 (1913): 207–15.

55. The dedication of the Kosciuszko statue in 1904 in Chicago's Humbolt Park contained the traditional multivocal quality of commemorations. About one hundred thousand Polish-Americans gathered to watch young girls dressed in both native and American costumes unveil a heroic version of the Polish patriot. Humbolt Park and the site of the statue continued to serve as a public gathering place for Polish civic gatherings for many years thereafter. See Joseph John Parot, *Polish Catholics in Chicago, 1850–1920* (DeKalb, Ill.: Northern Illinois University Press, 1981), 173; Victor Greene, *For God and Country: The Rise of Polish and Lithuanian Ethnic Consciousness in America* (Madison: State Historical Society of Wisconsin, 1975), 137; *Chicago Record-Herald*, Sept. 12, 1904, p. 3; The claim that the United States was the "second fatherland" was made by an official of the Polish National Alliance in the *Washington Post*, May 12, 1910, p. 2.

56. Dorothy Spicer, *Folk Festivals and the Foreign Community* (New York: The Woman's Press, 1932), 11–13; John Higham, *Strangers in the Land: Patterns of American Nativism, 1860–1925* (New Brunswick, N.J.: Rutgers University Press, 1955), 236.

57. Allen H. Eaton, *Immigrant Gifts to American Life* (New York: Russell Sage Foundation, 1932), 88–89; *New York Times*, Oct. 16, 1921, p. 16.

58. *New York Times*, Oct. 21, 1921, p. 9; Oct. 25, p. 17; Oct. 29, p. 12; Nov. 1, p. 19; Nov. 8, p. 18.

59. Ibid., Oct. 30, 1921, p. 17.

60. Ibid., Nov. 2, 1921, p. 17; Nov. 11, p. 13.

61. Richard Weiss, "Ethnicity and Reform: Minorities and the Ambience of the Depression Years," *Journal of American History* 66 (Dec. 1979): 566–85. Gary Gerstle has suggested that the extensive Americanism campaigns of the 1920s penetrated ethnic subcultures in part because the concept of the nation as "a huge family" attracted existing communal sentiments in ethnic workers. He goes on to argue that a decade later these workers transcended ethnic ties to form a powerful class-based movement because they had learned how to use patriotic language and symbolism for their own ends. Thus, they did not simply accept patriotic lessons uncritically. Gary Gerstle, "The Political Culture of Ethnic Workers in Twentieth-Century America," unpublished paper delivered at the Social Science History Association Meeting, New Orleans, Oct. 31, 1987.

62. "America's Making in Connecticut, A Pageant of the Races," program in Northwest Territory Centennial Celebration Records, box 2, R.G. 148, National Archives.

63. *Golden Jubilee of His Eminence William Cardinal O'Connell, Archbishop of Boston* (Cambridge, Mass.: The Riverside Press, 1935), 3–4.

64. Ibid., 13–17.

65. Ibid., 38–39.

66. Ibid., 59–62.

67. Ibid., 64–76.

68. For an excellent discussion of the influence of ethnic leaders on immigrant commemoration see Rudolph Vecoli, "'Primo Maggio' in the United States: An Invented Tradition of the Italian Anarchists," in *May Day Celebration*, ed. Andrea Panaccione (Venice: Marsilio Editori, 1988), 55–81.

69. Anthony D. Smith, *The Ethnic Origins of Nations* (Oxford, Eng.: Basil Blackwell, 1986), 174–76.

Chapter Four
Commemoration in the City

1. *Fifteenth Census of the United States, 1930, Populations* 3, part 1 (Washington, 1932), 61–63.

2. *Indianapolis Star*, July 4, 1903, p. 3; July 3, 1905, p. 3; July 4, 1905, p. 4; July 5, 1905, p. 1.

3. Ibid., July 4, 1903, p. 3; July 3, 1905, p. 1; July 3, 1910, p. 1; July 4, 1910, pp. 1, 4.

4. Ibid., May 30, 1910, p. 4.

5. *Indianapolis News*, May 14, 1902, p. 3; May 15, 1902, pp. 2, 4, 6; The *News* also reported on May 15, 1902, p. 9, that Indiana received the largest amount of veterans benefits in the nation in 1900. Max Hyman, ed., *Hyman's Handbook of Indianapolis* (Indianapolis: M. R. Hyman, 1909), 53, 56–58.

6. *News*, May 30, 1918, pp. 1, 3; *Star*, May 31, 1918, pp. 1, 2, 9.

7. *News*, July 3, 1918, pp. 1, 12; *Star*, July 4, 1918, p. 8.

8. On the Ku Klux Klan in Indianapolis see Kenneth T. Jackson, *The Ku Klux Klan in the City, 1915–30* (New York: Oxford University Press, 1967), 156–58; Judith Endelman, *The Jewish Community in Indianapolis* (Bloomington: Indiana University Press, 1984), 124.

9. *News*, May 30, 1929, pp. 1, 19; May 30, 1931, pp. 1, 2; Nov. 11, 1931, sec. 2, p. 1; May 30, 1932, p. 2.

10. *Star*, Nov. 11, 1929, pp. 1, 10. Arguments over the ultimate disposition of the bodies of the American dead in World War I reflect a similar public division over the nature of patriotic expression. Many officials in the federal government and elsewhere wanted to leave the war dead in Europe in American cemeteries as a symbol of a victorious nation and American world power. Most ordinary citizens, however, did not want to make any more sacrifices for the nation and wanted the bodies of their friends and loved ones brought home. See the discussion on this matter in G. Kurt Piehler, "American Memorialization in the Two World Wars," unpublished paper delivered at a conference on "Public Memory and Collective Identity," Rutgers University, March 1990.

11. Robert and Helen Lynd, *Middletown: A Study in American Culture* (New York: Harcourt, Brace, 1929), 222, 488–91; *Star*, Nov. 12, 1919, pp. 1, 12; Richard Morris Clutter, "The Indiana American Legion, 1919–1960" (unpub. Ph.D. diss., Indiana University, 1974), 110–16.

12. *Star*, July 4, 1927, p. 3.

13. Ibid., p. 1.

14. Ibid., July 5, 1927, p. 1.

15. Ibid.,, July 4, 1927, p. 3.

16. *Star*, Nov. 11, 1937, p. 1; Nov. 12, 1937, p. 1.

17. *News*, July 3, 1942, sec. 2, p. 1; July 4, 1942, p. 1; July 5, 1944, sec. 2, p. 1.

18. Ibid., July 4, 1947, p. 1; Nov. 12, 1947, p. 12; July 4, 1952, p. 10.

19. Ibid., July 4, 1969, pp. 1, 14; *New York Times*, May 25, 1971, p. 24; May 31, 1971, p. 8. This merger of the city and the suburbs was not complete. Schools, law enforcement, and some taxing authorities were not joined.

20. *Star*, July 4, 1970, pp. 10, 15.

21. *Star*, May 31, 1968, pp. 13, 14. About 20 percent of the statements were devoted to servicemen.

22. Ibid., May 29, 1969, pp. 1, 10, 12; May 30, 1969, p. 2; May 29, 1971, pp. 1, 2.

23. Ibid., May 29, 1976, pp. 1, 9; July 5, 1976, p. 8. A downtown festival of July 4, 1976, included a mixture of civic and entertainment events such as places where citizens could sign scrolls of reaffirmation to the Declaration of Independence and presentations of various kinds of music.

24. James H. Kennedy, *A History of the City of Cleveland* (Cleveland: The Imperial Press, 1896), 520–53.

25. *Cleveland Plain Dealer*, July 4, 1894, sec. 2, pp. 1–2; George E. Condon, *Cleveland: The Best Kept Secret* (Garden City, N.Y.: Doubleday, 1967), 79.

26. *Plain Dealer*, July 4, 1894, sec. 2, pp. 1–2.

27. Ibid.

28. Ibid.; Condon, *Cleveland*, 79–80.

29. *Plain Dealer*, July 5, 1894, pp. 1, 3, 5, 8.

30. Ibid., July 4, 1918, pp. 1, 12; July 5, 1918, pp. 1, 4. On the widespread Americanization program in Cleveland during the entire era see "Report of the Work of the Cleveland Americanization Committee" (Cleveland: Cleve-

land Americanization Committee, 1918); Edward M. Miggins, "Becoming American: Americanization and the Reform of the Cleveland Public Schools," in *The Birth of Modern Cleveland, 1865–1930*, eds. Thomas F. Campbell and Edward M. Miggins (Cleveland: Western Reserve Historical Society, 1988), 345–73. Miggins makes a good point when he suggests that Americanization efforts in the city changed in 1918 from a focus on "social uplift" to one that attempted to secure social unity to win the war. However, it could be argued that the goal of social unity and civic order was always part of the Americanization effort.

31. The charge that the riot may have been fomented by business interests in the city is found in Oakley C. Johnson, *The Day is Coming: The Life and Work of Charles E. Ruthenberg, 1882–1927* (New York: International Publishers, 1957), 144. On the riot itself see *Plain Dealer*, May 2, 1919, pp. 1–2; May 3, 1919, p. 1. Another account describing police brutality in the Cleveland riot can be found in Frank Marquart, *An Auto Worker's Journal: The UAW from Crusade to One-Party Union* (University Park, Pa.: Penn State University Press, 1975), 22–23.

32. *Plain Dealer*, Nov. 12, 1919, p. 1; "Official Program of 125th Anniversary Celebration of Cleveland" (Cleveland, 1921).

33. To an extent professionals such as Weidenthal and others who were influential in the cultural gardens represented a drift away from the fixation of individualism and acquisitiveness that had characterized the middle class under nineteenth-century capitalism. They were certainly interested in individual gain but also in providing services to society in a responsible way. It is possible that this alteration in thinking led to something of a change in the emphasis this class placed upon memory. They spoke less of material progress, for instance, and may have been more prone to celebrate the nation than simply material progress as a means of emphasizing unity and deemphasizing the celebration of the achievements of the competitive marketplace. The ethnic middle class carried the additional agenda, of course, of asserting ethnic pride and memories in some form that would be acceptable to both their followers and their peers in the larger society. On professionals in general see Thomas L. Haskell, "Professionalism versus Capitalism: R. H. Tawney, Emile Durkheim, and C. S. Peirce on the Disinterestedness of Professional Communities," in *The Authority of Experts*, ed. Haskell (Bloomington, Ind.: Indiana University Press, 1984), 180–225. Clara Lederer, *Their Paths Are Peace: The Story of the Cleveland Cultural Gardens* (Cleveland: Cleveland Cultural Gardens Federation, 1954), 9–19.

34. "Cleveland Cultural Gardens Federation Minutes," Jan. 31, 1941, Cleveland Cultural Gardens Federation Records (CCGFR), box 1, Western Reserve Historical Society (WRHS); Lederer, *Their Paths Are Peace*, p. 19.

35. "Cleveland Cultural Gardens Federation Minutes," Jan. 13, 1933; Jan. 27, 1933; Apr. 28, 1933, box 1, WRHS. The occupations of ethnic representatives were obtained from the *Cleveland City Directory* (1932).

36. Lederer, *Their Paths Are Peace*, pp. 47–49; *Cleveland News*, Oct. 14, 1935, clipping in CCGFR, box 5.

37. *Cleveland News*, May 30, 1937; *Catholic Universe Bulletin*, June 27, 1947; *Plain Dealer*, Oct. 28, 1934, clippings in CCGFR, box 5.

38. Lederer, *Their Paths Are Peace*, pp. 91–92; *Jednota*, Sept. 24, 1952, p. 7.

39. Lederer, *Their Paths Are Peace,* pp. 76–77.

40. *Plain Dealer,* June 26, 1939, clipping in CCGFR, box 5.

41. "Cleveland Cultural Gardens Federation Minutes," Dec. 12, 1941; Jan. 9, 1942, CCGFR, box 1.

42. *Cleveland News,* July 25, 1942, and *Plain Dealer,* Sept. 27, 1942, clippings in CCGFR, box 2.

43. Lederer, *Their Paths Are Peace,* pp. 61–63, 92.

44. *Plain Dealer,* July 22, 1946, pp. 1, 7.

45. Lederer, *Their Paths Are Peace,* pp. 26–27; *Plain Dealer,* Sept. 15, 1952, clipping in CCGFR, box 5.

46. *Plain Dealer,* July 5, 1942, p. 1.

47. Ibid., May 30, 1969, sec. AA, pp. 4–5; May 31, 1968, p. 12.

48. Ibid., July 4, 1976, sec. A, p. 3; sec. AA, p. 4.

49. Michele H. Bogart, *Public Sculpture and the Civic Ideal in New York City, 1890–1930* (Chicago: University of Chicago Press, 1989), 221, 226, 259–76.

Chapter Five
Memory in the Midwest before WW II

1. Peter S. Onuf and Andrew R. L. Cayton, *The Midwest and the Nation: Rethinking the History of an American Region* (Bloomington: Indiana University Press, 1990), 103–18.

2. Harlow Lindley, ed., *The Indiana Centennial, 1916* (Indianapolis: Indiana Historical Commission, 1919), 17–27; James Woodburn, "The Indiana Historical Commission and Plans for the Centennial," *Indiana Magazine of History* 71 (Sept. 1975): 245–68.

3. Lindley, ed., *The Indiana Centennial,* 82–83, 90.

4. Ibid., 317–19.

5. Ibid., 139–41.

6. Jessie P. Weber, comp., *The Centennial of the State of Illinois, Report of the Centennial Commission* (Springfield, Ill.: Illinois State Journal, 1920), 13–17.

7. Ibid., 23–25.

8. Ibid., 31–33.

9. Ibid., 322–23, 367–69.

10. Ibid., 94–95, 244–46.

11. *Illinois State Journal,* Oct. 4, 1918, p. 1; Oct. 8, 1918, pp. 1, 9.

12. Lewis Atherton, *Main Street on the Middle Border* (Bloomington, Ind.: Indiana University Press, 1954), 186, 204–7.

13. *Galena Gazette,* June 30, 1876, p. 2.

14. Ibid., July 9, 1874, p. 2.

15. *Michigan Pioneer and Historical Society Collection* 6 (1983): 309.

16. For a discussion on how the natural landscape can serve as a link to the past see Henry W. Lawrence, "Historic Change in Natural Landscapes: The Experimental View," *Environmental Review* 6 (Sept. 1982): 14–37.

17. Carl Sandburg, *Always the Young Strangers* (New York: Harcourt, Brace, 1952), 356ff.

18. Ibid.; Sandburg, *Complete Poems* (New York: Harcourt, Brace, 1950), 79–88.

19. Sherwood Anderson, *Mid-American Chants* (New York: Hill and Wang, 1918), 11, 16.

20. James Oliver Robertson, *American Myth, American Reality* (New York: Hill and Wang, 1980), 143–46; John Mack Faragher, *Sugar Creek* (New Haven, Conn.: Yale University Press, 1986), 222.

21. Ross Lockridge, "Our Great Historic Hoosier Memorials: I: Our Hoosier Lincoln Memorials," *Indiana University Alumni Quarterly* 17 (April 1930): 133–45; Lockridge, "Our Great Historic Hoosier Memorials: II: Quarto-Millennial Celebration of the Coming of LaSalle—Our First Historic Hoosier," ibid., 18 (Jan. 1931): 1–12; clipping of *St. Louis Post-Dispatch*, Mar. 17, 1929, box 10, George Rogers Clark Sesquicentennial Commission Records, R.G. 148, National Archives. *New York Times*, July 6, 1930, sec. 3, p. 2; Sept. 4, 1933, p. 13; Sept. 5, 1933, p. 16; *Vincennes Sun*, Feb. 25, 1929, p. 16; Edwin C. Bearss, *George Rogers Clark Memorial* (Washington, D.C.: National Park Service, 1970), 5–8.

22. *Vincennes Commercial*, Feb. 20, 1927, p. 1; Jan. 26, 1930, p. 3; C. B. Coleman to Frank Ball, Oct. 18, 1932, box 8, George Rogers Clark Sesquicentennial Commission Records; Bearss, *George Rogers Clark Memorial*, pp. 9–12.

23. *Vincennes Sun*, Feb. 29, 1928, p. 1; clipping of *Valley Advance* in George Rogers Clark file, History Branch, National Park Service, Washington; Bearss, *George Rogers Clark Memorial*, p. 15; Lockridge, "Our Great Historic Hoosier Memorials: III: The George Rogers Clark Memorial," *Indiana University Alumni Quarterly* 18 (Oct. 1931): 482.

24. 69th Cong., 2d sess., *Hearings Before the Joint Committee of the Library, George Rogers Clark Memorial* (Washington, 1927), pp. 1–2.

25. *Vincennes Commercial*, Feb. 25, 1928, p. 1; Feb. 26, 1928, p. 1; *Valley Advance*, Mar. 18, 1975, clipping in George Rogers Clark file, History Branch, National Park Service; A. E. Demaray to C. H. Hamke, June 12, 1940, ibid.; *Vincennes Sun*, May 28, 1928, p. 10; Bearss, *George Rogers Clark Memorial*, pp. 21–23. Smith, influenced in part by his experience with the Clark memorial, became a leader in the movement to establish a memorial to national expansion and the pioneer movement in St. Louis in the 1930s that resulted in the construction of the St. Louis arch.

26. *Vincennes Sun*, Feb. 26, 1875, p. 1; Feb. 24, 1929, p. 12; Feb. 25, 1929, p. 16; Feb. 27, 1929, p. 1.

27. "Minutes of the Executive Committee," July 13, 1931; Sept. 26, 1931, box 1; and Mar. 20–22, 1931, box 3, Clark Memorial Commission Records.

28. "Historical Notes," *Michigan History Magazine* 16 (1932): 498–503.

29. Grant Wood, *Revolt Against the City* (Iowa City, Iowa: Clio Press, 1935), 21–37.

30. Karal Ann Marling, *Wall to Wall America: A Cultural History of Post-Office Murals in the Great Depression* (Minneapolis: University of Minnesota Press, 1982), 9–20, 204–22.

31. "Final Report of the Northwest Territory Celebration Commission," typescript in box 32, Northwest Territory Celebration Commission Records.

32. L. A. Alderman, *Centennial Souvenir of Marietta, Ohio, 1788–1887* (Marietta, Ohio: n.p., c. 1887).

33. Undated news release in box 5, Northwest Territory Celebration Commission Records.

34. "Final Report of the Northwest Territory Centennial Celebration Commission," p. 26; E. M. Hawes to W. C. Taylor, Dec. 8, 1937, box 1, and untitled list of recommendations for celebrating the event (Dec. 19, 1936), Northwest Territory Celebration Commission Records.

35. Ibid.

36. *Steubenville Herald-Star*, Apr. 5, 1938, pp. 1, 9.

37. *Marietta Daily Times*, Apr. 6, 1938, p. 10; Apr. 7, 1938, p. 1; Apr. 8, 1938, pp. 1, 9. "Souvenir Program, Wagons West" (Marietta, 1938), copy in the Ohio Historical Society.

38. *Marietta Daily Times*, Apr. 7, 1938, 150th Anniversary Edition, p. 7; Apr. 8, 1938, pp. 1, 9.

39. Unpublished reports of receptions for the caravan are found in box 1, Northwest Territory Celebration Commission of Minnesota," box 33, ibid.

40. "Historic Parade, Bloomington, Ill., June 22, 1938," typescript in Illinois Survey Collection, University of Illinois.

41. "Freedom on the March," box 5, ibid.

42. "Final Report of the Northwest Territory Celebration Commission," p. 79.

43. Cayton and Onuf, *The Midwest and the Nation: Rethinking the History of an American Region*, 118–22.

44. Warren I. Sussman, *Culture as History* (New York: Pantheon, 1984), 190–95, 205–6. For a discussion of Michel Foucault and the discipline exerted by officials and "authorities" see Mark Poster, *Foucault, Marxism, and History* (Oxford, Eng.: Oxford University Press, 1984), 19, 53, 75–80, 83.

Chapter Six
Memory in the Midwest after WW II

1. See the speech of Ora Rice, 1948, box 8, Records of the Wisconsin Centennial Commission, State Historical Society of Wisconsin (SHSW); see also Clifford L. Lord and Carl Ubbelhode, *Clio's Servant: The State Historical Society of Wisconsin, 1848–1954* (Madison: State Historical Society of Wisconsin, 1967), 408.

2. Clifford Lord to Rice, Aug. 14, 1946, box 8, Records of the Wisconsin Centennial Commission, SHSW.

3. The radio scripts are located in box 8, ibid.

4. "Final Report of Wisconsin State Centennial Subcommittees" in Minutes and Reports, Records of Wisconsin Centennial Commission, Series 1657, SHSW.

5. Ibid.

6. Ibid.

7. Ibid.

8. "Memo to Chairmen of County Centennial Committees," box 8, Records of Wisconsin Centennial Commission.

9. "Final Report of Wisconsin State Centennial Subcommittees."

10. "Wisconsin Centennial of 1948: A Report of the Agricultural Committee," and "Wisconsin Centennial Expositions," news release, Aug. 23, 1948, box 8, Wisconsin Centennial Records; *Milwaukee Journal*, Aug. 12, 1948, p. 1; Aug. 13, 1948, p. 1.

11. "Minutes of Executive Committee of Wisconsin State Centennial Committee, Apr. 15, 1948, box 8, Wisconsin Centennial Commission Records. For another commemorative event that used symbols of the religious faith of pioneers to counter the threat of a "Godless communism," see accounts of the celebration at Cahokia, Illinois, in 1949; see *Cahokia: Anniversary Celebration, 1699–1949: The Birthplace of the Midwest Souvenir Program* (Cahokia, 1949), copy in the Illinois Historical Survey Program, Univ. of Illinois; *East St. Louis Journal*, May 18, 1949, pp. 1–2; May 19, 1949, p. 1.

12. *Wisconsin State Journal*, May 28, 1948, p. 1; May 29, 1948, pp. 1–4.

13. Ibid., May 29, 1948, p. 1. A copy of the speech of Governor Oscar Rennebohm, May 29, 1948, can be found in box 8, Records of the Wisconsin Centennial Commission.

14. Robert S. Harper, "Ohio Nineteen Fifty-Three," 2 vols.; typescript in Ohio Historical Society, 1, chap. 1.

15. *Suggestions for Celebrating Ohio's 150th Anniversary* (Columbus: Ohio Sesquicentennial Commission, 1952), 2–7.

16. Harper, "Ohio Nineteen Fifty-Three," 1, chap. 13.

17. Ibid., chap. 32.

18. *Toledo Blade*, June 11, 1953, p. 1; June 15, 1953, p. 1; June 16, 1953, p. 1; June 17, 1953, p. 1.

19. Harper, "Ohio Nineteen Fifty-Three," 2, chap. 25.

20. Ibid.

21. *Final Report of the Minnesota Statehood Centennial Commission* (St. Paul: Minnesota Statehood Centennial Commission, 1959), 39–57. The state did not neglect pioneers. Certificates were presented to residents over the age of ninety and a "Pioneer Portrait Hall" was erected on the state fairgrounds.

22. Ibid., 1–2.

23. Ibid., 4–7.

24. Ibid., 9–11.

25. Ibid., 15–17.

26. To acknowledge ethnic diversity officials from many lands that had supplied immigrants to Minnesota were invited to the centennial celebration including Norway, Sweden, Denmark, Finland, Italy, Israel, and Austria. *Final Report of the Minnesota Statehood Centennial Commission*, 13–20.

27. Ver Lynn Sprague to Ralph Newman, Dec. 16, 1965, section R, Field Operations and section P, Records of Ralph Newman, Illinois Sesquicentennial Commission Records, Illinois State Historical Society (ISHS).

28. "Remarks of Ralph G. Newman, Organization and Planning Conference," Apr. 18, 1966, and "Illinois Sesquicentennial Commission," section P, Illinois Sesquicentennial Commission Records.

29. *Southern Illinoisan*, May 27, 1968, p. 1; May 31, 1968, p. 3; May 16, 1968.

30. A copy of Godfrey's speech can be found in section A, Illinois Sesquicentennial Commission Records.

31. *Salem Times Commoner*, July 2, 1968, p. 1; *85th Annual Marion County Soldiers and Sailors Reunion, Souvenir Program* (Salem, Ill., June 24–29, 1968).

32. News release, Feb. 7, 1967, Records of the Illinois Sesquicentennial Commission.

33. *Illinois Sesquicentennial, 1818–1968, Final Report to the Governor, the General Assembly, and the People of Illinois* (Springfield, Ill.: Illinois Sesquicentennial Commission, 1972), 53–55.

34. "Illinois Sesquicentennial Commission, Arts Committee, Final Report," in section H, Illinois Sesquicentennial Commission Records.

35. "Illinois Sesquicentennial Conference, April 18, 1966," section P, Illinois Sesquicentennial Commission Records.

36. Reports of the activities of various counties are in section K, Illinois Sesquicentennial Commission Records.

37. *Final Report to the Governor, General Assembly, and the People of Illinois*, pp. 20–38. Indiana undertook a sesquicentennial celebration in 1966 similar to the one in Illinois. A state commission was created in 1957 that administered a celebration almost mystifying in the diversity of its activities. But the objectives were clearly articulated and included the celebration of the "rich" cultural, historical, and economic resources of Indiana, the stimulation of business and industry, and the promotion of tourism in the state. Planners also made a special effort in the 1960s to encourage local and national pride and patriotism. "The patriotic theme is not old hat," one planner wrote, "Patriotism and pride in our country, state, and county are the things which make programs of this sort successful. This is what we need to combat many of the forces which act against us." See "The Indiana Sesquicentennial Commission," *Indiana History Bulletin* 42 (1965): 123. See also William Wilson, "Hush-a bye Indiana," *American Heritage* 18 (Dec. 1966): 68–71, for a discussion of how local pride can distort communication about the past during a celebration such as the one in Indiana.

Chapter Seven
The National Park Service and History

1. Harlan D. Unrau and Frank Willis, "To Preserve the Nation's Past: The Growth of the Historic Preservation in the National Park Service During the 1930s," *The Public Historian* 9 (Spring 1987): 19–49; Barry Macintosh, *The Historic Sites Survey and National Historic Landmarks Program: A History* (Washington: National Park Service, 1965), 2; Conrad Wirth, *Parks, Politics, and the People* (Norman, Oklahoma: University of Oklahoma Press, 1980), 41; Ronald F. Lee, *Family Tree of the National Park System* (Philadelphia: Eastern Parks and Monument Association, 1974), 18–19; Alfred Runte, *National Parks: The American Experience* (Lincoln, Nebr.: University of Nebraska Press, 1987), 71–73.

2. William Robert Rambin, "Thomas Wood Stevens: American Pageant Master" (2 vols.; unpub. Ph.D. diss., Louisiana State Univ., 1977), 1:318–42. I would like to thank David Glassberg for this reference. David Glassberg, "History and the Public: Legacies of the Progressive Era," *Journal of American History* 73 (Mar. 1987): 957–80; Ethel T. Rockwell, "Historical Pageantry: A

Treatise and a Bibliography," *State Historical Society of Wisconsin Bulletin* no. 84 (July 1916): 5–9; Robert W. Rydell, *All the World's a Fair: Visions of Empire at American International Expositions, 1876–1916* (Chicago: University of Chicago Press, 1984).

3. Frederick Bittinger, *The Story of the Pilgrim Tercentenary Celebration at Plymouth in the Year 1921* (Plymouth, Mass., 1923), 35–43.

4. *Philadelphia Inquirer*, June 28, 1926, pp. 1, 4; June 29, 1926, p. 6; July 1, 1926, p. 7; July 6, 1926, pp. 4–8.

5.Edgar A. Guest, *Poems of Patriotism* quoted in *Celebrating a 300th Anniversary: A Report of the Massachusetts Bay Tercentenary of 1930* (Boston: Massachusetts Bay Tercentenary Commission, 1931), 23; Commonwealth of Massachusetts, *Material Suggested for Use in the Schools in Observance of the Tercentenary of Massachusetts Bay Colony* (Boston: Massachusetts Department of Education, 1930), 42–45.

6. See *The Yorktown Sesquicentennial* (Washington: Government Printing Office, 1932), 205–40.

7. *Washington Star*, Sept. 21, 1930, clipping in Vera Woods File, box 1, George Washington Bicentennial Commission Records (GWBCR), R.G. 148, National Archives. One cannot read the Washington press for the early 1930s without noticing the tremendous amount of attention given over to the building of historic landmarks and memorials in the nation's capital.

8. Sol Bloom's speech at the Betsy Ross house, July 14, 1931; copy in Vera Woods File, box 3, GWBCR.

9. Hal Rothman, *Preserving Different Pasts: The American National Monuments* (Urbana, Ill.: University of Illinois Press, 1989), 198–99.

10. *Report of the United States George Washington Bicentennial Commission*, 5 vols. (Washington: George Washington Bicentennial Commission 1932), 5:xii, 284, 442. See *Washington Star* Nov. 20, 1932 in Vera Woods File, box 2, GWBCR. Oliver McKee, "Super Salesman of Patriotism: A Portrait of Sol Bloom," *Outlook and Independent* 160 (Feb. 3, 1932): 139–46. Bloom's "salesmanship" is criticized in M. De F. Doty, "Glorifying George," *The Forum* 87 (1932): 345–48. Also see Karal Ann Marling, *George Washington Slept Here: Colonial Revivals and American Culture, 1876–1986* (Cambridge, Mass.: Harvard University Press, 1988), 325–35.

11. *Report of the George Washington Bicentennial Commission*, 5:3.

12. Unrau and Williss, "To Preserve the Nation's Past: The Growth of Historic Preservation in the National Park Service During the 1930s," 19–49; Horace M. Albright, *Origins of the National Park Service Administration of Historic Sites* (Philadelphia, 1971); Donald Swain, *Wilderness Defender: Horace M. Albright and Conservation* (Chicago: University of Chicago Press), 200.

13. Unrau and Williss, "To Preserve the Nation's Past: The Growth of Historic Preservation in the National Park Service During the 1930s," 31. The desire of the park service to use historic sites to attract more tourists and, thus, more government and public support is described in Hal Rothman, *Preserving Different Pasts: The American National Monuments* (Urbana, Ill.: University of Illinois Press, 1989), xv, 204–5.

14. Mackintosh, *The Historic Sites Survey and National Historic Landmarks Program: A History*; Lee, *Family Tree of the National Park System*, pp. 21–35; idem,

Interpretation in the National Park Service: A Historical Perspective (Washington, D.C.: National Park Service, 1986), 18; Unrau and Williss, "To Preserve the Nation's Past: The Growth of Historic Preservation in the National Park Service During the 1930s," 26, 31.

15. See "Memo for Director, NPS," Apr. 19, 1932; clipping of *Roanoke World News*, Apr. 25, 1932, and V. Chaterlain to Horace Albright, Feb. 25, 1932, in National Park Service Records, Central Files, box 651, R.G. 79, NARS.

16. Mackintosh, *Interpretation in the National Park Service: A Historical Perspective*, 7–14.

17. Ibid., pp. 19–23, 83. The NPS was also getting involved in 1933 in the Historic American Buildings Survey which was first established under the Civil Works Administration for the purpose of employing architects who made measured drawings of historic buildings to be deposited in the Library of Congress. Additionally, a historic sites survey was initiated in 1936 as a result of the Historic Sites Act of 1935 but was brought to a virtual standstill during World War II. See Mackintosh, *The Historic Sites Survey and National Historic Landmarks Program*, 13–31; "Minutes of the Board of the Historic American Buildings Survey," Jan. 1934, files 12–33, Dept. of Interior Records, R.G. 48, NARS.

18. "Suggested Statement of Principles and Standards Involving National Historical Areas, 1933," memo in Dept. of Interior Records, files 12–33; "National Resources Board Report," and V. E. Chatelain to A. Demaray, Apr. 23, 1933, in History Branch files, NPS, Washington, D.C.

19. Carlton C. Qualey, "A National Parks Historical-Educational Program," Aug. 21, 1933, memo in History Branch files, NPS, Washington, D.C.

20. Graham White and John Maze, *Harold Ickes of the New Deal* (Cambridge, Mass.: Harvard University Press, 1985), 104.

21. U.S. Cong., House Committee on Public Lands, *Preservation of Historic American Sites, Buildings, Objects, and Antiques of National Significance*, 74th Cong., 2d sess., 1935.

22. Lee, *Family Tree of the National Park System*, p. 48; Mackintosh, *The Historic Sites Survey and National Historic Landmarks Program*, 5–7; Charles B. Hosmer, *Preservation Comes of Age: From Williamsburg to the National Trust, 1926–1949*, 2 vols. (Charlottesville, Va.: University of Virginia Press, 1981), 1:578, 80; 2:926–34.

23. Hosmer, *Preservation Comes of Age*, 1:585–94.

24. "Minutes of the Advisory Board," Feb. 13–14, 1936, files 12–13, Dept. of Interior Records, R.G. 48, NARS. See Mackintosh, *Interpretation in the National Park Service*, 101.

25. "Minutes of the Advisory Board," ibid., and "Advisory Board Resolution," May 7, 1936, Dept. of Interior Records, files 12–36, R.G. 48, NARS.

26. Bumpus's remarks are contained in undated transcripts in the "American Planning and Civic Association File," History Branch, NPS, Washington, D.C.

27. Clark Wissler, *Man and Culture* (New York: Thomas Y. Crowell, 1923), 5, 34–35; Marvin Harris, *Cultural Materialism* (New York: Random House, 1979) 278–79; Ronald Lee, *Family Tree of the National Park Service* (Philadelphia: Eastern National Park and Monument Association, 1974), 46.

28. See Lee, *Family Tree of the National Park Service*, 44–46.

29. See the "Proposed Monuments" files in Central Classified Files, National Park Service Records, R.G. 79, NARS; Franklin D. Roosevelt to Harold Ickes, Feb. 6, 1939, "Policy File," History Branch, NPS, Washington, D.C.; Lee, *Family Tree of the National Park Service*, 71–72. See Herbert E. Kahler, "Ten Years of Historical Conservation under the Historic Sites Act," *Planning and Civic Comment* (Jan. 1946), 20–24.

30. L. G. Gardner to Douglass McKay, July 17, 1953, Dept. of Interior Records, Central Files, R.G. 48, NARS; Emil Leicht to Henrik Shipstead, Oct. 1, 1935, box 2940; "Cushing Memorial" file box 2933 B; "Emily Geiger" file, box 2997; Newton Druy to Frank Maloney, Apr. 15, 1948, box 2992; "Emigrant Canyon" file, box 2991, Central Files, National Park Service Records, R.G. 79, NARS.

31. A. E. Demary to Under Secretary of the Interior, Sept. 20, 1949, files 12–42, Dept. of Interior Files, R.G. 48, NARS. The Douglas home was eventually turned into a national site in 1962.

32. A. J. Wirtz to W. T. Bishop, Apr. 7, 1941, and Joseph Ellenbacher to Harry Truman, June 30, 1947, both in box 3000, ibid.

33. "Acquiring Shawnee Mission," report in box 3000, National Park Service Records, R.G. 79.

34. See "Atomic Bomb Monument" file, box 2982, ibid.

35. "Fort Stanwix" file, box 2996, ibid.

36. During the period that regional officials pursued a national monument at Cumberland Gap, civic leaders in Kentucky attempted to gain national recognition for forts and sites associated with Daniel Boone and pioneer settlement in the state. A statewide celebration in honor of the bicentennial of Boone's birth in 1934 attempted to create public support for the idea of a Pioneer National Monument Park that would incorporate sites associated with Boone. See the Pioneer Monument Association Records, 1933–40, Eastern Kentucky State University. I would like to thank Mr. Charles Hay for his assistance in finding this material. Also see "Fort Boonesborough" file, box 649, National Park Service Records, R.G. 79, NARS.

37. "Cumberland Gap" file, box 2932, National Park Service Records, ibid.

38. See Sharon A. Brown, *Administrative History, Jefferson National Expansion Memorial National Historic Site* (Washington: National Park Service, 1984), 83; copy in NPS History branch, Washington, D.C.

39. Merrill D. Peterson, *The Jefferson Image in the American Mind* (New York: Oxford University Press, 1960), 273–75.

40. Brown, *Administrative History, Jefferson National Expansion Memorial National Historic Site*, 1; "Minutes of the United States Territorial Expansion Memorial Commission," Dec. 19, 1934, box 2, Jefferson National Expansion Memorial Files, NPS History branch, Washington, D.C.

41. "Minutes of the United States Territorial Expansion Memorial Commission," 1–4.

42. Ibid., 4–12.

43. Ibid., Feb. 1, 1935; May 1, 1935.

44. Paul Ward, "Washington Weekly," *The Nation* 142 (Mar. 4, 1936): 267–68; *St. Louis Post-Dispatch*, Sept. 8, 1936, p. 1; Brown, *Administrative History*,

Jefferson National Expansion Memorial National Historic Site, 18–41. A description of the court cases that led to the acquisition of land for the project can be found in April Hamel, "The Jefferson National Expansion Memorial: A Depression Relief Project" (unpub. Ph.D. diss., St. Louis University, 1983).

45. Hosmer, *Preservation Comes of Age*, 1:630–35. Hosmer attributes Roosevelt's claim to material supplied by Luther Ely Smith.

46. Ibid., 626, suggests that the NPS "probably" would not have approved the plan without political pressure. Brown, *Administrative History, Jefferson National Expansion Memorial National Historic Site*, 31, 54; Peterson, *The Jefferson Image in the American Mind*, 360–61.

47. Gloria Peterson, *An Administrative History of Abraham Lincoln Birthplace National Historical Site* (Washington: National Park Service, 1968), 8–16.

48. Ibid., 20–28.

49. Ibid., 33–37.

50. Ibid., 74–86.

51. Thomas M. Pitkin, *General Grant National Memorial: Its History and Possible Development* (New York: National Park Service, 1959), 3–5; copy in History branch, NPS, Washington, D.C.

52. Ibid., 5–6.

53. Ibid., 69–70.

54. Ibid., 71.

55. Ibid., 75–84.

56. Ibid., 141–44; Charles Snell and Sharon A. Brown, *Antietam Battlefield National Cemetery, Sharpsburg, Maryland: An Administrative History* (Washington: National Park Service, 1986), 67, 146; Richard Meyers, *The Vicksburg National Cemetery* (Washington: National Park Service, 1968), 1–11.

57. Southerners built elaborate cemeteries for their dead as well in the late nineteenth century. See Mary H. Mitchell, *Hollywood Cemetery: The History of a Southern Shrine* (Richmond, 1985). Virginia State Library, 1985.

58. Wirth, *Parks, Politics, and the People*, 261, provides the following data on visitation and funding:

Fiscal Year	*Visitors (millions)*	*Funding ($ millions)*
1935	7.6	11.8
1955	56.5	32.9
1965	121.3	128.1
1973	222.3	221.7

59. Ibid., 166, 237–39, 255, 258.

60. Mackintosh, *Interpretation in the National Park Service*, 34.

61. "'Mission 66' For the National Park System," "Mission 66" file, History branch files, NPS, Washington, D.C.

62. Ibid. For an argument about the need to guard historic resources as well as environmental ones see Frank E. Masland, "The Conservation of Spiritual Values," in "Report of 'Mission 66' Frontiers Conference" (1961), ibid.

63. Frank Barnes, "Personalized Historical Interpretation" (June 1957), General Secretary file, ibid.

64. John Hussey, "The Role of History in the National Park System," "Mission 66" file, ibid. The heightened interest in interpretation at this time caused the NPS to support the publication of Freeman Tilden, *Interpreting Our Heritage* (Chapel Hill, N.C.: University of North Carolina Press, 1957).

65. Hussey, "The Role of History in the National Park System."

66. Ronald F. Lee, "Bringing History to the People" (1950), speech in box 6, Ronald F. Lee Papers and "Minutes, Advisory Board Meeting, Mar. 28–30, 1956, and Sept. 17–22, 1960, NPS Archives, Harpers Ferry, West Va.

67. Barbara Blumberg, *Celebrating the Immigrant: An Administrative History of the Statue of Liberty National Monument, 1952–1982* (Boston: National Park Service, 1985), 28–58. Enabling legislation was passed by Congress for the AMI in 1956 and a museum was opened in 1968 that was immediately criticized by minority groups for insufficiently portraying the history of blacks, Italians, Poles, and Jews.

68. "Memo to Director, NPS," June 18, 1968, "Urban Programs" file, NPS Archives, Harpers Ferry, West Va.

69. See Walter J. Hickel to John D. Ehrlichman, May 20, 1969; clipping of the *Wall Street Journal*, Feb. 3, 1956; and "Program Support Paper, Parks to the People," all in "Urban Programs" file, NPS Archives, Harpers Ferry, West Va.

70. "Program Support Paper, Parks to the People," "Urban Programs" file, ibid.

71. Robert S. Nathan et al., *Responding to the Urban Challenge: The National Park Service in New York City* (New York: Council on the Environment of New York City, 1972), i, 186–203.

72. Ronald A. Foresta, *America's National Parks and their Keepers* (Washington, D.C.: Resources for the Future, 1984), 142–48.

73. "Program Objectives," Oct. 24, 1970, "Centennial Philosophy" file, Ronald F. Lee Papers, series 3.

74. Ibid.

75. The NPS offered grants-in-aid to assist programs at National Historic Landmarks and National Register historic properties that exemplified the "ideals that shaped America's heritage." See "Statement of Heritage Bicentennial Activities of the National Park Service, Bicentennial Program file, History branch files, NPS, Washington, D.C.

76. "U.S.A., 1776–1796," document in ibid.

77. Scripts and videotapes of both productions are available for inspection at the NPS Archives, Harpers Ferry, West Va.

78. Edward Shils, "Tradition," *Contemporary Studies in Society and History* 13 (Apr. 1971): 130.

Chapter Eight
Celebrating the Nation, 1961–1976

1. Victor Gondos, "Karl S. Betts and the War Centennial Commission," *Military Affairs* 27 (Summer 1963): 51–61.

2. "Minutes of the Civil War Centennial Commission," March 1961, Records of the Civil War Centennial Commission (RCWCC), box 20, R.G. 79, National Archives.

3. Ibid., June 5, 1960.

4. Ibid., Jan. 6, 1959.

5. Gondos, "Karl S. Betts and the War Centennial Commission," 58. Administratively the commission was placed under the jurisdiction of the National Park Service.

6. "Minutes of the Civil War Centennial Commission," Jan. 5, 1960, RCWCC, box 20; "Executive Committee Minutes," May 23, 1958, and July 22, 1959, RCWCC, box 22.

7. "Minutes of the Civil War Centennial Commission," Jan. 5, 1960, RCWCC, box 20.

8. *New York Times*, Jan. 8, 1961, p. 1; U.S. Civil War Centennial Commission, *The Civil War Centennial: A Report to Congress* (Washington, D.C.: U.S. Civil War Centennial Commission, 1968), 10–11.

9. *New York Times*, Jan. 9, 1961, p. 1.

10. Ibid., Jan. 9, 1961, p. 23.

11. On September 22, 1862, Lincoln had issued a Preliminary Emancipation Proclamation prior to his proclamation of January 1, 1863, which declared slaves to be free in areas still in rebellion and not under federal control.

12. *New York Times*, Sept. 22, 1962, pp. 1, 50; *The Civil War Centennial Commission: A Report to Congress*, p. 18. Taylor Branch, *Parting the Waters: America in the King Years* (New York: Simon and Schuster, 1988), 399–400, 685.

13. *New York Times*, Sept. 22, 1962, p. 50.

14. Gondos, "Karl S. Betts and the War Centennial Commission," 64–65.

15. Ibid. Branch, *Parting the Waters*, pp. 399–400.

16. The National Park Service, like other government agencies, devoted a good deal of attention to the Civil War Centennial. It was able to add four new Civil War sites including Lincoln's boyhood memorial, and build new visitor centers at places such as Gettysburg. Congress, in fact, provided funds to improve and expand facilities at some thirty Civil War sites under NPS administration. The U.S. Army gave logistical support to several reenactments and created a mobile display on the contributions of the Civil War to the nation's military progress. The National Archives microfilmed large segments of its Civil War holdings and the United States Information Agency circulated books overseas related to the anniversary of the Emancipation Proclamation; see *The Civil War Centennial: A Report to Congress*, 30–36; "Minutes of the Civil War Centennial Commission," Dec. 6, 1960, RCWCC, box 20.

17. "Minutes of the Civil War Centennial Commission," Aug. 30, 1961, RCWCC, box 20.

18. Ibid., Dec. 4, 1961, box 21. *The Civil War Commission: A Report to Congress*, p. 2, referred to the actions of Betts and Grant by saying that they planned the Charleston meeting "with a deplorable lack of vigilance."

19. See "Centennial of the Civil War: Business Booms Like the Gettysburg Cannon," *Newsweek* 57 (Mar. 27, 1961): 76–77; "How Silly Can You Be," *America* 107 (July 7, 1962): 463–64; "The Civil War and Our Unity," *America* 107 (Nov. 10, 1962): 1048.

20. *The Civil War Centennial: A Report to Congress*, 1–2, 14; *Atlanta Constitution*, Apr. 8, 1961, clipping in "Florida Civil War Centennial Commission file," RCWCC.

21. The involvement of the park service is discussed in "Special Events" file, Branch of History, NPS offices, Washington, D.C. See especially Conrad Wirth to Regional Director, Region One, Aug. 14, 1961.

22. See Cleveland Amory, "First of the Month," *Saturday Review* 44 (Aug. 5, 1961): 4; "On to Appomattox," *Reporter* 25 (Aug. 17, 1961): 18; James I. Robertson to A. Adams, Oct. 2, 1963, RCWCC, box 74. Jay Anderson, *Time Machines: The Worlds of Living History* (Nashville: American Association for State and Local History, 1984), 143, reported that the national commission secretly reversed its policy against reenactments when it learned that President Kennedy enjoyed sham battles. In a letter to the author, Aug. 2, 1988, Robertson stated that Kennedy told him and Nevins that he was annoyed with reenactments and commercialism.

23. Commission awards are listed in "Meeting of Committee on Awards," RCWCC, box 23.

24. Ibid. See also the Records of the Civil War Centennial Jewish Historical Commission, American Jewish Historical Society, Waltham, Mass.

25. See correspondence in "Pennsylvania State Commission," RCWCC, box 86. Appropriations for state centennial commissions ranged from less than $3,000 per year in Missouri, Minnesota, and Michigan to $500,000 for four years in Mississippi and to over $2 million spent in Virginia.

26. Illinois newspaper clippings are located in the Illinois Civil War Commission Records, box 22, Illinois State Historical Society, Springfield.

27. Illinois Civil War Commission News Release, Apr. 6, 1958, ibid.

28. "Report of the Civil War Centennial Commission of Massachusetts," Dec. 29, 1959, RCWCC, box 78; News Release of the Indiana Civil War Centennial Commission," Mar. 19, 1960, ibid., box 78; Clyde Walton to U. S. Grant III, June 29, 1961, Illinois Civil War Centennial file, RCWCC, box 75.

29. "Minutes of the Illinois Centennial Commission," 1962, 1963, RCWCC, box 75. *Illinois State Journal*, May 1, 1965, p. 1; May 3, p. 15; May 5, p. 5.

30. Commonwealth of Massachusetts, *Reports of the Civil War Centennial Commission* (Dec. 29, 1959), pp. 16–20; copy in box 75, RCWCC.

31. See "Indiana Returns Confederate Flags," box 75, RCWCC.

32. See Ohio Civil War Centennial Commission, "Bulletin" (Jan. 1961), box 85, RCWCC.

33. "Pennsylvania Centennial Commission file, box 86, RCWCC.

34. At a reenactment of the battle at the 125th anniversary in 1988, "hostilities" concluded with the "combatants" removing their hats and kneeling in silence. As a lone bugler astride a white horse rode onto the field, spectators knelt "in silent prayer" as well; see *Indianapolis Star*, July 3, 1988, section F, p. 1.

35. *Alabama Journal*, Feb. 15, 1961, p. 4; *Montgomery Advertiser*, Feb. 17, 1961, p. 1; Feb. 19, 1961, p. 1. See also the *Richmond Times-Dispatch*, Oct. 26, 1959, p. 4. Branch, *Parting the Waters*, p. 391.

36. "Report of the Georgia Civil War Centennial Commission" (1966), box 74, RCWCC.

37. Virginia Civil War Centennial Commission, "Civil War Centennial, Final Report, 1965," box 90, RCWCC.

38. "Mississippi Civil War Bulletin," no. 4 (1960) and Mississippi Commission of the War Between the States, "Statement of Policy," box 80, RCWCC.

39. "Report of the Georgia Civil War Centennial Commission" (1965), box 74, RCWCC.

40. See copy of "Arkansas Civil War Centennial Newsletter" (Oct. 1961) and clipping of *Arkansas Gazette*, Jan. 19, 1956, box 79, RCWCC.

41. This material is drawn from the "News Letter" of the North Carolina Confederate Centennial Commission, 1962–65, box 85, RCWCC.

42. Ibid.

43. Virginia Civil War Centennial Commission, "Virginia Civil War Commission, Report" (1961), box 91, RCWCC.

44. Ibid.

45. Ibid. (1962).

46. *Washington Post*, Apr. 10, 1965, p. 3; The "Final Report, 1965" of the Virginia Civil War Centennial Commission is to be found in box 91, RCWCC.

47. American Revolution Bicentennial Administration, *The Bicentennial of the United States of America: Final Report to the People* (5 vols.; Washington, D.C.: American Revolution Bicentennial Administration, 1977), 1:51.

48. Ibid., Preface; Warner made a strong plea for patriotism in a speech to the Bicentennial Ethnic Racial Council. See American Revolution Bicentennial Administration Records, R.G. 452, "Transcript, Minority Ethnic Bicentennial Meeting, June 27, 1974," box 273, National Archives.

49. *Bicentennial of the United States of America*, 1:34.

50. Ibid., 4.

51. 89th Cong., 2d sess., House Doc. 408, "Joint Resolution to Establish the American Revolution Bicentennial Commission," Mar. 10, 1966.

52. *The Bicentennial of the United States of America: Final Report*, 1:244.

53. Ibid., 244–46.

54. "Planning Meeting of Civil and Patriotic Organizations, Philadelphia, Dec. 15, 1969," ARBC file, History Branch, National Park Service, Washington, D.C.

55. *The Bicentennial of the United States of America: Final Report*, 1:246; *New York Times*, July 4, 1976, p. 70.

56. *Washington Post*, Aug. 14, 1972, p. 1; Sept. 8, 1972, sec. C, p. 3.

57. *New York Times*, July 4, 1973, p. 70.

58. *The Bicentennial of the United States of America: Final Report*, 1:248.

59. *Washington Post*, July 4, 1976, sec. D, p. 1.

60. *The Bicentennial of the United States of America: Final Report*, 1:252.

61. Ibid., 76–77.

62. Ibid., 252–57. An American Indian group in Portland, Oregon, refused an invitation to join the Wagon Train because they felt it was like Germans inviting Jews to celebrate Hitler's rise to power; ibid., 130. The commercial aspects of the celebration were often criticized by those who felt the bicentennial should be above commercial exploits. Warner's general response was that the American people were fully able to decide what they wanted to buy and no one was forcing them. See ARBA Records, R.G. 452, "Commercialism File," box 63, NARS. A discussion of Pennsylvania's involvement in plan-

ning the Wagon Train can be found in a small file of material on the Pennsylvania Bicentennial Commission, Pennsylvania Historical and Museum Commission.

63. *New York Times*, Jan. 11, 1976, p. 18.

64. *Washington Post*, Apr. 11, 1976, pp. 1–3; *New York Times*, Feb. 9, 1973, p. 16.

65. People's Bicentennial Commission, *America's Birthday: A Planning and Activity Guide for Citizens' Participation During the Bicentennial Years* (New York: Simon and Schuster, 1974), 9–10.

66. Ibid., 123–25.

67. *New York Times*, Jan. 18, 1976, sec. 4, p. 18.

68. The activities of the PBC, by this point, provoked Senator James O. Eastland to convene the Senate subcommittee he chaired on Internal Security, a relic of the "witch-hunting" days of the 1950s. Eastland's group issued a report claiming that Congress had created ARBA in the hope that citizens would be given "a better understanding of our magnificent national history and would be able to draw a fresh inspiration from the examples of the founding fathers and the immortal documents of liberty which they have handed down to us." Eastland complained that the PBC had received more publicity than ARBA but that its views were closer to those of Castro and Mao than our founding fathers. "By muscling in on the Bicentennial observance," Eastland complained, "it seeks first of all to pervert its meaning and, secondly, to exploit it for the purposes of overthrowing our free society"; 94th Cong., 2d sess., Report of the Subcommittee to Investigate the Administration of the Internal Security Act and Other Internal Security Laws, "The Attempt to Steal the Bicentennial: The People's Bicentennial Commission" (Washington, 1976). See also *Washington Post*, May 15, 1976, p. 10.

69. *New York Times*, July 5, 1976, p. 18.

70. *Washington Post*, July 4, 1976, p. 11.

71. The activities of the Bicentennial Ethnic Racial Coalition can be traced in ARBA Records, R.G. 452, boxes 273–76, NARS. See especially "Transcript, Minority Ethnic Bicentennial Meeting, June 27–28, 1974," box 273, and "Final Report, Ethnic Racial Forum, Apr. 9, 1976, Boston," box 276.

72. *The Bicentennial of the United States of America: Final Report*, 3, identifies over sixty-six thousand celebration activities. For lists of the contents of time capsules see ARBA Records, R.G. 452, box 60, NARS.

73. *The Bicentennial of the United States of America: Final Report*, 3:3–17, 307–23.

74. Ibid., 359–408.

75. Ibid.

76. Ibid., 1:197.

77. Ibid., 128.

78. Ibid., 194–95.

79. Ibid., 3:309–14, 368–71. At Bishop Hill ethnic pioneers were still recalled. Traditional Swedish religious services were held and a "communal agrarian demonstration of the 1840s" was presented. Ties to the homeland

were evident with visits of Swedish royalty. In Decorah, Iowa, pioneer log structures were restored at the Norwegian-American museum; see ibid., 362, 452.

80. Ibid., 4–18, 307–20. This study does not make an attempt to analyze the entire variety of activities classified as bicentennial celebrations by ARBA. The scope and variety are enormous and many events were simply stamped with a bicentennial label but really had little to do with historic themes or with commemorating the past. Thus, parks were built or hospitals were expanded. These projects could contribute to future generations, one of the official thrusts of ARBA, and civic pride, an important goal of government planners, but really did not deal directly with the subject of public memory.

81. Ibid., 312–33, 360–408.

Conclusion
Subcultures and the Regime

1. Louis Hartz, *The Liberal Tradition in America: An Interpretation of American Political Thought Since the Revolution* (New York: Harcourt, Brace, and World, 1955), 11; George Lipsitz, *Time Passages: Collective Memory and American Popular Culture* (Minneapolis: University of Minnesota Press, 1990), xiv.

2. The stages of French national memory are summarized in Pierre Nora, "La Nation Memoire," in *Les Lieux De Memoire*, vol. 2, pt. 3; *La Nation*, ed. Nora (Paris: Gallimard, 1986), 647–58; Luisa Passerini, *Fascism in Popular Memory* (Cambridge, Eng.: Cambridge University Press, 1987), 117; George L. Mosse, *Fallen Soldiers: Reshaping the Memory of the World War* (New York: Oxford University Press, 1990), 70–106. David Glassberg makes good comparisons between commemorations in the United States and Germany in the 1930s in *American Historical Pageantry: The Uses of Tradition in the Early Twentieth Century* (Chapel Hill: University of North Carolina Press, 1990), 289, and argues that "folk symbolism" in the United States was not incorporated into mass political spectacle as it was in Germany. Additional accounts of vernacular culture resisting state manipulation of civic traditions are to be found in Mona Ozuf, *Festivals in the French Revolution* (Cambridge, Mass.: Harvard University Press, 1988), chap. 9, and Mikhail Bakhtin, *Rabelis and His World*, trans. H. Iswolsny (Bloomington, Ind.: Indiana University Press, 1984), 8–12.

3. Mosse, *Fallen Soldiers*, 212; Raphael Samuel, "Introduction: Exciting to be English," in *Patriotism: The Making and Unmaking of British National Identity*, 3 vols. (London: Routledge, 1989), 1:xviii-lx. Also see Michael Ignatieff, "Soviet War Memorials," *History Workshop* (Spring 1984), 152–60.

4. Todd Gitlin, "Postmodernism: Roots and Politics," in *Cultural Politics in Contemporary America*, eds. Ian Angus and Sut Jhally (New York: Routledge, 1989), 355. On the notion of cultural mixing see James Clifford, "Introduction," in *Writing Culture: The Poetics and Politics of Ethnography*, eds. Clifford and George E. Marcus (Berkeley: University of California Press, 1986), 2. Lipsitz, *Time Passages: Collective Memory and American Popular Culture*, 4–14.

5. In 1990, millions of Americans viewed a televised account of the Civil

War. The public discourse over the event revealed the continued power of both official and vernacular interests. The popularity of the war's history was grounded both in the power of the narrative of nation building and in dramatic readings of letters and diaries from the Civil War era that conveyed dimensions of the personal and firsthand experience of the war itself.

A Note on Sources

A FULL LISTING of the sources consulted in the preparation of this book would needlessly duplicate much of the notes. A few points should be made, however, about the materials that were most valuable and about the possibilities for future work in the area of public memory. Commemorative activities were frequently organized by public bodies and commissions that left voluminous records behind. Among the most helpful to me were the records of several commissions stored at the National Archives. These included the files of the Civil War Centennial Commission, The American Revolution Bicentennial Commission, The George Washington Bicentennial Commission, The George Rogers Clark Sesquicentennial Commission, and the Northwest Territory Sesquicentennial Commission.

Fortunately, the extensive resources of state historical societies include indispensable collections of centennial celebrations. Especially crucial to this study were records of state anniversary commissions at the State Historical Society of Illinois at Springfield, the Ohio History Center at Columbus, and the State Historical Society of Wisconsin at Madison. Although all records of such events could not be fit into this book, very interesting centennials are documented in the state historical societies of Iowa, Minnesota, and California where Spanish explorers and seekers of gold replaced the sturdy pioneers of the Midwest in public commemoration. It should also be mentioned that state historical societies are excellent places to survey a range of newspapers from various localities concerning any particular celebration.

My understanding of the National Park Service was pieced together from collections at a number of different locations. The National Archives contains records for the park service as does the National Park Service archives at Harpers Ferry, West Virginia. The Harpers Ferry center is a good source of recent activities and minutes of the advisory board and holds several films and video tapes concerning park service presentations of history. The park service offices in Washington, D.C., contain files pertaining to the history of most of its sites and can be used with the permission of office staff.

Published volumes of commemorative activities also hold much valuable information and can be incredibly comprehensive. Sometimes such accounts take the form of simple pamphlets. This was especially true for small, ethnic celebrations. But often they can run to several volumes and contain precise details of the organization of the event, public reaction, photographs, and the broad assortment of activity. Anyone interested in public memory in twentieth-century America should not ignore the official reports of the state centennials of Indiana (1916) and Illinois (1918), the George Washington Bicentennial Commission (1932), and the American Revolution Bicentennial Administration (1977).

Records of ethnic commemorations are not so easily found and have to be traced to small ethnic archives and research centers. The possibilities here are unlimited, but I found especially useful the Mennonite Archives in Newton, Kansas; the Swedish Immigration Center, Rock Island, Illinois; and the Norwegian-American Historical Association in Northfield, Minnesota. The Records of the Cleveland Cultural Gardens at the Western Reserve Historical Society contain a descriptive account of the attempt to negotiate a vast commemorative undertaking on the part of numerous ethnic groups.

Finally, much remains to be done in the United States before a fuller understanding of public commemoration and memory can be reached. Scholars in England and France have gone further in documenting the various ways in which individuals and organizations have discussed their past. The best general introduction for the way in which the past is used in the present is David Lowenthal, *The Past is a Foreign Country* (Cambridge University Press, 1985). For England see the three volumes edited by Raphael Samuel, *Patriotism: The Making and Unmaking of British National Identity* (Routledge, 1989). On France see especially the three volumes edited by Pierre Nora, *Les Lieux De Memoire* (Gallimard, 1984). Students of American history still must undertake histories of statuary and monuments, ethnic and other vernacular museums, ceremonies, cemeteries, and symbols which are only introduced in this book. Pioneering work was conducted by W. Lloyd Warner in *The Living and the Dead: A Study of the Symbolic Life of Americans* (Yale University Press, 1959). Recent attempts to expand the understanding of how memory has been used in American society include Michele H. Bogart, *Public Sculpture and the Civic Ideal in New York City, 1890–1930* (University of Chicago Press, 1989); Susan G. Davis, *Parades and Power: Street Theater in Nineteenth-Century Philadelphia* (Temple University Press, 1986); David Glassberg, *American Historical Pageantry: The Uses of Tradition in the Early Twentieth Century* (University of North Carolina Press, 1990); Michael Kammen, *A Machine That Would Go of Itself: The Constitution in American Culture* (Knopf, 1986); George Lipsitz, *Time Passages: Collective Memory and American Popular Culture* (University of Minnesota Press, 1990); and

Karal Ann Marling, *Wall to Wall America: A Cultural History of Post-Office Murals in the Great Depression* (University of Minnesota Press, 1982) and *George Washington Slept Here: Colonial Revivals and American Culture, 1876–1986* (Harvard University Press, 1988).

Index